THE ROOTS AND REACHES OF UNITED NATIONS ACTIONS AND DECISIONS

The Roots and Reaches of United Nations Actions and Decisions

by

MOSES MOSKOWITZ

SIJTHOFF & NOORDHOFF 1980
Alphen aan den Rijn, The Netherlands
Rockville, Maryland, U.S.A.

Library of Congress Catalog Card Number: 80-51741

ISBN 90 286 0140 6

Printed in The Netherlands.

TABLE OF CONTENTS

PREFACE

A growing preoccupation in recent years among many who have labored in one or another area of United Nations concern has been the relationship between the international Organization and the work of its hands. The central question posed has been whether the ideas, institutions and practices engendered by the United Nations can survive the intellectual torpor and moral retreat of the parent body. The possibility of an entire culture built around the United Nations collapsing in a state of such lassitude and withdrawal came into focus with the realization that the world body can pervert as much as it can redeem; the United Nations could not stumble without conviction from one contrivance to the next without prejudice to itself and to the international community.

Although opinion is deeply divided on the question of the efficacy of the United Nations, its relevance and its proper role in the larger world, the impact of the international Organization for good or evil can be ignored only at our peril. The United Nations remains a world arena in which words and resolutions have moral and political consequences. Like individual tesserae of a mosaic which are but little bits of colored glass or stone until they are put together in a given order, so the individual resolutions or decisions of United Nations bodies often make little sense until they are put together to make a pattern. No one who has witnessed the unfolding of international issues since 1945 can deny the United Nations its role as midwife to many problems and fairy godmother to others. "A resolution on record", Sir Kenneth Baily observed, may today, in a point of law, look like only a recommendation, or even a mere "voeu". But it is to be remembered that propaganda can create pressure; that pressure can create practice; and that practice can create law.*

Thus every counsel of prudence dictates the importance of universal concern for the welfare of the United Nations and its moral, political and intellectual integrity. To be sure, the United Nations cannot be faulted for lack of self-criticism or criticism proffered by others. The widening contradictions between promise and performance do not go unnoticed and warnings abound against the tendency of the world body to flirt daringly with damnation. Not a day passes without some reference being made at public and private meetings of United Nations bodies all over the globe to the existing deficiencies and hoped-for improvements in the structure and functions of the international Organization and its related agencies. The same can be said of the growing number of academic and nongovernmental forums devoted to international affairs. From time to time the General Assembly is formally seized with the question of Charter review, while ad hoc bodies of every type seek to probe different areas of United Nations responsibility and make recommendations. Yet we are no nearer than ever to a solution of the problem of United Nations decision making and other problems inherent in the structure and functions of the United Nations.

Perhaps the explanation is to be found in the suggestion that we do not address ourselves to the issues which hold the answer. Indeed, failure to address ourselves to those issues only encourages the United Nations to embroider opinions and events without conscience and to distort unpleasant realities with abandon. It also accounts for the difficulty of identifying a plausible perception of the world body that is either typical or representative, consistent or persuasive. While there is general agreement that the United Nations has long ago transcended the trim framework of the Charter, there is little agreement on whether it is an arena in which men and ideas are reshaping the

* Quoted by Heribert Golsong in his chapter in *International Law Tomorrow*: A Collection of Papers published by the Faculty of Law and Economic Science of the University of Neuchâtel; Neuchâtel, Editions Ides et Calendes 1974.

world, or a place that is at odds with much that is hopeful and creative; a forum addicted to commodious and expansive phrases, or a violent focus of contradictions. Hope and expectation, stress and emphasis, illusion and disappointment, are but some of the threads that weave the pattern of the United Nations.

The United Nations is difficult to define, difficult to quantify, and difficult to communicate. Much depends on the angle of vision and whether the world body is viewed from within or from without. It also depends upon the issues that may be high on the United Nations agenda at a particular moment, as well as upon the intensity with which they engage States Members materially, politically and emotionally. But sooner or later we must strike a balance between the dream of what might be and the accomplishment of what is. We can no more rivet our attention on the present failures of the international Organization without recalling its past successes, than dwell on its future possibilities without emphasizing its present limitations. Whatever the realities behind the claims and aspirations of the United Nations might be, we must try to separate facts from fiction and deduce the totality of the world Organization from the sum of its parts. Like archeology, the United Nations is not made out of the anomalous; it is made out of correlations painstakingly assembled from a multitude of sources.

The present volume addresses itself to a number of issues which have helped shape and define the permanent character of the United Nations and whose impact on the world body is likely to survive into the far future long after they have disappeared from the agenda of the international Organization. The several case studies, which span an era in which many of the patterns and conflicts of our day are rooted, record the pulsating evolution of the United Nations.

I welcome this opportunity to pay tribute to the Officers and Members of the Governing Board of the Consultative Council of Jewish Organizations, which I have the honor to serve as Secretary-General, and in particular to Mr. Justice Harry Batshaw (Montreal), Mr. Jules Braunschvig (Paris), Dr. Basil Bard, C.B.E. (London), Co-Chairmen, Mr. Marcel Franco (Mexico City), Vice-Chairman, and Mr. Alexander Salzman

(New York), Deputy Vice-Chairman. Their solid grasp of the realities behind the issues and rhetoric in the United Nations and their preference for the coherence and dignity of thoughtful reflection to indignation and outrage have served me in good stead. My gratitude to my wife for her encouragement, understanding and forbearance. The views and judgments expressed in this volume are the author's, for which he bears sole responsibility.

New York, N.Y. September 1979 *Moses Moskowitz*

Chapter I

THE POLITICAL ORDER OF THE UNITED NATIONS

The United Nations can neither be captured nor dismissed in one all-encompassing act of commission or omission. Neither can it be judged as an undifferentiated whole; to do so is to fail to penetrate to the naked core of its meaning. The world Organization operates on many fronts with varying degrees of effectiveness at one and the same time, through organs and agencies with distinctive goals and methods of their own and with unique records of achievement. There is no nation in the world today, regardless of size, population, wealth or power, that is not in one way or another affected by, and in turn does not affect, the United Nations. And just as no nation can long evade the reach of the world body, so the international Organization cannot be insulated against the moral and material consequences of a country's acts or policies. The fate of international peace and security can be decided in any field of human endeavor, anytime, anywhere.

For all its difficulties and contradictions, limitations and doubts, the United Nations has for more than three decades discharged vital negotiating and pacifying functions in the international community and has served as an instrument for the promotion of human welfare. Although unable to address itself forcefully to the problem of collective security, the United Nations has successfully intervened in many situations to forestall conflict and ameliorate disputes, while its soldiers have manned truce lines in critical areas of the globe. Functionally, the organs and agencies through which the United Nations has been conducting its diverse activities have overwhelmingly been engaged in economic, social and technical tasks, thereby enlarging human society beyond the confines of the domestic hearth.

But the United Nations is also a battleground of conflicting social and political ideologies, as well as of opposing national interests. All shades of opinion, from passion for things as they were to irrepressible drives for things as they might be, ultimately find a voice in the United Nations; the United Nations serves as a sounding board of world-wide dimensions which amplifies every untoward sound, while its public debates are massive projections into the open of the many problems which plague man, as well as their underlying causes. If the world body is to be judged, it must be not solely by the success or failure in furthering its principal objectives but by the will and the processes through which it permits improvement and reform.

We need not indulge in the pious belief that the United Nations must be morally pure and right-minded before it can meet the demands of the times; moral choice is rarely between absolute right and wrong, but one of balance. But we cannot celebrate the virtues of the international Organization without reckoning with its flaws. The worst service we can render to the United Nations is to encourage exaggerated notions of its nature and functions and to strain to elevate it to the reaches of heaven. The United Nations will always remain earthbound. Its history knows virtue as well as ignominy; truth as well as deceit; purpose as well as drift. It depends on what phase of United Nations development is addressed, on what issues and nations are involved, and on the frame of reference in which questions are posed and answered. While we cannot expect an organization commanding only such power as is placed at its service by more than 150 independent sovereign Member States automatically to transform ancient feuds into ready-made formulas of agreement and to resolve the complex problems which agitate the world, the United Nations cannot bow to realities to the point of accommodating itself to partisan pursuits without destroying its usefulness, nor tolerate the perversion of the language of the Charter without abandoning its role as arbiter of international conduct.

To construct a peace in which Powers, great and small, do not challenge each other's interests and to induce change by mutual consent the United Nations must lay claim to a universal trust and allegiance that cannot be conceded to an organization in which trends, morals and language shift like desert sand over abiding human truths; whose range is often narrow and obsessional, and which leans on the fine art of selective commission or omission. When the mainstay of the United Nations is integrity and credibility its prop, any blemish is necessarily thrown into bold relief. The comment made by the nineteenth-century French writer Charles Peguy on the Dreyfus Affair aptly applies to the United Nations. "A single injustice", he wrote,

> a single illegality, especially if it be officially confirmed, a single insult offered to justice and to right, especially if it be generally, nationally, conveniently accepted, is enough to dishonor and disgrace an entire nation.[1]

The Charter dedicated the United Nations to be "a center for harmonizing the actions of nations" in pursuit of certain common aims. The goals were clearly set forth as the promotion of international peace and security; collective action against aggression, peaceful settlement of international disputes; co-operation for economic and social progress in larger freedom and promotion of human rights for all; observance of international law and justice; and the advancement of dependent territories toward self-determination and self-government. Of these the maintenance of international peace and security is the United Nations' primary and continuing task. In the words of the International Court of Justice,

> The primary place ascribed to [the maintenance of] international peace and security is natural, since the fulfillment of the other purposes—developing friendly relations; promoting economic, social, cultural and humanitarian progress and respect for human rights; and acting as a harmonizing center—will be dependent upon the attainment of that basic condition.[2]

In fact, the great changes which have taken place since the Second World War—the proliferation of nuclear and thermonuclear power, decolonization, the growing recognition of the imperative need for economic and social development, and the expanding international concern with human rights—have radically changed the political context in which States find themselves in dispute with other States, and give added emphasis to the keeping of the peace as the paramount objective of the United Nations. Dag Hammarskjold was intolerant of any suggestion that there might be a substitute for the efforts of the international body to bring international conflict under the rule of law. In an address to the Consultative Council of Jewish Organizations in New York on 30 November 1953, the late Secretary-General said:

> There is a tendency on the part of some whose main interest in the United Nations is its activity in the field of human rights to leave aside the dangerous political issues that threaten international conflict. After all, they argue, we are concerned in the long-range program of peace aimed at eradicating the basic causes of war. Others must concern themselves with the present crisis. There is danger in this line of thinking. It is true that the provisions in the Charter aimed at the creation of a universal system of collective security have so far been largely frustrated by the conflicts in our world and by the fear and suspicions which surround them. But this very fact leaves vulnerable all efforts aimed at the international promotion and protection of human rights.
>
> The right with which the ordinary man or woman today is most concerned is the *right to peace*. For him that sums up a great many rights—the rights to life, the right to freedom, the right to security. All these are swept away by modern war in its up-to-date manifestation. The Universal Declaration in Article 28 proclaims: Everyone is entitled to a social and international order in which the rights and freedoms set forth in this Declaration can be fully realized. I take this to mean: human rights cannot be realized *in vacuo*. The realization of human rights requires a social and international order. The more that order is governed by the rule of law, the greater the opportunity for the full realization of human rights. But destroy that, even the rudimentary international order we have today, and you destroy the minimal basis of human rights.
>
> We are therefore confronted not so much by a dilemma as by a dual imperative. The international promotion of human rights should be as much the concern of the statesman as of the moralist as an end in itself and as part of the means for creating a society that will sustain peace. Equally, the immediate business of preserving peace through rigid adherence to pledges under the Charter and through the utilization of the machinery of mediation and arbitration must be as much the concern of the moralist as the statesman, both as an end in itself and as a necessary condition for man's realization of his right to fulfil himself as a human being.[3]

Twenty years later, similar sentiments were expressed by Secretary-General Kurt Waldheim when he voiced fear lest the tendency to regard the value of the United Nations solely in terms of its economic, social and humanitarian activities might lead people to forget its principal function—the establishment of a secure peace. Addressing a conference on "The Future of the

Secretariat" held in May 1973 in New York under the joint auspices of the United Nations Institute for Training and Research and the Institute on Man and Science, the Secretary-General declared:

> There are many who take the view that the effectiveness of the UN in such fields as economic and social development, human rights, etc., should be considered as important which to some extent compensates for its relative lack of effectiveness in the political field. While I recognize the solid work of the UN in these fields, I personally hold that if the UN is not effective in the political field it will be difficult for the UN to command the confidence not only of the Member States, but of the "peoples of the UN". . . . For this reason I attach the greatest importance to improving the effectiveness of the UN in the political field.[4]

These are reactions to tendencies which have always been strong in the United Nations to regard the world body more as a source of material assistance and the promotion of economic and social justice than as a source of security against aggression. As General Carlos Romulo of the Philippines, one of the original signers of the Charter in 1945, suggested to the twenty-ninth General Assembly in 1974;

> Few will deny that the United Nations has devised ingenious procedures to overcome the inherent limitations of the present Charter. It had broadened the scope of its activities to cover a wide spectrum of issues which the founders of the Organization never anticipated. Still, for our time, the Charter fails to reach the heart of the matter, which is the disturbing division between the developing and developed countries, or, to put it more bluntly, the few rich and the many poor. Never in the history of the United Nations has that division been more apparent than it is today.
>
> The paramount need of the United Nations is a Charter which provides the institutional means for reconciling the two sides, for breaching the gap between them, and for inducing them to cooperate, instead of deepening the distrust in which they hold one another. On these terms alone, if no other, there is, I submit, little to be lost if we place the provisions of the Charter under continuing review, to study how they work and have worked in the past and, above all, to explore the possibility of bringing them more in accord with present realities.[5]

The admonitions addressed by the two Secretaries-General have deep roots in the reality of the United Nations as primarily a political, not technical, organization; its success or failure ultimately depends on its record of political achievement, of resolving disputes and reconciling adversaries. Thus, while the United Nations has many functions, overall it stands and falls on its primary function as defined in Article 1(1) of the Charter,

> To maintain international peace and security, and to that end to take effective collective measures for the prevention and removal of threats to the peace, and for the suppression of acts of aggression or other breaches of the peace . . .

Yet, while the principal norm of international law in our time is the injunction of the Charter in Article 2(4) that:

> All Members shall refrain in their international relations from the threat or use of force against the territories or political independence of any State, or in any manner inconsistent with the purposes of the United Nations,

the ancillary requirement that they settle their disputes by peaceful means has achieved little significance as an independent obligation. The principle of peaceful settlement of disputes is a necessary consequence of the renunciation of the threat or use of force in solving contentious problems. As the development of international law reduces the possibility of the legitimate use of force by States, the need for international machinery capable of centralizing the application of the law increases. But without the obligation to seek the peaceful settlement of disputes the principle of the non-use of force is bound to diminish in importance. Thus, although there have been a number of instances where armed conflict or the spread of hostilities were averted by the timely intervention of the United Nations, in few cases had any real effort to find a solution been made by the Security Council, the General Assembly, or by any other United Nations body.[6] The States Members of the United Nations, Secretary-General Kurt Waldheim has noted, had not availed themselves of the services of the new bodies set up after 1945, while limitations had been encountered by the Security Council and the General Assembly in thirty years of general concern with peaceful settlement of disputes.[7] As of 24 March 1978, the Special Committee on the Charter and on the Strengthening of the Role of the Organization had before it fifty-one proposals for the peaceful settlement of disputes, including proposals for a declaration and a convention which would reaffirm the obligations to settle all disputes by peaceful means, and for special instruments to define such disputes.[8] The proliferation of proposals for improving the capacity of the United Nations for the peaceful settlement of disputes reflects not only the disturbing situation in the world, but also the weakness shown by the United Nations in this crucial area of international relations.

Clearly, nations remain reluctant as ever to submit their differences to third-party settlement. But if they prefer direct negotiations to mediation, arbitration or conciliation, it is not necessarily because such negotiations afford the parties in dispute the widest latitude to pursue their national goals and to exercise their persuasive powers to advance their interests; it is very much a consequence of the political alignment in the contemporary world which leaves little room for impartiality and objectivity. This is especially true of the United Nations, where actions and reactions bear directly upon the prospects of successfully involving third parties in the process of settlement of international disputes. The United Nations is far from being an organized international community of members acting together in equal dignity and mutual tolerance to create a better life for humanity. It is not an organization, as the late U Thant once hoped, "which has no 'face' to lose and no victory of its own to win . . . serving all nations but dominated by none, which has the continual obligation to avoid disaster and misery and to provide a more productive future for all peoples."[9] The United Nations is essentially an instrument of multilateral diplomacy, which the States Members use or abuse to promote their national interests; it has yet to rise above partisan interests and conflicting passions to become a body of manifest and unarguable impartiality, while its judgments have yet to be balanced in a commitment to justice. Addressing the Board of Directors of Reuters in New York on 8 March 1978, Secretary-General Kurt Waldheim said:

> The decisive element in virtually all undertakings of the U.N. is the attitude which Governments adopt towards their obligations under the United Nations Charter and towards the world Organization which is the physical embodiment of that Charter. In most nation States, the citizens have a clear idea both of their obligations to the State and of the rights which they enjoy and to which they are entitled. But in the United Nations we have not yet reached the point where most Governments accept, as a matter of course and in all situations, their rights and their obligations under the Charter.

> Because power politics remains the prevalent mode of international behaviour, we still lack a consistent and reliable system for the maintenance of international peace and security based on the respect of all nations for the Charter and for the decisions of the Security Council. The United Nations tends to be brought into critical situations too late or not at all, and its decisions are often disregarded if they interfere with national policies.[10]

Member States of the United Nations are rarely equally detached from both sides of a conflict and without vested interests of their own to hold high the illuminating torch of objectivity. The ease with which principles are abandoned for expediency and practical necessities elevated to dogma, as well as the multiple perversions of the vocabulary of idealism, are enough to sap confidence in the ability of the United Nations for sustained and purposeful action; the propulsive tendency of the international Organization to allow the widest range of ambiguity to words and deeds and to tolerate the torture of facts to justify self-commitment to abstract judgments are more than enough to strain the credibility even of the seemingly unimpeachable. A large dose of willing suspension of disbelief is needed to give credence to much that issues forth from the forums of the United Nations. Nothing less than a blind leap of faith is necessary to entrust one's fate and future to the mercies of the world body.

Surely the susceptibility to exploitation for partisan purposes is the United Nations' most vulnerable point; it accounts in large measure for the fact that the international Organization has been more an arena for waging conflicts than for solving them. The popular causes which consume so much of the time and energy of the United Nations are not necessarily the great tides of history; nor must the extremism in the world body be equated with the pursuit of moral certainties. The moral passions which agitate the United Nations are often willful and imperious and are sustained mainly by the zeal and the political interest of those who would transform sectional and national goals into universal policy. The strident debate in full public glare only serves to fuel fevers and biases that reach beyond the immediate question of merit into the world of fantasy and make believe. For the United Nations is not a parliament where conflicts of interest are acted out within a common framework of national loyalties and values and where all contenders are heirs to a mutual fate; it is not an association of States that represents a common heritage of law and political institutions, of cultures, administration and like-mindedness of general approach. The United Nations is a diplomatic forum practicing a parliamentary procedure which often tends more to aggravate than reduce international tension and conflict. The insistence on outvoting an opponent rather than seeking his agreement provides neither substantive nor procedural restraints upon the majority, nor protection for the minority against injustice and abuse.

Parliamentary procedures are designed to promote a maximum of negotiations and agreement. Within an organized national society the test is law making and legislation; on the world stage it is, or ought to be, peace making. The need for realistic and practical decision making in the United Nations as a whole, lest it produces the opposite result, led the late Dag Hammarskjold to note:

> Since the "legislative" processes of the United Nations do not lead to legislation, and the power of decision remains in the hands of the national governments, the value of public debate in the United Nations can be measured only by the degree to which it contributes to the winning of agreement by the processes of diplomacy. If public debate contributes to winning consent either immediately or in the long run, it serves the purposes of peacemaking. If it does not so contribute, then it may be useless or even harmful.[11]

Thus the United Nations is and can be a "dangerous place", as Professors Yesselson and Caglioni say in their preface to the book by the same name. "We do not mean", they write,

> that it is a good institution in need of a few reforms, or that it is usually ineffective, or that it changes nothing. It is a weapon in international relations and should be recognized as such. As part of the armory of nations, the United Nations contributes as much to peace as a battleship or an atomic bomb. Disputes are brought into the United Nations in order to weaken an opponent, strengthen one's side, prepare for war, and support a war effort. Analyses that project illusions are irrelevant, unrealistic, and dangerous . . .[12]

Only by recognizing that the actions and decisions of the United Nations are demonstrably shaped by political bias can we hope to dissolve the mystifying sympathies or animosities that thrive in the international body and to see through the strange omissions and disturbing emphases in which it abounds. The United Nations is a "dangerous" place if only because it is presumed to transcend the limits of partisan interest and to act in harmony with its international values when, in fact, the States Members remain captive to their conflicting national interests and varied moral codes. As we shall see in the chapters that follow, the General Assembly and other organs of the United Nations have become increasingly ex parte forums of irresponsible posturing, where passions are free to rage without restraint of consequence, without responsibility of power, without a sense of common allegiance and without a transcendental solidarity. Deceptively disguised behind the rhetoric of pious intentions or dispassionate grief, the United Nations can position itself as guardian of the most sublime principles and at the same time erode the basis of human brotherhood and international solidarity. Very often the actions and decisions of the international Organization are outrageously contrary to a well-instructed conscience and betray more an awareness of what it is that the United Nations seeks to destroy than what it ought to be trying to create. The ease with which national resentments and racial animosities are carried over into international causes only produces disorientation and distorted perceptions, while the dispensation of judgments with the inflexible certainty of embittered infallibility provokes neither relief nor catharsis. The United Nations is a place where heroes can do no wrong and villains can do no right, and where texts are wrenched out of their orbits to fit the ellipses of the Members' own making. In the process of seeking to reconcile the contradictions inherent in the Charter, the United Nations has often tended to compromise beyond the point of prudence and has created a situation which permitted aggressors to preach law and offenders against justice to masquerade as protagonists of the rights of man.

"It seems", the author of a well-reasoned case study of United Nations violations of natural justice concludes,

> that there are certain issues before the United Nations from time to time on which passions are so inflamed and self-interest so strong that the formulation of conclusions by the ordinary processes of objective in-

vestigation, analysis, and deduction is excluded. Positions, having been taken up on the basis of pure emotion or self-interest, are sought to be justified by a process of rationalization which in its extreme form may rely on false or distorted evidence, unsubstantiated conclusions from evidence, or pure assertions. . . .

International affairs in general, and the United Nations in particular, provide an environment in which rationalizing back is not difficult, where accurate and timely information is hard to obtain, and where skilful diplomacy or sheer voting power can secure the exclusion of inconvenient arguments, the conversion of a doubtful assertion into a resolution possessing legal force, or the incorporation of misleading evidence into the report of a body entitled to respect and enjoying wide publicity.

Disregard of the principles of justice not only tends to diminish respect for the organs of the United Nations but also undermines confidence in the system of international law itself, which is in large measure developed and administered by those organs.

If the organs of the United Nations are to secure the respect without which their resolutions on political or legal questions can never be more than scraps of paper, their integrity must be above suspicion. The members of the United Nations must cease to use the Organization for the promotion of their self-interest by political or legal sharp practice and endeavor, when sitting as members of a United Nations body, to develop a spirit not of judicial detachment but at least of fairness, objectivity and accuracy in which all governments and peoples, whether weak or strong, popular or unpopular, may place their trust. . . .[13]

Beyond that, the emergence of blocs and the development of bloc-voting and the way large majorities are formed of States whose combined population represents but a small fraction of mankind and whose burdens incurred by their votes are minimal, leaves little room for accommodation and compromise. On this point, the comments made by the representative of the Netherlands in 1968, when he discussed the need for improving the institutional machinery and working methods of UNCTAD, is most appropriate. Said the representative of the Netherlands:

The group phenomenon is so well known that it need not be analyzed here. It is important to stress that the working methods of the "Group of 77" and of "Group B" have led to often rigidly formulated group positions, which tend to be based on the extremes within each group. As a modified Gresham's Law one could say: extreme positions drive out moderate ones. Maximum demands confront minimum offers. Moreover, the group positions have, once arrived at, turned out to be changeable only with the greatest difficulty. This group rigidity has played havoc with the traditional

> method, according to which the most directly involved in a problem strive to work out a compromise and, during and after the working out of a compromise, endeavor to convince their allies and friends that the compromise is reasonable. The participation of some countries in an effort to work out a compromise does not prevent them from entering into intimate consultations with allies. It must be concluded that UNCTAD's best interests would be served if the groups functioning in UNCTAD, principally the "Group of 77" and "Group B" would be willing to assist a return to the traditional approach holding out better prospects for obtaining concrete results.
>
> To this end it should be agreed to modify the application of the group system in the permanent machinery of UNCTAD by limiting group positions to some broad lines on any issue or problem so as to prevent that too-rigidly-held group positions—or as is frequently the case—the absence of group positions become a blocking factor in their own right. From the outset contacts between individual members of different groups should be encouraged.[14]

Six years later Swedish Ambassador Olof Rydbeck, speaking in the General Assembly on the subject of strengthening the role of the United Nations, said:

> A tendency which has become increasingly obvious in the United Nations, particularly during the last few years, is the increased and broadening cooperation within groups of countries with common fundamental interests. Sweden welcomes this development. These various groupings have considerable practical advantages in an organization with as many members as the United Nations. They also contribute to clarifying quickly what are the most important problems within each separate block of negotiations. In addition to this, these groupings can constitute a framework for working out common stands and how these positions can best be strengthened.
>
> However, there is also a risk that controversies may be deepened and accentuated for no real reasons. A stand which has been taken becomes difficult to give up or change, even if political and practical reasons make it advisable. It is our opinion that, in order to counteract such negative effects, Members and groups of Members should to a larger extent than at present make use of the possibilities that exist to consult with each other and with other Members or groups of Members.[15]

The largest single grouping in the United Nations is that of the nonaligned nations. Its vocation was described by President Abdelaziz Bouteflika of Algeria in his acceptance speech upon election to the presidency of the twenty-ninth General Assembly as follows:

> The movement of the nonaligned nations was born of the awakening awareness of the flaws in that international system, controlled as it was by the great Powers. Its primary objective was precisely to guarantee to small countries safety against the abuses of such a regime. The movement of nonaligned nations is constantly being strengthened in the crucible of its difficult undertaking; it is as close to an ideal on which it depends as to an international reality which it cannot ignore. . . .
>
> Policies used to be decided without us, against us, despite us. But we have conquered the right to make ourselves heard, to be allowed to participate actively and helpfully. It is true we are merely at the first stages of the inevitable movement of ideas. But the ideas are moving, and they show us a foretaste of the architecture of tomorrow's society. . . .
>
> The development of the movement of the nonaligned in the course of the last few years must be considered a phenomenon whose importance and ramifications yield in no way to those of the detente that has taken place in the relations between the two super-Powers. The new dimensions it has acquired and the dynamic which is constantly shown by it make it a weighty participant in world affairs. . . .
>
> . . . Its acts are based upon the solidarity of the countries of the Third World and thus are intended above all to bring into relations among nations this new factor of justice and humanity which the prodigious development of the power of some had obscured. . . .[16]

That each Member State should look to its own national interests when deciding to vote for or against a particular proposal is not unnatural; that like-minded nations and their allies should unite to give voice to the views they hold in common and to score against their adversaries is understandable. Neither the Charter nor the canons of traditional international law and diplomatic practice bar governments, separately or jointly, from exploiting to their advantage the actual and potential opportunities afforded by membership in international organizations. But the United Nations cannot work its wonders in conditions in which those who invoke the Charter do not know the virtue of self-restraint in international affairs. The guiding and compelling motive of self-interest seems to exist in an overwhelming degree in the United Nations, where it is aggravated by the fact that governments not only act in accordance with the interests of their respective countries, but often also in accordance with the interests of the group of States to which they belong. Frequently, too, governments act in accordance with the decisions of the group caucus.

The proclivity of States Members to overtax their power of judgment and to yield to their own sympathies lies astride all efforts to rescue the world body from its own excesses. The warning the late U Thant made in his annual report to the General Assembly in 1971 against the irresponsible use of the vote has only been reinforced by the passage of time. The General Assembly, the late Secretary-General wrote,

> offers the smaller and the medium Powers not only a voice, but also a way of influencing the course of events far in excess of what was previously available to them. To really exercise this influence, however, the majority must make it plain that they will listen to both sides of a case and not only to the larger faction. The majority must prove that they will seek a realistic way out of difficulties rather than resort to condemnation or threats.
>
> It would be a grave pity if the smaller and medium Powers throw away their opportunity and fail to establish some collective credibility through a more realistic approach to what they can and cannot do. Such failure would strengthen the criticisms of the United Nations which are increasingly heard and which could, in the long run, destroy the Organization. On the contrary, if the opportunity is grasped by those concerned, the Organization can look forward to a future bright with hope and success. The General Assembly, in particular, could become increasingly effective over the whole field of United Nations operations, including the maintenance of peace and security, primary responsibility of which is vested in the Security Council. The Assembly also has responsibilities in this field, however, and any balanced sober recommendations which it can adopt will surely not go unheeded even in the most powerful nations of the world.[17]

"The nonaligned Group", Sri Lanka's Ambassador Hamilton Shirley Amerasinghe and Chairman of the Group told the 1974 General Assembly,

> is today more united, numerically stronger, and better placed than it ever was to exert its influence on the course of international relations in the political, economic, and social spheres and thereby to fortify the United Nations in all efforts directed towards the application and enforcement of the principles and purposes of the Charter. If we are to fulfil this high mission, we must be wary of besmirching our credentials by the least manifestation of partisanship. The nonaligned Group must treat all nations as friends while dissociating itself from, and striving united to secure the abolition of, policies and practices repugnant to the ideals and objectives of nonalignment.[18]

U Thant's admonition, like so many others before and after, has gone unheeded: United Nations resolutions and decisions have only continued to add to the strain the international Organization had long ago put on simple truths.[19] Since votes are what characterize United Nations actions, the swelling number of resolutions which are products of deeply-held emotion rather than soundly-based reason and which substitute wishful thinking for recognizable reality, provides persuasive evidence of a state of mind that demands attention and holds a claim that cannot be denied. Partisan peeves and animosities find strong echoes in resolutions adopted by the General Assembly and other organs of the United Nations; but even those that are of good intent and might serve as high water marks of human endeavor often outdistance the capacity of the international Organization to implement them. Frequently, these resolutions tend to ignore the differing framework of the national structures and juridical systems of the Member States; they lack the element of balance which should be the hallmark of a body charged with the high responsibilities laid down in the Charter. "We shall never be equal to what the world expects of us and to the tasks entrusted to us by the Charter", French Ambassador Luis de Guiringaud told the General Assembly on 6 December 1974,

> if we cannot organize our interdependence by reconciling our interests. Since no decision can be applied in this sphere if it is not backed by those who have State power, the clash of sovereignties . . . thus emerges into the full light of day. There are only two possibilities: either we adopt texts in which a majority will find political comfort but which remain inoperable; or we try to reach real agreements which will be binding on all the parties concerned and which will subsequently be reflected in the policies and decisions of Member States. The latter course is possible only if the groups mainly concerned negotiate patiently in appropriate conditions of equality and after sufficient preparations. Unfortunately, that is not the case because, I must say frankly, of certain wanderings we have noted off the true course of the inter-State relations with which we are and shall remain concerned, such aberrations are more and more manifest in the manner in which the majority, wittingly or unwittingly, conducts our negotiations on a number of essential issues. I wonder, like U Thant, whether the present majority is really making it plain that they will listen to both sides of a case and not only to the larger faction.
>
> The procedure employed in certain committees—particularly the Second Committee—make that doubtful. A private club seems to be emerging which monopolizes the scene, deciding what contacts are to be made, what methods used, raising insoluble problems, rounding up unconvinced

cosponsors in the hope of wresting from the various minorities ambiguous concessions which are inevitably meaningless when it comes to implementing the recommendations, because they are found unacceptable to the States asked to give them effect. We are thus always on the edge of clashes likely to lead to dangerous confrontations. Thus we are likely to provoke indifference, incomprehension or the actual hostility of countries, without which, nothing important can be done.[20]

United States Ambassador John Scali put it more bluntly when he warned that

> Each time this Assembly adopts a resolution which it knows will not be implemented, it damages the credibility of the United Nations. Each time this Assembly makes a decision which a significant minority of members regard as unfair or one-sided, it further erodes vital support for the United Nations among the minority. But the minority which is so offended may in fact be a practical majority, in terms of capacity to support this Organization and implement its decisions. Unenforceable, one-sided resolutions destroy the authority of the United Nations. Far more serious, however, they encourage disrespect for the Charter, and for the traditions of our Organization.
>
> No organization can function without an agreed-upon framework of rules and regulations. The framework for this Organization was built in the light of painful lessons learned from the disastrous failure of its predecessor, the League of Nations. Thus, the United Nations Charter was designed to ensure that the important decisions of this Organization reflected real power relationships and that decisions, once adopted, could be enforced. . . .
>
> The function of all parliaments is to provide expression to the majority will. Yet, when the rule of the majority becomes the tyranny of the majority, the minority will cease to respect or obey it, and the parliament will cease to function. Every majority must recognize that its authority does not extend beyond the point where the minority becomes so outraged that it is no longer willing to maintain the covenant which binds them. . . .
>
> We are all aware that true compromise is difficult and time-consuming, while bloc voting is fast and easy. But real progress on contentious issues must be earned. Paper triumphs are in the end expensive even for the victors. The cost is borne, first of all by the United Nations as an institution, and in the end by all of us. Our achievement cannot be measured in paper. . . .
>
> If the United Nations ceases to work for the benefit of all its Members, it will become increasingly irrelevant. It will fade into the shadow world of rhetoric, abandoning its important role in the real world of negotiation and compromise.[21]

Clearly, the voting in the United Nations, in the words of Ambassador C. W. A. Schurmann, former permanent representative of the Netherlands,

> is not determined by judgements about rights and wrongs in any conflict or proposal, not even always by national interest. In many cases what determines the vote of a delegation is the general view (or interest) of any of the groups to which it happens to belong: Communist or non-Communist, rich or poor countries, Western, Latin American, African and Asian groups and various others.[22]

And there is no way of barring any organ of the United Nations from adopting resolutions and taking decisions within its generally recognized sphere of competence which it deems proper, and no way of challenging their propriety and constitutionality. As Professor Salo Engel suggested, under the Charter there are only limited, if any, possibilities for judicial or political review of the constitutionality of action by a judicial or a political organ.[23] A State Member which considers itself aggrieved by the actions of any organ of the United Nations and is unable to summon the necessary votes to bend the views of the majority in its favor, has no other recourse than submission, resignation or withdrawal; it is as if a citizen or corporate body could make no appeal to a court of justice for redress of wrongs, and as if the sole power of reference on the constitutionality of a legislative act lay with the very legislative body that is responsible for it. Whatever impact United Nations resolutions and decisions may have on international issues, they all too often work havoc with the principles they address and have the erosive effect of attrition on the countries at which they are aimed. The sweeping resolutions adopted by the General Assembly and other United Nations organs for the promotion of ostensibly worthy causes contribute to the crystallization of moods and tempers which are hostile to the States concerned and inimical to their vital national interests.

It is not juridical doctrine that determines the authority of United Nations resolutions and decisions. Law is not the governing principle of the world body,[24] and if the position it occupies is an ambivalent one, it is because of the basic revolutionary attitude of many States Members which are more concerned with seeing the law changed than with seeing their rights enforced; they are bound by law to the forms and procedures of a formal, conservative legal process, but have political sympathies with a vision of revolution. Perhaps the Foreign Minister of Benin was not wide of the mark when he told the General Assembly on 10 October 1978 that:

> Throughout the world today, the dominant and irreversible trend of the struggle of the people is towards revolution. In Asia, in Latin America and, more particularly, in Africa, the situation is characterized by the struggle of countries and peoples to snap the chains of imperialist domination, to put an end once and for all to reactionary social and economic structures inherited from colonialism and neocolonialism and to take their destiny into their own hands.[25]

The real justification for the many United Nations resolutions and decisions must be sought outside the scope of juridical arguments. The order of the Charter is a political one and it is the political force placed at their service, the power alignment behind them, their objectives and concrete interests that determine the weight of United Nations decisions. The tendency of States to draw together in the international Organization in voting blocs on the basis of their special interests and their estimate of parliamentary realities has placed States Members at the mercy of blocs which command sufficient votes to initiate, prevent or abort action of any kind. Thus, while the flexibility to respond to change and dynamics afforded by the political rather than jural order of the Charter may be welcome to an organization of such heterogeneous membership and cultural differences as is the United Nations, it is all too often achieved at the expense of third parties and the moral integrity of the world Organization.

We have noted at the beginning that the United Nations can neither be captured nor dismissed by one all-encompassing act of commission or omission. By the same token, its salient characteristics can neither be gleaned from an analysis of its functions nor deduced from the records of its achievements or failures. What takes place at the United Nations is the consequence of an entire manifold of interlocking causes, which beckon us to search for constants that are valid beyond the vagaries of individual events. Failing that, the best way perhaps in which we can hope to record the pulsating reality of the international Organization is to focus on case studies which seek not only to illustrate and illuminate the more pronounced traits of the United Nations, but to peer past the details of action into the structure of the world body. While, as times goes on, the themes that monopolize our attention today are bound to get off the active agenda of the United Nations along with other seemingly perennial issues, the events they had set in motion, the problems they had engendered and the ideas they had inspired are such that they can illuminate events rather than be outdated by them. Also, while in time the problems themselves may disappear, their underlying causes will always remain relevant. We now turn to the first of the several case studies.

NOTES

1. Notre Jeunesse, 1910; 2nd ed., 1933, Editions Gallimard, 15 rue Sebastien, Bothin, Paris, p. 240.
2. Advisory Opinion of 26 July 1962 on Certain Expenses of the United Nations, p. 21.
3. Department of Public Information, Press Release SG/356, 30 November 1953, pp. 3–4.
4. Office of Public Information, Press Release SG/SM/1694, ORG/714, p. 3.
5. A/PV.2243, p. 52.
6. From time to time Governments have called urgent attention to this problem. See, for example, Canada's observations of June 1978 on General Assembly resolution 32/106 of 15 December 1977 entitled "Comprehensive Review of the Whole Question of Peace-keeping Operations in All their Aspects", suggesting that the establishment of a peace-keeping operation should be linked to an agreement for a political settlement, or at least a reasonable expectation of a negotiated settlement. Canada also suggested that whenever possible the Security Council should include in the terms of the peace-keeping operation the mode of settlement, be it in the form of mediation, good offices or direct negotiations between the parties concerned (Comprehensive Review of the Whole Question of Peace-keeping Operations in All their Aspects, A/AC.121/28, pp. 4–5).

A similar suggestion was made by the United Kingdom, which urged that more attention should be paid to the relationship between the functions of observer missions or peace-keeping forces and the promotion of an enduring and just settlement in the areas in question (ibid., p. 22).

A variety of proposals have been advanced by various States Members at meetings of the Special Committee on Enhancing the Effectiveness of the

Principle of the Non-Use of Force in International Relations. For example, Finland suggested that any pledge to refrain from the use of force would have only limited effect unless it was universally recognized and accompanied by a commitment to settle disputes by peaceful means alone. The prevention of the use of force should be accompanied by an improvement in the means of cooperation and in procedures for the peaceful settlement of disputes (A/AC.193/SR.9, p. 5). Ecuador maintained that it was of the utmost importance that peaceful settlement of disputes be made obligatory on a global basis, not only as a responsibility of the parties to a dispute, but as a duty of the international community (ibid., p. 2). In general, a widely-shared view is that the fact that the United Nations had not been able to establish an efficient system for the peaceful settlement of disputes constitutes a major shortcoming of the world Organization.

7. A/10289, *passim*.

8. Report of the Special Committee on the Charter of the United Nations and on the Strengthening of the Role of the Organization, 1978. A/33/33, pp. 63–69.

9. United Nations Day address, 1964. Office of Public Information, Press Release SG/SM/174, 24 October 1964, p. 5.

10. Office of Public Information, Press Release SG/SM/2543, 8 March 1978, pp. 1–2.

On another occasion, Secretary-General Waldheim, addressing the Biennial Convention of the United Nations Association of the United States in New York on 18 April 1977 said:

> The fact that the Security Council held more meetings last year than ever before in its history may demonstrate that in the minds of Governments at least there seems to be no alternative to the admittedly imperfect procedures of the United Nations in time of global crisis. However, I would be less than frank with you if I were to pretend that the influence of the Security Council is commensurate with the number of meetings it holds. There is, in fact, a growing anxiety among the Members about the capacity of the Security Council, in the present political circumstances, to fulfil the task entrusted to it by the Charter, the maintenance of international peace and security. In my opinion, no problem facing the United Nations is more vital than strengthening the effectiveness of the Security Council. The ways in which this body is used, and the respect, or lack of it, for its decisions, should be given the closest attention by all Member States (OPI Press Release SG/SM/2434, p. 5).

11. Introduction to the Annual Report of the Secretary-General on the Work of the Organization quoted by former Assistant Secretary of State for International Organization Affairs of the United States, Joseph J. Sisco in an address before the United Nations Association in New York, 19 September 1965. Department of State, Press Release No. 226, p. 5.

12. Abraham Yeselson and Anthony Caglione, *A Dangerous Place: The United Nations as a Weapon in World Politics*, Grossman Publishers, New York, 1974, p. x.

13. Michael Stephen, *Natural Justice at the United Nations: The Rhodesia Case*, American Journal of International Law 67 (3) July, 1973, pp. 489–490. The study concerns the refusal of the Security Council and the General Assembly to give the Smith regime an opportunity to lay its case before the United Nations, even though there were precedents for it. For a similar study concerning the refusal of the International Court of Justice to accede to South Africa's application for seating a Judge ad hoc in the advisory proceedings regarding Namibia in 1971, see Michla Pomerance's article *The Admission of Judges ad hoc in Advisory Proceedings: Some Reflections in the Light of the Namibia Case*, ibid., pp. 446–464. On the subject of Judges ad hoc, see Leo Gross, *The International Court of Justice: Considerations of Requirements for Enhancing its Role in the International Legal Order*, ibid., 65 (2) April, 1971, pp. 295–301.

14. TD/B/175/Add.3, 3 September 1968, p. 7.

15. A/PV.2307, pp. 63–65.

16. A/PV.2233, pp. 26–38.

17. Introduction to the Report of the Secretary-General on the Work of the Organization, 1971, A/8401/Add.1, pp. 95–96.

18. A/PV.2263, p. 32.

19. For example, speaking to the subject of strengthening the role of the United Nations, the representative of the German Federal Republic warned that

> an organization able to safeguard peace and to promote international cooperation can never implement its decisions unless it also takes account of the interests of the minority. That requirement would be fulfilled if in draft resolutions the majority renounced use of intransigent and immoderate language, which only aggravates existing conflicts. I should also like to stress that confident cooperation and the effectiveness of the United Nations are considerably reduced when rules of procedure are abused for political purposes . . . (A/PV.2307, 1974, p. 38–40).

20. A/PV.2307, pp. 31–32.

21. Ibid., pp. 47–56.

22. *Two Kinds of Diplomacy*. An Address by Ambassador Carl W. A. Schurmann at the Sixty-third Annual Meeting of the American Society of International Law, Proceedings, Vol. 63, April, 1969, p. 249.

23. See, for example, Professor Salo Engel's address at the 59th Annual Meeting of the American Society of International Law, entitled *Procedures for the De Facto Revision of the Charter*, Proceedings, 1965, pp. 108–115.

24. See, for example, Professor Maxwell Cohen's address at the 54th Annual Meeting of the American Society of International Law entitled *Reflections on the Law and the United Nations System*, Proceedings, 1960, pp. 243–253.

25. A/33/PV.29, p. 107.

Chapter II

FLEXIBILITY AND PRINCIPLE

The United Nations, as we have seen, is a political, not jural, order. Indeed, the glory of the Charter and its relevance derive precisely from its nature as an instrument of infinite accommodation and its ability to slice through life in pursuit of its aims uninhibited by a tradition which rejects change. There is merit to the suggestion that the viability of the United Nations depends not so much upon the consistency with which it applies the law of the Charter as upon its ability to make decisions dictated by time and circumstance. "A great source of strength in the United Nations", Ambassador James T. Wadsworth told a meeting of the American Association for the United Nations in 1957,

> is its flexibility. In the beginning many people thought we could write laws to fit all circumstances and thus build our structure of peace on a base of legal precepts, to which all men would give allegiance. But it has become apparent that in the world as we know it today there is no common agreement on basic concepts of right and wrong—or even on the meaning of words. In these circumstances attempts to codify ideals and render them into laws usually end up by giving propaganda advantages to those who are the most cynical, the most propaganda-minded and the most eager to deceive their fellow-men.[1]

The history of the United Nations confirms that the Charter has in fact been a flexible instrument, susceptible of growth and development to the extent that the Member States have been prepared to see it grow and develop. It also bears out the fact that

> most interpretations of the Charter leading to the development of the United Nations system have been made politically by political organs rather than juridically by the International Court . . . Political interpretation has enabled the organization on many occasions to free itself from its

> own rules and limitations and had often permitted action when strict legal interpretation would have foreclosed or hobbled it.[2]

Surely the institutional development of the United Nations has long ago transcended the tidy original mold of the Charter. Not only has the international Organization been transformed into an institution more than thrice its original size but the areas of its concern and involvement have expanded vastly in number and substance; they range from outer space to the depths of the seas and embrace virtually everything that lies in-between in the political, economic, social, cultural, humanitarian, scientific and technological spheres.[3] It is the result of pressures brought to bear upon the world body by developments abroad, especially the immensely rapid and widespread awakening of political consciousness and racial nationalism; the vast increase in population, and the equally vast demands for raising the standard of living for all peoples everywhere. These developments have subjected the United Nations to severe strains and demanded an effort that was not foreseen at San Francisco. The United Nations could not remain passive and survive.

Survive it did. The question is whether in responding to challenges the United Nations merely succumbed to pressures which converged upon it, or sought to reach the right compromise between competing interests and values by making decisions likely to advance the principles and purposes of the Charter. It is not merely a question of measuring means against predictable ends, but one of determining whether a consensus, decision or course of action was intended to harmonize the interests of the States Members for the promotion of the common good, or to press partisan viewpoints in the interests of one nation or group of nations. To be sure, it is no easy task to find reasonable balancing points between opposing views in conflicts which obstruct international cooperation. However, competing as the visions of the common good might be, the principles and purposes of the Charter are sufficiently clear to serve as universal criteria of judgment. The Preamble and Article 1 of the Charter, together with several provisions in Article 2, are precise enough to clarify the obligations of Member States and their consequential commitments.

Alas, while the United Nations was able through the continuous interpretation of the Charter in its daily encounter with the real world to enlarge the areas of its concern and to move further and further into the field of action, its flexibility also encouraged far-reaching changes in interpretation of the Charter without recourse to formal amendments.[4] In the absence of a self-regulating instrument that would resist inequities and injustices, the United Nations evolved into an organization where an automatic majority seems to reign supreme, without law and without judgment. Events over the past three decades bear witness to the dominating and decisive presence in the United Nations of practices and procedures that are unfettered by the constraints of the Charter and uninhibited by the more traditional forms of diplomatic discourse, and of a majoritarianism that is without internal rules and external accountability. These have emerged as major instruments of global policy making. When political expediency and the constellation of votes determine the evolution of international issues, the ultimate triumph of the United Nations in resolving conflicts among nations within the context of law, morality and international orderliness is placed in jeopardy.

The rise of so-called parliamentary diplomacy in the United Nations followed the collapse of all hopes for accommodation between the great Powers in an atmosphere of consultation as envisaged in 1945. When the Cold War made it impossible for the Soviet Union and the United States to deal directly with each other within the framework of the Security Council, the emphasis shifted to the veto-less General Assembly, where complex devices of parliamentary government became the order of the day. The advantages first lay with the United States, which could count on a loyal majority of old allies. The United for Peace resolution of 1950, initiated by the United States, was perhaps the single most daring attempt to alter the constitutional character of the United Nations. It drew the sting from the Soviet veto by mobilizing the United Nations' reserve powers and authorizing the General Assembly to vote for executive action whenever the Security Council was unable to act.[5]

But it did not take long before it was realized that if the General

Assembly were to become an effective and responsible instrument of parliamentary diplomacy its procedures and practices would have to be tailored accordingly. Speaking in the House of Lords on 18 December 1961, the Earl of Home, United Kingdom Secretary of State for Foreign Affairs, said:

> In the eighteen months that have passed since I have been Foreign Secretary I have persistently warned the country and the United Nations of the dangers which would result in the United Nations by reason of the fact that the balance of responsibility as it was laid down in the Charter has been upset. I can express these apprehensions and anxieties quite simply, one country, one vote is an ideal and a very good idea, but if that vote is not used with wisdom, discretion, tolerance and restraint, then the United Nations could become nothing less than a demonstration of power without responsibility.[6]

Earlier, Senator Mike Mansfield of the United States, a Member of the United States Delegation to the thirteenth session of the General Assembly in 1958, told an audience at Montana State College that

> The General Assembly is neither organized nor empowered to discharge executive functions. . . . Ways must be found to streamline and simplify the procedure of all United Nations bodies. . . . Ways must be found either to restore the integrity and the functions of the United Nations Security Council so that it can act with reasonable decisiveness on dangerous political questions or, alternatively, ways must be found to produce in the General Assembly a more accurate relationship between votes and the international responsibilities of the Member Nations. These changes are essential if the United Nations is to play its full part in building and maintaining world-wide stability.[7]

As a parliament, the General Assembly is bound to reflect the desires and goals of the majority; majority rule is everywhere regarded as the axiom of democratic government. Yet the principle of voting by majority, which makes sense in a homogeneous political context, is ill-adapted to the world of profound political and cultural schisms as represented by the United Nations. In the United Nations, for example, negotiations with an opponent rather than outvoting him might perhaps be a more promising procedure for resolving differences and agreeing upon common objectives. But the General Assembly has never seemed to have learned the importance of tempering politics by a clear-eyed awareness of its limits; its stance has been determined not by objective situations, but by the way the facts present themselves to a particular majority. As it acquired a taste for action and as it evolved sophisticated and not-so-sophisticated means of influencing world events, the General Assembly's powers and judgment became severely overtaxed. By 1960 the changes in the membership of the United Nations, the rise of blocs and groupings around common characteristics, interests and affinities of all kinds, as well as the emergence of new issues, combined to destroy the premise upon which the strengthening of the General Assembly's widened competence rested. The Soviet Union, which had been in a position of minority, could now make common cause with the newly-emerged nations to outvote the United States. Colonialism, self-determination, economic development and social justice were issues into which the Soviet Union could not only inject itself with profit, but they also gave it an advantage over the United States and its allies. The Soviet Union's anticolonialist posture as guardian of the true Marxist-Leninist faith, for example, was steadily broadened until it came to embrace Arab grievances as well, and the swirling minority of the past became a solid majority which exercised sweeping parliamentary power in the General Assembly and other organs and agencies of the United Nations.

The concentration on themes of great political and emotional intensity gave birth to aberrant interpretations of the Charter that have frequently overridden respect for law and for the common purposes inscribed in that basic document of the world Organization. The history of the decolonization campaign in the United Nations, for instance, holds many examples of grievous assaults on the integrity of the Charter and of the efforts to alter the terms by which it was understood and experienced. Ideas and principles have come to be employed as adversaries and their scope and content diminished or enlarged in accordance with the exigencies of the moment. Surely by the end of 1960 the end of colonial empire was at hand; nothing could have altered the course of history as the call for freedom echoed throughout the colonial world of old. Yet the issue of colonialism continued to monopolize the attention of the United Nations with undiminished intensity of feeling and commitment; governments and politicians continued to ride their hobby-horses long after the road had given out. Anticolonialism became one of the most potent ideologies pressing upon the international Organization.

Perhaps one of the principal reasons which explains the survival of anticolonialism as a living issue is the fact that its rhetoric, more than that of any other issue, lends itself to adaptation to fit new circumstances. The colonial revolution had been carried forward under the banner of national self-determination and social justice, and until these have been fully realized to the satisfaction of the Third World, colonialism will continue to be invoked to confront the developed nations in the global struggle for economic equality. Anticolonialism has also proved to be a convenient rallying cry for nations new and old. The existence of colonial regimes is not contrary to the Charter; in fact, the Charter lays down certain principles to govern colonial regimes, even while it looks forward to the ending of colonialism. But from the very beginning the term colonialism assumed a perjorative connotation and the debate on the subject in the United Nations proceeded on the assumption that the existence of a colony violated the letter and spirit of the Charter. The new nationalism that emerged after World War II, aided and abetted by doctrinaire anticolonialists, viewed the whole Western experience as a monolithic and unmitigated evil and even as a living and menacing threat, so much so that it led to a reading of the Charter to permit the unilateral use of force to combat the evil. It was clear that the struggle for decolonization was turned into a position to be won and maintained for greater revolutionary purposes.

Of that there can be no doubt. The Declaration on the Granting of Independence to Colonial Countries and Peoples, which Premier Nikita Krushchev presented as a birthday gift to the United Nations on the occasion of its fifteenth anniversary in 1960,[8] sought to make illegal what had long since become sinful. In reality, however, the Declaration and the creation the following year of a special committee to oversee the operation of the decolonization program inspired by it,[9] were more expressive of the dominating belligerence of the Soviet Union's strident anticolonialist posture than of objective needs; there was no special reason for a solemn announcement of a public commitment in the process of fulfilment. Having for years tried with studied intent to build up its image as champion of the colonial peoples, the Soviet Union strove to freeze that image into the popular conscience and to reap all the benefits that might accrue from it.[10]

The true nature and purpose of the Declaration becomes clearer when it is recalled that at the time it was placed on the agenda of the fifteenth session of the General Assembly in 1960, 1,500 million of the roughly 1,600 million colonial people at the end of World War II had, by Premier Krushchev's own admission, won their freedom. There is nothing in the lengthy memorandum the Soviet Premier submitted on 23 September 1960 for consideration by the General Assembly that pointed to the existence anywhere in what remained of the old colonial world of a situation that called for urgent and extraordinary measures to accelerate the decolonization process in order to save the 100 million people then still under colonial domination from impending catastrophe.[11] The hue and cry was raised by the Soviet Union and bore all the earmarks of a politicoideological ploy. "The States Members of the United Nations submitting this Declaration", the memorandum averred,

> are of the opinion that every Government which is for peace and progress in deeds, and not in words should respect the rights of all nations without exception in their demands for equality, justice and independence. Either these demands will be recognized by all States or the oppressed peoples, with the support of their numerous friends throughout the world, will take their destiny in their own hands and will win liberty and independence, breaking down all the artificial barriers erected in their way by the colonialists. The primary duty of all nations is to extend a helping hand in the sacred struggle for independence and against colonialist domination.[12]

Resolution 1514(XV) was adopted on 14 December 1960 by a roll-call vote of 89 in favor, none against and 9 abstentions. Those abstaining were: Australia, Belgium, Dominican Republic, France, Portugal, Spain, South Africa, United Kingdom and United States. Although the Soviet text of the Declaration was not put to the vote as a whole after its first three substantive paragraphs were rejected, its spirit and much of its letter permeated the Afro-Asian text which was finally adopted and remained an integral part of it. They are perhaps best embodied in paragraph 5 of the Declaration which enjoins that,

> Immediate steps shall be taken, in Trust and Non-Self-Governing Territories which have not yet been attained independence, to transfer all powers to the peoples of those territories, without any conditions or reservations, in accordance with their freely expressed will and desire, without any distinction as to race, creed or color, in order to enable them to enjoy complete independence and freedom.

The Declaration is one of the most striking examples of the tendency of the General Assembly to make new law and to impose it on the States Members of the United Nations. Some of the Declaration's provisions are unquestionably new law which is not to be found in the Charter or in traditional international law. Surely paragraph 3 of the Declaration providing that

> Inadequacy of political, economic, social and educational preparedness should never serve as a pretext for delaying independence;

Paragraph 4, providing that,

> all armed action or repressive measures of all kinds directed against dependent peoples shall cease in order to enable them to exercise peacefully and freely their right to complete independence, and the integrity of their national territory shall be respected;

and Paragraph 5, providing for the immediate transfer of all powers to the peoples in territories which had not yet attained independence, are revisions of parts of Articles 2(7), 73(a) and 73(b) of the Charter, as is Paragraph 7 of the Declaration which states unequivocally that all States must "observe faithfully and strictly . . ." the present Declaration.[13] This was a bold attempt on the part of the General Assembly to modify existing law governing the acquisition and loss of territory and giving the United Nations supervisory and guidance power, as well as legislative power, with respect to colonial questions. The General Assembly went to the maximum limit of its own interpretation of the Charter in securing compliance with its resolutions and decisions.

That a document which is not formally binding upon the international community was able to shape a doctrinal position involving the destiny of peoples and nations and to impose it unbidden on the larger world is a tribute to the power of propaganda in the service of a great Power. That the Declaration has become a siren voice whose attraction a large part of humanity has found it difficult to resist may be explained, as Professor Stoessinger put it, by the fact that,

> Although the record demonstrates that Western colonialism is largely a phenomenon of the past, the new nationalism acts as if it were very much alive. Indeed, as we have seen, in the life of the new nations the past often lives on with a fierce intensity. . . . Hence the struggle over colonialism, too, is intensified by great divergencies between image and reality.[14]

But the moral ambivalence of the Declaration is as obvious as its ideological origins are unmistakable. At issue is the application of the right of peoples to self-determination. Referred to as a principle in Articles 2(1) and 55 of the Charter, it entered the canon of rights on the wave of decolonization and was elevated to the status of primordial law. In large measure the recognition which the Charter accords the principle of self-determination confirms the acceptance already accorded to community interest in nonindependent peoples in post-World War I treaties. In the United Nations, however, this interest was catapulted to a major governing principle of contemporary international relations and became a battle-cry for all who were impatient of political, economic and social change in the colonial world.[15]

As defined in the Declaration and in the International Covenants on Human Rights, self-determination is a right belonging to all peoples by virtue of which

> they freely determine their political status and freely pursue their economic, social and cultural development.

It is a complex concept, consisting of a variety of notions and susceptible of different forms of application. As Professor Rupert Emerson noted,

> . . . while self-determination lends itself to simple formulation in words which have a ring of universal applicability and perhaps of revolutionary slogans, when the time comes to put it into operation it turns out to be a complex matter hedged in by limitations and caveats.[16]

Self-determination also varies with the definition of the peoples which stand to benefit from its exercise and with the territories involved. At the end of World War I, for example, self-determination was limited to a relatively closely-defined category of peoples and territories in Eastern Europe, the Balkans and the Middle East, and applied to ethnic communities, nations or nationalities primarily defined by language and culture; the justification for the claim to self-determination was the subjection of ethnically-different peoples to alien rule. Where, as was the case in much of Central Europe, people of different language and national consciousness were mixed together in such an incredible mosaic of unassimilated minorities as to render the exercise of self-determination impractical, special protection accorded to minorities served as a corollary and corrective to self-determination.[17] In the new dispensation after World War II, ethnic identity became totally irrelevant to the claim to self-determination; the decisive, ordinarily sole consideration has been the existence of a political entity in the guise of a colonial territory. It has neither a corollary nor a corrective.

The most ardent and the most eloquent champions of self-determination in the United Nations have carried on their struggle within the context of anticolonialism; the debates on the issues in United Nations bodies proceeded on the assumption that the very existence of colonies was contrary to the Charter. This, as has been noted, was a misreading of the basic text of the international Organization. As was suggested by the representative of Sweden in the Third Committee of the tenth session of the General Assembly in 1955,

> The Swedish delegation did not consider that Articles 1 and 55 of the Charter represented a codification of the right of peoples to self-determination. They could not be construed as proclaiming a general right which could be exercised by any country or any nation in order to alter its status by breaking its ties with the metropolitan country. They meant that relations between Member States should be based on the mutual obligation to respect their right of self-determination. Having regard to the circumstances in which the Charter was drafted, it was impossible to claim that the authors of the Charter had intended to produce an instrument with which to settle colonial problems. The provisions of Article 2(7) confirmed that view. If the principle of self-determination was to be given the status of an inviolable right, there would have to be explicit provisions to that effect either in the Charter or in another legal instrument, and the conditions in which that right could be exercised would have to be clearly defined.

> In the view of the Swedish delegation, the notion of self-determination was expressly recognized by the Charter, not as a right but as a guiding principle. Article 76 provided for progressive development towards self-government or independence. The United Nations was of course required to intervene if a colonial dispute was likely to threaten international peace and security, but fortunately the experience of the past ten years has shown that colonial peoples had been able to achieve independence in a climate of peace and understanding without the need for United Nations intervention . . .[18]

Sweden's was one of the last moderate voices heard in the General Assembly on the subject of self-determination. The wave of the future was resolution 637 A (VII) of 16 December 1952, which declared:

> The States Members of the United Nations shall recognize and promote the realization of the right to self-determination of the peoples of Non-Self-Governing and Trust Territories who are under their administration and shall facilitate the exercise of this right by the peoples of such territories according to the principles and spirit of the Charter of the United Nations in regard to each territory and the freely expressed wishes of the peoples concerned, the wishes of the people being ascertained through plebiscites or other recognized means, preferably under the auspices of the United Nations.
>
> The States Members of the United Nations responsible for the administration of Non-Self-Governing and Trust Territories shall take practical steps, pending the realization of self-determination in preparation thereof, to ensure the direct participation of the indigenous population in the legislative and executive organs of government of these territories, and to prepare them for complete self-government and independence.

In reality, of course, decolonization did not necessarily follow the path prescribed by the General Assembly in its resolution of 1952; people were rarely consulted and the African States followed the arbitrary boundaries of the colonizers. More than an offense to the sensibilities of those who would uphold the integrity of the Charter, the distortion of the meaning and intent of Articles 2(1) and 55 of the Charter and the insistence upon equating self-determination with the right to statehood engendered tragic problems which have been unfolding since the end of World War II. In the haste to bring freedom and independence to the colonial peoples, a grave and lasting injustice was done to millions the world over not only outside the colonial sphere, but within the colonial sphere itself. "The noble principle of self-determination", Egypt's member of the Sub-Commission on the Prevention of Discrimination and the Protection of Minorities, Ahmed Khalifa said in a statement in the Sub-commission on 6 September 1978,

> has sometimes been used to "atomize" the world into small countries which were unable to stand on their own feet. A national flag and a figurehead was all that was needed to create a State.[19]

On the other hand, many peoples, nations and nationalities which met objective criteria for entitlement to self-determination were barred from asserting their claims by the overwhelming concentration on decolonization, while the wilful disregard of the ethnic factor in the determination of the boundaries of newly-established States was as cruel a negation of self-determination as colonialism itself.[20]

The right to self-determination is a regulative principle that either applies universally or it is no principle at all; it must be honored at home as well as abroad. But the Declaration of 14 December 1960 recognizes self-determination as valid only within the context of colonialism as defined by a majority in the General Assembly. Outside that context, the right of self-determination is practically outlawed. By declaring unconditionally that

> any attempt aimed at the partial or total disruption of the national unity and the territorial integrity of a country is incompatible with the purposes and principles of the Charter of the United Nations,

resolution 1514(XV) has for many years inhibited the United Nations from even as much as paying nodding attention to the racial, religious, linguistic and ethnic diversity in the world and thus begin the complex and demanding task of uncovering a reality that partisan interest has so long obscured. The United Nations cannot studiously close its eyes to the existence of problems which preceded colonialism and are likely to survive long after the memory of colonialism has faded into the pages of history. For it is precisely within the domain of established States that the right of self-determination is deeply engaged, is often crucial and permanently relevant. Thus, far from being an instrument of imaginative sympathy, the Declaration is ultimately contemptuous of deep concerns felt by a world made turbulent by ceaseless and accelerated change.

It is clear that the sponsors of the Declaration did not try to gauge the long-term consequences of their initiative, nor relate its effects to the total purpose of the United Nations. By narrowing international concern to classic forms of colonialism, the Declaration served to distort the true perspective of self-determination and the proportions of the problems it engendered and helped create dilemmas to plague future generations. Addressing the 1968 annual meeting of the American Society of International Law Evgeny, E. Nasinovsky, the then Legal adviser to the Permanent Mission of the U.S.S.R. to the United Nations, said:

> The principle of self-determination, that came into being as a program demand of the popular masses who fought against social and national oppressions, became, ever since the emergence of the Soviet State, a major principle, the basis for the construction of national and state institutions in the country. It also became a major principle in the foreign policy of the Soviet State which, ever since its inception, has steadfastly been carrying it into effect and working for its international recognition and confirmation in international law. Inclusion in the U.N. Charter of provisions on the right to self-determination is a major success in this respect. Thanks to the initiative and skill of Soviet diplomacy the right of nations to self-determination has also been given extensive treaty confirmation in such acts as the International Covenant on Civil and Political Rights, and the International Covenant of Economic, Social and Cultural Rights. Such treaty confirmation of the major principle of international law was effected despite the resistance on the part of the Western powers. Steadfastly upholding the principle of self-determination of peoples, the U.S.S.R. has invariably sought this principle to be applied to the peoples of colonial and dependent countries.
>
> The Declaration on Granting Independence to Colonial Countries and Peoples, which has been adopted on the initiative of the the Soviet Union, is a testimonial of the international recognition of the principle of self-determination of peoples which should be unreservedly applied with regard to the peoples of colonial and dependent countries. Hence the recognition of the legality, within the framework of international law, of the struggle of colonial countries for their freedom and independence, for exercising their (inalienable) right to self-determination. Hence the recognition of the fact that colonialism contradicts international law, and recognition, as a logical consequence thereof, that colonialism constitutes an international crime, a

crime against humanity, and this has been recognized in well-known decisions of the United Nations.

Thus we may say that once the principle of self-determination of nations propounded by the Soviet State, has become one of the most important principles of international law, it has begun to play a major role in the great social movement of contemporary life, in an epoch-making liberation of hundreds of millions of people of colonial and dependent countries from the yoke of colonialism.[21]

The move from rejection of colonialism to support of its overthrow by force of arms is not an automatic step. But it was inevitable as it was unavoidable. The fierce anticolonialism which had gripped the United Nations soon became a handmaiden of larger political forces and enabled the Soviet Union to hold out practical hope of making the anticolonialist commitment come true and to draw upon a much-vaunted tradition. For example, among the conditions for admission to the Communist International laid down by the second Congress of the Comintern in July 1920, was the active support of liberation movements in the colonies by words and deeds. Section 8 of the program read:

> on the question of colonies and oppressed nations, the Parties of countries whose bourgeoisie possesses colonies and oppresses other nations should adopt a particularly clear attitude and line of action. . . . Any Party wishing to belong to the Third International has a duty mercilessly to expose the machinations of its imperialists in the colonies, and support with deeds as well as words any movement of liberation in the colonies, demanding the expulsion of its own imperialists, and in the hearts of workers at home rousing a true sense of fraternity for the working populations of colonies and oppressed nations, and instigating protest movements against all forms of oppression of colonial peoples, in the armies of their own countries.[22]

In November 1957, on the occasion of the 40th anniversary of the Revolution of 1917, the Soviet Communist Party boasted that:

> The existence of the Soviet Union and other socialist States who resolutely defend the Leninist principle of self-determination of peoples, considerably facilitates the struggle of the oppressed peoples for national independence and against colonialism. . . . The people which yesterday were still colonies or semicolonies and who have now chosen the path of independent development, may rely upon the altruistic aid of the Soviet Union and other socialist countries in the struggle to consolidate their economic and political independence against imperialist plots and ventures.[23]

The decision of the General Assembly in 1965 to recognize the legitimacy of wars of liberation and liberation movements[24] and its sanction five years later of their use of "any means at their disposal" to achieve their ends[25] were momentous in their implications; they added up to an official encouragement to extremists to take the path of violence and bloodshed to vindicate their claims. By absolving the liberation movements from the injunction of Article 2(4) of the Charter against the threat or use of force and by enjoining all States to provide material and moral assistance to the national liberation movements in colonial territories, the United States committed itself deeper and deeper to the twisted logic that professes to rationalize the murder of innocents as a response to social injustice, and to a reading of the Charter which virtually invites the unilateral use of force against colonialism and eventually, as we shall see, against racial discrimination.

In his presidential address to the 1969 annual meeting of the American Society of International Law Oscar Schachter, former Director of the General Legal Division of the United Nations noted:

> . . .For the older generation the elimination of armed conflict has been the primary objective of international law. The prohibition against force, as in paragraph 4 of Article 2 of the Charter, is seen as the cardinal tenet of existing international law. Much of the resources and energy of the international legal community, official and private, has gone into bolstering and extending that tenet. Yet in recent years, at first almost imperceptibly, we have witnessed a countertrend toward the justification and, one might say, the licensing of international violence. The countertrend has been closely associated with the efforts to eliminate racism and with the movement for decolonization and national independence. In those contexts, attitudes have crystallized in the direction of legitimizing the use of armed force to change the existing situation. Interpretations have been advanced—not limited to extremist groups—that the Charter provisions on self-defense and on self-determination provide adequate legal authority for the use of armed means to overthrow oppressive regimes in power. Nor have these views been limited to theory. . . .[26]

While international law does not restrict revolution within States or revolution against colonial authority, it does restrict what third parties may lawfully do in support of insurrection. "It is these restrictions", former Secretary of State of the United States, Dean Rusk, observed,

> which are challenged by the doctrine and violated by the practice of "war of liberation". It is plain that acceptance of the doctrine of "wars of liberation" would amount to scuttling the modern international law of peace which the Charter prescribes. And acceptance of the practice of "wars of liberation" as defined by the Communists, would mean the breakdown of peace itself.[27]

The role assigned to the Declaration and to all resolutions flowing from it has been to call upon States to take action which not all were ready to take and to provoke efforts to secure implementation until it shaded into enforcement. The creation pursuant to General Assembly resolution 1654(XVI) of November 1961 of the Special Committee on the Situation with regard to the Implementation of the Declaration on the Granting of Independence to Colonial Countries and Peoples,

> to examine the application of the Declaration, to make suggestions and recommendations on the progress and extent of the implementation of the Declaration . . . and to carry out its task by employment of all means which it will have at its disposal within the framework of the procedures and modalities which it shall adopt for the proper discharge of its functions,

followed by repeated requests upon States Members to withhold assistance from colonial regimes, betrayed a pattern clearly aimed at stripping those regimes of their protective armor and breaking their will. The acquiescence of the overwhelming majority in these decisions, not so much out of conviction but because the lines were drawn between an inexorable will and an inadequate resistance, prepared the ground for the recognition and support of the so-called liberation movements.

This technique of aggressive violence known today as war of liberation has been ideologically defined as an extension of the class struggle and has been sanctioned as just war. It is part of the heritage bequeathed to the world by the October Revolution of 1917 and its paternity is proudly acknowledged. Thus in November 1960, while the text of the decolonization Declaration was being hammered out in the halls of the United Nations, the leaders of eighty-one Communist Parties who had met in Moscow issued a manifesto in which they declared:

Communists have always recognized the progressive, revolutionary significance of national liberation wars; they are the most active champions of national independence. The existence of the world socialist system and the weakening of the position of imperialism have provided the oppressed people with new opportunities of winning independence.[28]

The draft program of the Soviet Communist Party which Premier Nikita Krushchev submitted for approval by the 22nd Congress in October 1961 devoted much space to the emerging nations and declared that the alliance with former colonial peoples was a cornerstone of Soviet Party policy. "The socialist countries", we read;

are sincere and true friends of peoples fighting for their liberation and of those who have freed themselves from imperialist tyranny and render them all-around support. They stand for the abolition of all forms of colonial oppression and vigorously promote the strengthening of the sovereignty of the states rising on the ruins of colonial empires.

The C.P.S.U. considers fraternal alliance with the peoples who have thrown off colonial and semicolonial tyranny to be a cornerstone of its international policy. This alliance is based on the common vital interests of world socialism and the world national-liberation movement. The C.P.S.U. regards it as its internationalist duty to assist the peoples who have set out to win and strengthen their national independence, all peoples who are fighting for the complete abolition of the colonial system.[29]

Reaffirming its internationalist duty to render all assistance to the "peoples' struggle for final liberation from colonial and neocolonial oppression" the Communist Party of the Soviet Union, in the Report of its Central Committee delivered by Premier Leonid Brezhnev to the 23rd Congress on 29 March 1966, declared:

... The successes of the national liberation movements are inseparably bound up with the successes of world socialism and the international working class. The firm and unbreakable alliance of these great revolutionary forces is the guarantee of the final triumph of the cause of national and social liberation.[30]

Throughout, the Soviet Union has sought to secure international juridical recognition of the right of dependent and colonial peoples to struggle in arms for independence and to confer legitimacy upon liberation movements. While in the political sense, the Soviet Union and its allies and proxies argued, the struggle against colonialism had already been legalized by the decisions of the General Assembly and the Security Council, as well as by the "heroic sacrifices made in the cause of liberation", no modern formulation of the principles of international law was complete without a clear statement of the duty of States to refrain from repressive measures against colonial peoples struggling for independence and of the right of every such people to seek and receive assistance from other States.[31] They also argued that without those components no formulation of the principle of self-determination was acceptable.

It is difficult to assess the degree of earnestness with which the Soviet Union pursued its quest for juridical recognition of the rights of liberation movements accorded them by the General Assembly and other organs of the United Nations.[32] The ambivalence shown by nations toward a juridical definition of the right of self-determination explains their hesitation to confer juridical legitimacy upon the use of force by liberation movements.[33] They are both rooted in a pragmatism few dare ignore, including the Soviet Union. The years that have elapsed since the adoption of the decolonization Declaration of 1960 have not been able to erase all doubts surrounding the metamorphosis of self-determination from a political directive in 1945 to an institution of public international law in the course of barely a generation. It was by assertion, not by analysis, that the Declaration proclaimed the right of all peoples to self-determination; there is nothing in the Declaration to substantiate the claim by reference to any conventional source of international law or established international practice, nor to an authoritative interpretation of the Charter. As time went on, the Soviet initiative emerged ever more clearly as but a projection of politically-determined values extrapolated from postwar realities—the surge of anticolonialism, whose slogans and indoctrinating phrases blunted the perception of even the most objective mind. However well the Declaration may have served as an instrument of decolonization, States have been reluctant to go to the length of investing it with a juridical authority to sanction the use of force in the assertion of the right of self-determination lest it opens a Pandora's box to swell the ills of mankind.

In fact, the insistent effort to invest the Declaration with Charter-like authority, and to broaden the definition of colonialism in such a way as to embrace the racial situation in southern Africa and the Middle East dispute, compelled attention to the propulsive tendency of the United Nations to expand beyond legitimate boundaries. Thus it came to pass that, unlike the situation which obtained before the adoption of the Declaration, after 1960, scholars, diplomats and trained observers began to show greater concern for the question of the constitutionality of United Nations actions and decisions and the presence or absence of recourses available to aggrieved States Members. As Rosalyn Higgins related in her address to the sixty-fourth Annual Meeting of the American Society of International Law in 1970 on the subject of the United Nations and law making,

> In the early 1960s, when I first became interested in the subject, the proposition that the political organs of the United Nations were engaged in law making was regarded as novel. The view that political bodies developed law was variously described as pioneering or unorthodox, according to the viewpoint of the commentator. In the decade that has since elapsed, there have been many significant contributions to the literature which examine the extent, scope and limitations of this law-making activity. The greater change, perhaps, has been the gradual acknowledgement that, on the one hand, the basis of law is not solely contractual, and, on the other, that there is more at issue than a question of the formal legislative competence of the organs under discussion.[34]

In the final analysis, there is little need of risking the consequences of conferring legitimacy upon the use of force by liberation movements in open defiance of the Charter. From the practical point of view, it is the blessing bestowed upon these movements by the General Assembly that weighs in the scales. Its consequences are many and far-reaching. Already it has led to the widespread recognition of terrorism and violence carried out by liberation movements as legitimate instruments of rebellion and protest and both right and laudable. Terror has become increasingly an internationally-accepted political weapon yielded indiscriminately by so-called liberation movements of all kinds which are immune to the familiar peaceful procedures for settling conflicts. The inability of the United Nations to deal with the problem of international terrorism resolutely and effectively is due in no small measure to the attitude and action of States Members which are more concerned with safeguarding the freedom of action of the groups or movements with which they identify than with upholding the integrity of the Charter. The exceptions to the prohibition of the use or threat of force are expressly set forth in the Charter; they do not include threats to peace inherent in the doctrine of "just wars of liberation". Not surprisingly, Professor Albert A. Friedlander has commented,

> given the sovereignty explosion and prevailing international alignments, there has been almost a total lack of agreement within the world community on either the cause or the cure of the terrorist phenomenon. The cult of violence has become a ritual substitute for the use of reason in the political arena. Although there is widespread acknowledgement of the necessity for measures to deal with political terrorism, there has been almost no sense of international urgency towards creating viable judicial procedures and implementing legal controls. Until such time as a remedial consensus is reached, the politics of power will continue to make a mockery of the law of nations. . . .
>
> To say that randomized terror-violence utilized as a politicolegal strategy for ostensibly revolutionary ends can be condoned and even encouraged, simply because there is no peaceful or legitimate remedy for redress, is to replace the rule of law with the ancient credo of might makes right. . . .[35]

NOTES

1. United States Mission to the United Nations, Press Release No. 27-830, 24 October 1957.

2. Jack C. Plano and Robert E. Riggs, *Forging World Order*, Macmillan Co., New York, 1967, p. 55.

3. One need only consult the agenda of any recent regular session of the General Assembly to realize the scope of United Nations preoccupation. The Provisional Agenda of the 33rd session of the General Assembly in 1978, for example, lists 126 items (See A/33/100).

4. See, for example, Professor Salo Engel, *Procedures for De Facto Revision of the Charter*, op. cit., *passim.*

5. Under the resolution, adopted on 2 November 1950 by 52 votes to 5, with 2 abstentions, if there appears to be a threat to or breach of the peace or an act of aggression and the Security Council fails because of lack of unanimity among its permanent members to exercise its primary responsibility,

The General Assembly may be summoned at twenty-four hours' notice:
It may then make recommendations for collective measures by Member States, and
These recommendations may, in cases of a breach of the peace or act of aggression, include the use of armed force.

Furthermore,

A Peace Observation Commission was set up to observe and report on any area of tension where peace was likely to be endangered;
Member States were recommended to maintain elements within their national armed forces trained, organized and equipped for United Nations service, and
A Collective Measures Committee was established to study methods which might be used to maintain and strengthen world peace. (For a comprehensive review of the attitudes of the States Members to the resolution and of their expectations, see the *United Nations Bulletin* IX (10) 15 November 1950, pp. 498–523.)

6. From a release issued by the United Kingdom Mission to the United Nations.
7. United States Mission to the United Nations, Press Release No. 2033, 22 October 1958, p. 3.
8. For text, see Resolution 1514(XV).
9. The Special Committee on the Situation with Regard to the Implementation of the Declaration on the Granting of Independence to Colonial Countries and Peoples was established by the General Assembly pursuant to its resolution 1654(XVI) of 27 November 1961.
10. Cf. p. 48.
11. See Request for Inclusion of a New Item in the Agenda of the Fifteenth Session of the General Assembly: Item Proposed by the Union of Soviet Socialist Republics, Annex II. For text see A/4502/Corr. 1, 23 September 1960.
12. Ibid., p. 7.
13. The great majority in the United Nations would probably agree with the views of the Mexican representative on the Special Committee on the Charter of the United Nations and the Strengthening of the role of the Organization that, in practice, Chapters XI and XII of the Charter had been amended by the adoption of resolution 1514(XV) and the establishment of the Special Committee in 1961 (A/AC.182/SR.22, 28 February 1978, p. 3). See also Yassin El-Ayouty's *The United Nations and Decolonization*, The Hague, 1971, in which he argues that the adoption of the Decolonization Declaration marked the full-scale repudiation of colonialism and that the "delicate and legal balance of Chapter XI had become irrelevant", through a series of political interpretations of the Charter which brought about the internationalization of the colonial issue toward which the Afro-Asian bloc had consistently worked.

From time to time this thesis is challenged as a matter of principle. See, for example, the comment of the representative of the United States on the Mexican statement cited above (ibid.). See also Mr. Robert Rosenstock's statement in the Sixth Committee of the 32nd General Assembly in 1977, in which he took exception to the International Law Commission's commentary in its report on its 29th session in Geneva suggesting that the United Nations had developed the principle of permanent sovereignty over natural resources, by passing resolution 3201 entitled: Declaration on the Establishment of a New International Economic Order, and resolution 3281 entitled Charter of Economic Right and Duties of States (for portions of the statement see American Journal of International Law 72 (2) April, 1978, pp. 377–378).

14. *The Might of Nations: World Politics in Our Time*, Random House, New York, 1961, p. 413.

15. It may be of interest to note the reaction of the late Jamil Baroody, long-time representative of Saudi Arabia at the United Nations, who took the late Secretary-General Dag Hammarskjold to task for having referred to self-determination as a principle in a statement made on 11 October 1955 in the Third Committee (for the text of the Secretary-General's statement, see A/C.3/L.466; for Ambassador Baroody's comments, see A/C.3/SR.633, p. 4).

16. *Self-Determination*, American Journal of International Law 65 (3) 1971, p. 469.

17. See Jacob Robinson, *Were the Minorities Treaties a Failure?*, Institute of Jewish Affairs, New York, 1943, Ch. 3.

18. A/C.3/SR.641, pp. 6–7.

19. Office of Public Information, Press Release HR 1680, 2 September 1978, p. 2.

20. *Freedom at Issue*, published by Freedom House, New York, in the January–February 1978 issue cites the size and place of nationalities throughout the world which for one reason or another have been unable to exercise their right to self-determination as follows:

	Population (millions)	**Location**
Achehnese	2	Indonesia
Arabs of Chad	1.5	Chad
Armenians	2	U.S.S.R. (plus scattered millions)
Assamese	10	India
Aymara	1	Bolivia
Azerbaijani	4	U.S.S.R.
	5	Iran
Baluchis	2	Pakistan (and Iran)
Bamileke	1.5	Cameroon
Bantu of Rhodesia	6	Rhodesia
Bantu of S. Africa	14	S. Africa
Bashkir	1	U.S.S.R.
Basques	1	Spain (and France)
Batak	2.5	Indonesia
Berbers (various)	5	Algeria
	5	Morocco
Bosnian Muslims	1	Yugoslavia
Bretons	1	France
Buginese	3	Indonesia
Byelorussians	7	U.S.S.R.

	Population (millions)	**Location**
Catalonians	5	Spain
Chuang	8	China (Mainland)
Croats	4.5	Yugoslavia
Edo	3	Nigeria
Eritreans	1.5	Ethiopia
Estonians	1	U.S.S.R.
Ganda	2	Uganda
Georgians	3	U.S.S.R.
Gujerati	25	India
Hausa-Fulani	25	Nigeria
Hui	4	China (Mainland)
Ibibio	3.5	Nigeria
Ibo	14	Nigeria
Ilocanos	4	Philippines
Kannada	25	India
Kanuri	4	Nigeria
Karens	3	Burma
Kazakh	4.5	U.S.S.R.
Kirghiz	1.5	U.S.S.R.
Kongo	2	Zaire
	2	Angola (and Congo)

	Population (millions)	Location
Kurds	2	Iraq
	2	Turkey
	1	Iran
Latvians	1.5	U.S.S.R.
Lithuanians	2.5	U.S.S.R.
Luba-Kasai	1.5	Zaire
Luo	1	Kenya
Makassarese	2	Indonesia
Malayalam	20	India
Marathi	45	India
Mayans	4	Mexico (and Guatemala)
Mende	1	Sierra Leone
Miao	2.5	China (Mainland)
Minahassans	1	Indonesia
Minangkabau	5	Indonesia
Moluccans	1	Indonesia
Montagnards	1	Vietnam
Nilotics of Sudan	4	Sudan
Nkole	1	Uganda
Nupe	1	Nigeria
Oriyan	20	India
Oromo (Galla)	2–10	Ethiopia
Ovimbundu	2	Angola
Palestinian Arabs	2	Israel, Jordan, Lebanon, Syria
Pampangans	1.5	Philippines
Papuans	1	Indonesia
	1	Papua-New Guinea
Punjabi (India)	17	India
Quebecois	5	Canada
Quechua	5	Peru, Bolivia
	1	Ecuador

	Population (million)	Location
Scots	5	United Kingdom
Shan	1.5	Burma
Sidamo	2.5	Ethiopia
Sindhis	9	Pakistan
Slovaks	4.5	Czechoslovakia
Slovenes	1.5–2	Yugoslavia
Soga	1	Uganda
Sundanese	16	Indonesia
Taiwanese	14	China (Taiwan)
Tamil	40	India
	2.5	Sri Lanka
Tatars (various)	4	U.S.S.R.
Telegu	50	India
Teso	1	Uganda
Tibetans	3	China (Mainland)
	2	India, Pakistan, Nepal, Bhutan
Tigrinya	3	Ethiopia
Timorese	1	Indonesia
Tiv	8	Nigeria
Turkmen	1.5	U.S.S.R.
Uighur	4	China (Mainland)
Ukrainian	35–40	U.S.S.R.
Ulster Scots	1	United Kingdom
Uzbek	9	U.S.S.R.
	1	Afghanistan
Visayans	10	Philippines
Welsh	2.5	United Kingdom
Yi (Lolo)	3	China (Mainland)
Yoruba	16	Nigeria

21. *The Impact of Fifty Years of Soviet Theory and Practice of International Law*, Proceedings, Vol. 62, p. 193.

22. Quoted by Florent Peetersin in his article "Anticolonialism in World Policies", *World Justice*, IV (2) December, 1962, p. 172.

23. Ibid., p. 173.

24. Resolution 2105(XX) of 20 December 1965. Operative paragraph 10 reads:

> *Recognizes* the legitimacy of the struggle by the peoples under colonial rule to exercise their right to self-determination and independence, and invites all States to provide material and moral assistance to the national liberation movements in colonial Territories.

25. Resolution 2708(XXV) of 15 December 1970. Operative paragraph 5 reads:

> Reaffirms its recognition of the legitimacy of the struggle of the colonial peoples and peoples under alien domination to exercise their right to self-determination and independence by all the necessary means at their disposal and notes with satisfaction the progress made in the colonial Territories by the national liberation movements both through their struggle and through reconstruction programs.

26. *The Generation Gap in International Law*, Proceedings, 1969, p. 232.
27. Proceedings, 1965, p. 251.
28. For text, see *The New York Times*, 7 December 1960.
29. For text see *The New York Times*, 1 August 1960.
30. *23rd Congress of the Communist Party of the Soviet Union, 1966*, Novosti Press Agency Publishing House, Moscow, p. 41.
31. It may be noted that a working paper prepared by the Secretary-General in 1971 for the International Law Commission entitled *Survey of International Law* (A/CN.4/245) contains no reference to liberation movements, liberation wars or self-determination.
32. See A/AC.193/SR.1 for debate in the Special Committee on Enhancing the Effectiveness of the Principle of the Non-Use of Force in International Relations, which was established by the General Assembly in December 1977 at the urging of the Soviet Union which had prepared a draft treaty on the subject. Introducing the draft treaty the Soviet representative gave the assurance that

> nothing in the Draft Treaty was prejudical to the right of colonial peoples to independence and freedom, in accordance with the Charter, or to their right to wage a struggle towards those ends and to seek and receive support in accordance with the principles of the Charter . . . (A/AC.193/SR.3, p. 6).

Apparently this did not satisfy many Afro-Asian delegations which insisted upon explicit reaffirmation of the legitimacy of the struggle of peoples against colonialism, imperialism, racism and expansionism (see, for example, the statement by the representative of Senegal, A/AC.193/SR.10, p. 6). The Soviet Union was clearly put on the defensive. Replying to the observations made in the general debate the Soviet representative said that

> with regard to the question of the right of colonial peoples to wage a struggle for their freedom and independence, the draft treaty would in no way restrict that right, which was based on the Charter and on the Declaration on the Granting of Independence to Colonial Countries and Peoples.

In addition, he called attention to the fact that the Preamble of the draft treaty referred to a number of United Nations resolutions which upheld the legality of the struggle of the colonial peoples for their freedom and independence (A/AC.193/SR.13, p. 14).
33. It may be noted that similar efforts were made in 1970 in connection with the drafting of the Declaration on the Principles of International Law concerning Friendly Relations and Cooperation of States. There is no reference in the Declaration to the legitimacy of wars of liberation and liberation movements. The General Assembly reaffirmed its sentiments on the subject in resolution 2708(XXV) after the adoption of the Declaration.
34. Proceedings, 1970, p. 38.
35. *Terrorism and Political Violence: Do the Ends Justify the Means?* by Albert A. Friedlander, Chitty's Law Journal 24(7) 9 July 1976, p. 243.

Chapter III

HIGH-SOULED IDEALS AND MUNDANE OBJECTIVES

Next to colonialism, a generic term which subsumes a wide variety of notions and concepts, the racial policies of South Africa have been the second dominating theme in United Nations discourse. The struggle against racism in South Africa early assumed the quality of a moral passion which, like all moral passions, as Lionel Trilling observed, are more wilful and more imperious than self-seeking ones. Harnessed in the service of a political cause, such passions are capable of riding to the limits of dramatic tension. We have seen how the United Nations, in its impatience to hasten the translation of the promise of decolonization into an immediate reality, has pushed beyond the bounds of slogans and rhetoric to challenge the vital interests of States. The campaign against *apartheid* in South Africa, which has been conducted with a zeal that even a saint might decry, is a further example of the evocation of high-souled ideals to promote mundane objectives while mocking the loftiness of the pursuit by the methods employed. South Africa has become the scene of an evangelical-political polarization of absolute good and evil, where everything and anything done to combat the evil is automatically made lawful. The imperatives of morality have been combined with the devices of politics in a campaign to establish a non-racial and democratic South Africa and to create an egalitarian society by any means and at whatever cost.[1]

The response of the United Nations to the situation in South Africa has evolved into a servitude to a single reality to the point where judgments, relationships and actions come of necessity into conflict with all other rationales. After decades of public discussion of South Africa's racial policies and their overwhelming condemnation, individually and collectively, there seems to be little room left for qualitative questions. The case against South Africa appears to be unmarred by any doubts and it admits of no discriminating reappraisals. The world is determined to bring that unhappy land to heel, even if it means setting the country ablaze with racial war.

While the thrill of having catapulted the *apartheid* issue to the center of world attention may have wiped out all doubts as to the consequences of the deep involvement of the United Nations in the internal struggle of South Africa, the fact remains that the intervention of the world body, mounted on the swelling tide of African nationalism, has helped release pent-up passions of centuries to wreak terrible vengeance. There is a fundamental difference between opposing a policy and actively warring against it; by mobilizing its own resources and world public opinion to compel compliance with the decisions of a majority working its arbitrary will in the General Assembly, the United Nations has been acting as midwife to force and revolution. Observers of the United Nations scene who cannot accommodate their convictions to the mood and temper of the moment or suppress their conscience in the interest of the smooth working of the establishment, find it difficult to make peace with an international policy that demands compliance by some States with the highest standards of conduct and conscience while blinking at the enormities committed by others.

"Racial discrimination", Dr. Helen G. Edmonds of the United States told the Third Committee on 27 October 1970,

> exists in many parts of the world, even though not widely publicized. It may and does exist in the form of discrimination against minorities of different national origins in the same country where color is not the primary determinant. Often we are so obsessed with color as the determining factor that we overlook discrimination among people of the same color but with different national and racial origins. If we fail to see our mote in our own eye because we are so busy identifying the beam in our brother's eye, then all of our lengthy deliberations on the topic will have been in vain. Members of the Committee cannot be deluded into taking comfort that because *apartheid* is not part of the laws of their countries, they are free of guilt of racism and racial discrimination. And with Member States who claim perfection in this area when supportive evidence is to the contrary, we seriously wonder if self-examination can bc accomplished.[2]

The oft-stated and avowed reason for the United Nations preoccupation with South Africa has been the basic contradiction between *apartheid* and the principles and purposes of the Charter and the Universal Declaration of Human Rights. For example, the arguments of the more than fifty representatives of States Members who participated in the Security Council's debate in October 1974 on the General Assembly's request for a review of the relationship between South Africa and the United Nations in favor of South Africa's expulsion, were predicated on the abhorrence of the unequal treatment of peoples within a society and of minority rule which discriminates against the majority.[3] South Africa was asked to submit to the principle of majority rule in a land of many racial groups with little feeling of solidarity and without a common loyalty.

There is no question but that *apartheid* constitutes a unique record of discrimination and prejudice that challenges the self-respect of all Africans and offends the sensibilities of people everywhere. Not only is racial discrimination in South Africa enshrined in the legislative and legal structure of the State, but its theory has been consecrated as a philosophy of government. Yet this does not necessarily confer legitimacy on the demand made upon the South African Republic to make the unprecedented sacrifice for the cause of human rights and racial equality. Nor does it justify propelling the United Nations to extremes in pursuit of moral certainties; to do so is to pervert the mission of the international Organization and to distort its perspectives. The United Nations has not been given a mandate to go to the edge of disaster in order to set things right within Member States and it cannot, without deploying its resources beyond the point of wisdom and humanity, step into the role of guardian standing firm at the gate of purity while encampments of sin, old and new, are teeming all around it. To be sure, there is no comparable instance in the records of the United Nations of such passionate response to oppression as in the case of *apartheid* and of such determination to uphold human rights as in the case of South Africa; all the techniques of diplomacy, pressure and propaganda at the command of the world body have been deployed in defense of human dignity and human equality. Alas, the campaign against South Africa's racial policies is not a reflection of a striving, though imperfect, moral sense. Neither is it a triumphant assertion that the defense of human rights takes precedence over any other consideration.[4] At its ideal best, the campaign against *apartheid* makes the point that sensational events and sensational actions have more success than rational arguments in pushing forward the process of reform; at its worst, the campaign affords international politicians an opportunity to advance their favorite ideologies and to hammer their chisels into the cracks of inter-State relations opened wide by the action of the United Nations.

As will be seen, the anti-*apartheid* campaign developed over the years in response to pressures from the Third World and gained momentum as the Third World's impact and influence on United Nations decisions were being felt with increasing force. But the vast majority of those who called for freedom, human rights and racial equality in South Africa hardly conceded them to their own peoples. Governments whose domestic record would not stand up to a moment's scrutiny acquired respectability by denouncing South Africa, while others sought to exploit the situation to channel undifferentiated, emotional anti-Western feelings into lasting political gains. To black Africa the campaign against *apartheid* has been a fight to put an end to white rule in South Africa and to hasten the accession of the black majority to political power. To the Arab world, as will be seen later on, the deliberate identification of the struggle of black against white with its own struggle against Israel and the equation of Zionism with racism has been a potent propaganda ploy to gain unwitting allies in a partisan cause. To the Soviet Union and its allies and proxies, the campaign against South Africa is still another front in the unrelenting war against colonialism and neocolonialism, imperialism and foreign domination, and all other durable verbal relics in the Communist arsenal. And to many others all over the world who feel offended by South Africa's racial policies, the fight against *apartheid* provides a royal road on which to ride their hobby-horse.

Clearly, behind the surface of high principle is a staged propaganda exercise of massive proportions. It is not enough that the evil of *apartheid* is presented as a notion so-self-evident that people can yield to it without taking thought; the notion is reinforced by attributing to it characteristics which provide a broad target to all who are eager to promote a particular point of view. In recent years, for example, the racial issue in South Africa has been increasingly proffered as a struggle for decolonization, with the right of self-determination and national freedom as basic principles underlying its implementation; the battle cry has been the replacement of the white minority-ruled Republic of South Africa by a black majority-ruled Azania.

"As a colonial people", the observer at the United Nations from the African National Congress of South Africa told the General Assembly at the opening of the debate on *apartheid* in plenary on 26 October 1976,

> we not only assert our right to rebel against the colonizer; we assert also our right to determine for ourselves the means and methods to use to liberate ourselves and our country, as well as our right to determine what to do with our liberation. We have a vision of, and we fight for, a future South Africa in which national oppression will be abolished once and for all, in which racism in whatever form it rears its ugly head will be suppressed with all the might of popular power. We fight to restore power to the hands of the people. . . .
>
> We state now . . . that an incontrovertible part of the demands of our people is that there shall be one united and democratic South Africa. We will never abandon our birthright to the ownership and control of the whole territory of our country nor countenance any attempt to Balkanize it and to set its peoples one against another in tribal, racial or national conflicts. . . .[5]

The observer for the Pan Africanist Congress of Azania put it more bluntly when he said:

> The Pan Africanist Congress reminds us in all solemnity that the African liberation movement has made our people a pledge that should never be made lightly. We have promised to lead the people in armed struggle. Our credibility can be sustained only if we live up to our responsibilities. The mass organizations at home have strikes and demonstrations in hand. Our task is to lead the people in their war.[6]

These statements by representatives of liberation movements officially recognized by the Organization of African Unity are a far cry from the day when Madame Vijayalakshmi Pandit, leader of the Indian Delegation to the seventh session of the United Nations General Assembly in 1952, pleaded in the ad hoc Political

Committee for a United Nations study of the situation in what was then the Union of South Africa, with a view to finding an equitable solution to the racial problem in that land. "The purpose of the countries which have brought this matter before the bar of world opinion", Madame Pandit stated,

> is not to arraign or condemn the Union Government but to take note of the present situation and to study it with a view, if possible, to assisting and helping the South African Government to solve it on a rational and humanitarian basis in conformity with the principles of the Charter. There can be no solution by the continued domination of one race over others but only on a basis of mutual tolerance and understanding. The longer policies of persecution and discrimination are carried out, the more difficult will be the task of finding a fair and just solution of the racial question in that distracted country.[7]

It was daring for Sweden's Foreign Minister Osten Unden to suggest that it was right and proper for the United Nations to discuss the racial situation in South Africa, and even adopt a resolution on the subject, by virtue of the fact that the promotion of human rights and fundamental freedoms was an international obligation and hence a matter of international concern.[8] "Article 1, Paragraph 3 of the Charter", Mr. Unden said,

> declares that the purposes of the United Nations are inter alia to encourage "respect for human rights and for fundamental freedoms for all without distinction as to race, sex, language or religion." This is a program for the work of the United Nations, a declaration of aims for the future; but the Member States of the organization have not undertaken to carry this program into effect at once. It is not possible to maintain, that a Member State which in its legislation has not given effect to the principles of equality between the sexes or of equal rights for the races, has violated its obligations under the Charter. Nor does the Declaration of Human Rights, adopted by the General Assembly of the United Nations, contain any binding obligations for the Member States.
>
> But the fact that respect for human rights has been proclaimed as one of the purposes of the United Nations, must be considered to entail at least so much of an obligation for the Member States that they should not be able to prevent a debate of these questions, a debate which reasonably also should be permitted to dwell upon the policies of the various Member States with regard to the respect for human rights. This debate should also be allowed to lead to the adoption of recommendations, as provided for in Article 62, Paragraph 2, which I quoted previously.[9]

No one, the representative of Pakistan suggested, contested South Africa's right to pass such laws as it wished; all that was at issue at the moment, he added, was whether or not laws that involved human rights were matters within the competence of the General Assembly to discuss and resolve.[10] The decision came on 20 November 1952, when the ad hoc Political Committee, by a vote of 45 to 6, with 8 abstentions, rejected a South African motion that would have denied that competence to the General Assembly. Voting in favor of the South African motion were, in addition to South Africa itself, the United Kingdom, Australia, Belgium, France and Luxembourg. The Netherlands, New Zealand, Peru, Turkey, Venezuela, the Dominican Republic and Greece abstained.[11]

Crusades once launched develop their own momentum. "Today", to quote from the statement made by the Permanent Representative of Yugoslavia in the Security Council on 23 March 1977,

> the elimination of *apartheid* and racial discrimination is a priority and urgent task for the United Nations and the international community. The basic principle underlying the implementation of that task is the right of peoples to self-determination and freedom. Racism, *apartheid* and oppression in Southern Africa represent a violation of fundamental human rights and principles of justice and freedom and humanity and constitute a threat to peace and international security.[12]

In the most strongly-worded resolution in thirty years since the question of South Africa's racial policies was first placed on its agenda in 1946, the General Assembly virtually voted South Africa out of the human estate. Resolution I, the ninth in a series of ten resolutions on South Africa adopted on 9 November 1976, denounced the Pretoria regime as illegitimate and reaffirmed the status of the liberation movements recognized by the Organization of African Unity—the African National Congress of South Africa and the Pan Africanist Congress of Azania—as the authentic representatives of the people of South Africa. The resolution further reaffirmed the legitimacy of the struggle of the people of South Africa and their liberation movements for the "seizure of power by the people" and the exercise of their inalienable right to self-determination by "all possible means", including armed struggle. It recalled that the policy of *apartheid* constituted a crime against humanity and declared the situation in South Africa a grave threat to international peace and security and, as such, subject to action under Chapter VII of the Charter of the United Nations. Finally, the resolution called upon France, the United Kingdom and the United States not to "misuse" their veto power in the Security Council by shielding the Government of South Africa, but to join the majority in enabling the Council to declare the situation in South Africa a threat to international peace and security and to invoke mandatory sanctions against the Pretoria regime.[13]

The 1976 debate on South Africa conveyed a dire intimation of finality setting in that unhappy land. Ever since then the talk at the United Nations has been increasingly of the approaching liberation of South Africa and the dawning of the day when "the destiny of South Africa would be decided by all the people of South Africa, irrespective of race, color or creed, and above all by that great majority of the population which has been oppressed, and its liberation movements."[14] While much of this optimism has been bolstered by objective developments in southern Africa, especially the collapse of the Portuguese Empire, the defeat of South African troops in Angola, the accession of Angola and Mozambique and other Portuguese territories to national independence, the surrender, at least in principle, of Rhodesia to majority rule and the rising militancy of the black population in South Africa itself, it is the impressive array of numbers moving as one against the Pretoria regime that makes the point beyond refutation.

The United Nations has affirmed its will to force the pace of history and is unlikely to relent until all of Africa has been satisfied that righteousness has triumphed. Meanwhile, whatever the tally of human suffering under the uniquely cruel system of *apartheid* might be, the intervention of the United Nations in South Africa for the purpose of altering its internal order teems with profoundly significant political, constitutional, juridical and moral questions that strike at the heart of international organization and are full of portent for the future. The war against *apartheid* has been both seed and soil of doctrines which sanction ends giving way to means and law being subordinated to policy in an atmosphere of real or contrived emergency.

"Certain words, like imperialism, colonialism, or racism", former U.S. Ambassador John Scali told a New York audience, "take, after endless repetition, a coloring which precludes meaningful discussion. These words lose their ability to transmit ideas; they convey only emotions."[15] *Apartheid* is one of those words whose meaning has been blurred by the banality of the rhetoric it provokes. *Apartheid* is an Africaans word that translates loosely as separateness and traces its origins to the strict Calvinism of the Dutch settlers who arrived at the Cape in 1652 and who regarded the preservation of the diversity of the human species as fundamental theological dogma.[16] Territorial separation of the races is the first principle of *apartheid* as systematized and codified in 1948, when the Nationalist Party came into power under the leadership of Dutch-born ideologue Hendrik Verwoerd. This principle applies equally to separation between black and white and between black and black; the so-called homeland policy, or Bantustan principle, purports to offer the major historical, regional, racial, tribal or ethnic entities in South Africa an opportunity to preserve and develop their respective national identities in sovereign freedom or under a federal or cantonal system.[13] In the opinion of the Party in power,

> The divisions which exist in South Africa today came about naturally and historically, through sociological affinities and not as a result of an ideology. We believe that the objectives of self-determination for all our peoples will not be best achieved by attempting to force all of them into an artificial unity. Too often has the world seen the tragic consequences of attempts to force unity upon two or more divergent peoples, and we see it still today.
>
> A policy such as ours, which is designed to avoid disaster, to eliminate friction between the different peoples, to eliminate domination of one group by another, and to give to every man his due, can surely not be said to run counter to civilized concepts of human dignity and freedom.
>
> Our policy is not based on any concepts of superiority or inferiority but on the historical fact that different peoples differ in their loyalties, cultures, outlook and modes of life and that they wish to retain them.
>
> Nor is our policy inflexible; it postulates a certain broad direction the end of which is sovereign independence for the peoples concerned. There is no question, whatsoever, of forcing together peoples who do not wish to be

joined. Equally, there is no question of keeping apart people who wish to come together. The real point is, therefore, not one of objective but of method; the best practical way of ensuring self-determination and human development. We believe, particularly in the light of events elsewhere in the world, that our approach is better calculated to achieve the common objective than the alternative of forcing the various peoples of South Africa into an artificial entity which will lead to friction and strife not only between white and black but also between black and black. . . .[17]

We need not minimize the evils of *apartheid* or excuse the inequities and inhumanities which the system produces in order to recognize that the white population in South Africa faces a very real and agonizing problem of preserving its own historical and cultural identity against the pressure of an overwhelming black majority. The tangled, ill-omened racial conflict epitomized by the policy of *apartheid* reaches deep into the subconscious of white South Africa, where fear of being engulfed by a tidal wave of black humanity has been a haunting reality. For the struggle in South Africa is a struggle for power and identity, no less than a struggle for social equality; it is a fight for the enthronement of the majority. And majority rule conjures up a black political monopoly in a unitary State which, most white South Africans believe, would spell their physical and cultural annihilation. The new generation of blacks is roused, poised and awaiting its moment. Unless an unclouded vision is brought to bear on the situation in South Africa which takes account of the issue of survival of the white population and of the community conditions essential to its survival, the United Nations will never begin the complex and demanding task of uncovering the world which cliché and caricature have so long obscured. The solution it seeks must never be repetitious of the problem it is meant to solve.

Apartheid is first and foremost a massive attempt to rationalize a system created by a diminishing white minority deeply conscious of its beleaguered existence and determined to defend its privileged position as a guarantee of its national and cultural survival. The sense of being a beleaguered group runs through the whole history of the people who now rule South Africa. More than 150 years ago they left their homeland on the Cape of Good Hope and trekked north in search for freedom from the British, only to be overwhelmed by them in the Boer War of 1899–1902. In between, they fought for hearth and home and the right of self-determination not only against the British Empire, but also against all intruders into their new homeland in the Orange Free State and the Transvaal. The cultural patterns that have for centuries defined all human relations among the Afrikaners cannot readily be adapted to accommodate all the profound changes which have taken place in South Africa since the beginning of the century. What may be reality to the outside world is the abandonment of basic principles to the majority of the white population in South Africa.

Unlike Nazism, *apartheid* is not the expression of a scientifically precise, cynically cold-blooded manipulation of the fierce, mass anxieties of a distressed society. To be sure, to the extent that it is coercive and bars all possibilities of escape into personal choice, *apartheid* is absolutely immoral. The long, terrible burden of racial laws and the fear, the physical pain, the humiliation and degradation which they beget, marks the system as cruel beyond description; the sheer headlong inhumanity deliberately and programmatically pursued by an immense bureaucracy which affects both black and white makes it also tyrannical. But the fact that *apartheid* is an attempt to avert the shattering transformation of South African society decreed by the aspirations of the black majority shapes it into a human tragedy of monumental proportions. The aspirations of the majority are like a rising tide that never recedes; it is no longer likely that the black majority will readily agree to trade its claim to political and social rights in all of South Africa for a homeland or homelands in a fraction of the country. The representatives of South Africa's blacks left no doubt as to their intentions regarding so-called independence; they are not willing to abdicate their birthright as South Africans and to forfeit their share of the wealth they helped create by their labor.[18] Nemesis may not yet have delivered the coup de grace, but the contradictory forces that rack South African life are already rushing toward resolution in the public arena, if not in peace then in violence. The differences must not be minimized or robbed of their diametrical opposition by an illusory dream of peaceful coexistence.

Addressing a seminar on *Why Invest in South Africa* on 20 June

1977 in New York, South Africa's Foreign Minister, R. F. Botha warned against creating an apocalyptic prospect by ignoring or minimizing his Government's efforts at a solution of the racial problem. "We in South Africa", he said,

> can accept criticism. . . . But there is one thing we cannot accept . . . and I must be emphatic about it: we are not going to negotiate our own suicide. We are a nation in Africa; we are white Africans. We have earned the right to live and survive here and govern ourselves, through hard work and toil. I don't know how much more a nation must do to prove it is a nation and has the right to live and survive and maintain its identity, and not just because we are white, but because we ought to be entitled to enjoy and preserve that which is justly ours. We will not abdicate our sovereignty over ourselves, not now and not tomorrow. It is my sincere belief that an overwhelming majority of the American people although highly critical of many aspects of the application of the policies of the South African Government, do support our right to survive as a nation. I do not believe that the U.S. Government has received a mandate from the American people to follow a policy which will lead to the extinction of our nation as a nation. . . .[19]

The United Nations bears a burden that ought to lie on the conscience of those who have encouraged doctrinaire opponents of all things South African and who painted a picture of the South African regime as being totally without redeeming feature. The assertion that *apartheid* was an absolute evil that brooked no comparison between it and other tyrannies entrenched itself in the halls of the United Nations to such a degree that it blinded even the best-intentioned to the full range of choices of a solution to the racial problem in South Africa; as has been suggested above, to oppose *apartheid* became a sentiment so firmly established and unconsidered that it would neither be challenged nor examined. Appealing to the United Nations Charter, the world body spoke of a humane, egalitarian and individualistic society in an *apartheid*-free South Africa, ignoring all evidence to the contrary and insensitive to the need of reconciling the embarrassment of reality with the clichés of expectation, not only in South Africa, but in the world at large which was rumbling with centrifugal forces everywhere. While there is no sin in high standards, the peril of paralysis lurks in impossible standards. At no time did the United Nations question whether there was reason to expect in South Africa a fusing of the heterogeneity of the races which make up the people of South Africa on the basis of absolute equality in political, economic, social and cultural life and, if not, what alternatives presented themselves that were not abetted by simplistic ideology.

The ultimate question in South Africa cannot properly be addressed through a contest of votes in the General Assembly. A just solution to South Africa's dilemma lies within South Africa itself; it cannot be imposed from without. There is a clear and present danger in upsetting the delicate balance between what the United Nations can do and what States will not accept as obligatory. Attempts by international organizations to enlarge their role, like refusals of States to honor their commitments, are equally detrimental to the orderly development of international cooperation. To assert that the organized international community has arrived at the stage where it can intervene in the domestic affairs of States to right wrongs, redistribute political and economic power and enforce international rules of conduct is to fly in the face of reality. Few can subscribe to the logic of a system that excludes from international purview a situation like that which obtained, for example, in Lebanon during 1975–76 where civil war of a kind claimed 50,000 dead and 100,000 wounded, created more than one million refugees and wrought material destruction of overwhelming proportions,[20] while it mobilizes international political, moral and material resources to encourage and promote the establishment of an integrated polity in white-dominated South Africa. Even if the campaign against *apartheid* were a pure reflection of a stern, uncompromising moral ferocity seething within the breasts of people against a governmental policy that offends the new spirit of nations, it would still have been very difficult to justify United Nations efforts to enforce a solution to complex problems of human behavior. Neither would it have excused the procedural excesses and the sacrifice of legality to public expectations which have accompanied the campaign against *apartheid.*

The metamorphosis of *apartheid* from an offense against human rights to a crime against humanity and a threat to international peace and security shows how far Governments are willing to go in pursuit of their objectives by stirring up an indignation so extreme as to lose all moral discrimination. In the process, they have ignored with abandon barriers of law, custom and procedure aimed at keeping within bounds the complex forces of power politics, ideology, national interests, idealism, hopefulness and vision, which make the problems of the United Nations so stubborn, intractable and often compelling. By rejecting as early as 1946 a Belgian proposal for an Advisory Opinion from the International Court of Justice on the application of Article 2(7) of the Charter to the question of South Africa's treatment of persons of Indian origin,[21] and by opposing thereafter the submission of the domestic jurisdiction clause to a legal test,[22] the political organs of the United Nations reserved for themselves the freedom to invoke or not to invoke a Charter provision which is crucial to the proper functioning of the international organization and which has grown in importance with the passing years. Contrary to a common belief, it would appear that the more the need for international cooperation is being recognized and matters long regarded as strictly domestic become internationalized, the greater is the emphasis on nonintervention in the domestic affairs of States and on their sovereign equality. Article 2(7) which bars such intervention, is more than ever relied upon to serve not only as a restraint on arbitrary power to protect the weak against the strong, but also as a necessary safeguard against increasing pressures for the internationalization of national issues at the whim and caprice of undisciplined or fortuitous majorities for different aims and purposes.[23]

Indeed, the States Members have never yielded to the political organs of the United Nations the right to make authoritative interpretations of Article 2(7); they have jealously safeguarded intact their power of autointerpretation of the clause they regard as the most conspicuous symbol of State sovereignty. Replying to a question at a press conference in 1976 as to whether he was afraid to risk rebuke by showing the same concern for human rights in Soviet-bloc countries as shown in Chile, Secretary-General Kurt Waldheim said:

> ... I am against the violation of human rights everywhere in the world, wherever they may occur, not only in Chile. You mentioned Chile; therefore I mention it. But violations of human rights exist in other parts of

the world; we know it very well, and we do what we can. What the public, unfortunately, does not always understand is that we have our limitations.

I can make statements, and I have made many statements in this regard. If you go through my record you will find them. But we also have a Charter, Article II, Paragraph 7, which forbids us to intervene in the domestic affairs of a Member State. So we are always in the dilemma that, on the one hand, we have the Human Rights Declaration, the Covenants, and so on, which give us a title to do something about this. For that purpose we have the Human Rights Commission, of course, which is looking into these problems. We have the possibility to make public statements. On the other hand, we also have the limitation of Article II, Paragraph 7. I did not write the Charter. I can only say these are the limitations, and we here in the United Nations, whether it is the Human Rights Commission or the Secretary-General himself, have to operate between these two concepts which exist and which have to be kept in mind.

So to accuse us of not doing enough in this regard is not justified, because we have our limitations. And I want to add this: We have no executive power. We can only appeal; we can try to convince, but we cannot force anybody to do anything.[24]

The complete absence in Article 2(7) of any reference to an instance competent to give an authoritative interpretation and pass on its applicability was a deliberate decision at San Francisco to leave to the States Members full freedom to judge what is and what is not a matter essentially within their domestic jurisdiction. A serious effort to endow the International Court of Justice with the requisite power was defeated. Also defeated was a Belgian proposal which would have given the General Assembly the sovereign competence to interpret the provisions of the Charter. There is nothing on record in the United Nations to support the view that the States Members have surrendered their right and freedom of autointerpretation, directly or indirectly. "The futility of arguing against State autointerpretation", Professor J. S. Watson writes,

became obvious in the light of the fact that the Organization has in most cases no legal basis for enforcing its decisions. If it cannot bind a member to carry out a resolution directed against it, then it serves no purpose to claim that it does have magisterial competence in interpreting Article 2(7), since the practical impact of the whole process is nil. Target States have not considered themselves bound by the subsequent resolutions, with the result that they have effectively retained their power of autointerpretation. Thus, insisting that the Organization is legally entitled to interpret Article 2(7) is

> tantamount to demonstrating that it is powerless, a position that contributes little to a nascent legal system. . . .
>
> . . . A State that votes against a resolution on the ground that the resolution infringes upon its domestic jurisdiction or that of another State is quite clearly protesting the exercise of authority in that regard by the Organization. Thus the resolution in question, while it might be binding on those States that voted in favor of it, cannot be said to create a rule of customary law, especially a rule of customary law binding upon the objecting target State. Likewise, other States voting negatively, cannot be said to have acquiesced in the general proposition that in such instances the Organization is competent. To this the advocates of the customary approach would doubtless reply that over a period of time, as a result of many resolutions, a core of customary law is distilled. But this does not deal with the problem; it simply puts it out of focus by diverting attention away from the issue of consent.
>
> . . . The true test of the continuing validity of Article 2(7) is to be found not in the arguments in the legal literature or in the debates of the General Assembly and the Security Council but rather in the behaviour of states that are the unwilling targets of UN resolutions and have objected on the basis of domestic jurisdiction to any form of supranational intervention. When these states begin to comply with the Organization's resolutions against their political interests and because of a feeling that they must comply, then Article 2(7) will truly have been made redundant.[25]

As the resolutions on South Africa became increasingly more specific and the collective measures they recommended struck ever closer at the heart of the Republic's social order, the question of their legality and procedural propriety began to loom larger and became more compelling. Behind the persistent quest to win Security Council acceptance of the view that *apartheid*, along with forcibly maintained colonial rule, satisfied the conditions required for collective enforcement action even if they were not, strictly speaking, encompassed in the traditional concept of a threat to the peace, breach of the peace and act of aggression, is no less a desire to buttress the legal case against South Africa than to hasten the end of *apartheid*. For the logic behind the General Assembly's decisions was never put to the test and the decisions themselves never met the most difficult of the counterarguments; the authority invoked by the General Assembly for its actions against South Africa has been the authority of its own past decisions.[26] This led to the development of an atmosphere in which tactics took the place of goals, while analysis rested more on indiscriminate condemnation than on judicious sympathy. More and more conventional categorizations were used as substitutes for inquiries and studies, which soon lost much of their probative value to the basic problems at hand. The subject of *apartheid* never really gained a recognizable conceptual framework within which to organize both the essential factual information and analytical discussion.

Legitimacy cannot be built by sacrificing principle to public expectations. The open and implied assertion that the Charter had given third parties a contractual interest in South Africa's treatment of its black majority owes little to fact or legal theory.

"The idea that the Charter", Professor Roberto Ago, Special Rapporteur of the International Law Commission on State Responsibility, writes:

> legitimizes the application, by third States, of enforcement measures involving the use of force against States practicing *apartheid* or maintaining colonial domination over other countries is seriously questioned by a considerable number of States. The same is true of the idea that the Charter legitimizes the provision of armed aid by a third State to a people struggling for liberation from alien domination. Some Governments doubt whether the General Assembly—or even the Security Council—has the power to remove by recommendations alone the prohibition on the use of force established by the Charter in all cases, with the exception of self-defence and participation in action undertaken, on its own "decision", by the Security Council. Nor do the States in question subscribe to the idea of including in the legal definition of "self-defence", as the term is used in Article 51 of the Charter, armed action undertaken by a people to free itself from *apartheid* or colonial domination. Accordingly, they cannot agree that a possible intervention in the combat by another State be presented as participation in "collective self-defence", again as the term is used in Article 51. Lastly, these same States have great difficulty agreeing with all the attendant consequences—to regard the relations between a State and a people under its colonial domination as "international relations", in the sense in which the term is used in Article 2, Paragraph 4, at least until that people has acquired the limited international legal capacity which international law attributes to insurrectional movements under certain conditions.
>
> It is clearly not for us to take sides in these differences of opinion which divide States on delicate legal points. At this stage, our task is limited to examining the objective conclusions which may be drawn from attitudes adopted by States, particularly within the framework of the United Nations. The differing views described above do not seem to invalidate the

main conclusion, namely that the international community as a whole now seems to recognize that acts such as the maintenance by force of *apartheid* and colonial domination constitute internationally wrongful acts. On the other hand, these differences of opinion make it impossible to conclude that there exists a similar agreement on the part of all essential sectors of the international community as to the type of "action" or "measures" which may legitimately be taken to meet those situations. It must also be recognized that the point of view of the group of States experiencing the difficulties mentioned in the previous paragraph has considerable weight in the Security Council. This explains the caution with which the Security Council has proceeded in the matter and also the fact that, despite repeated appeals by the General Assembly, in only one case—that of Southern Rhodesia—has the Council decided to apply enforcement measures in accordance with Chapter VII of the Charter, and then only measures which did not involve the use of armed force. Furthermore, it must be said that in this field, the General Assembly itself has never gone beyond identifying any of the situations concerned as cases of a "threat to the peace". In such cases it is no doubt harder to contemplate the application of enforcement measures involving the use of armed force. Cases of "a breach of the peace" or "an act of aggression" thus apparently belong to a category apart, even in the view of those States which have advocated the adoption of the most advanced resolutions by the General Assembly.[27]

There is no dearth of examples of United Nations bodies tilting a variety of amending decisions against South Africa. Whatever their immediate outcome might be, they almost invariably serve as bases for fresh attempts and fresh hypotheses. For example, the decision of the Economic and Social Council at its thirty-sixth session in 1963 to suspend South Africa from participation in the work of the Economic Commission for Africa[28]—the first instance of suspension or expulsion of a Member State from a permanent subsidiary organ of the United Nations—served as a premise for the attempt five years later to suspend the South African Republic from the United Nations Conference on Trade and Development (UNCTAD). At the 1238th meeting of the Second, or Economic, Committee of the twenty-third General Assembly in 1968, Upper Volta moved the suspension of South Africa from UNCTAD "until it shall have terminated its policy of racial discrimination and until that fact has been duly confirmed by the General Assembly."[29] The Upper Voltan draft resolution was rushed to a vote even before the Committee had an opportunity to consider the opinion of the Legal Counsel requested by Denmark. It was adopted by a vote of 49 to 22, with 23 abstentions.[30]

The Legal Counsel's opinion cast serious doubts on the constitutionality of the Upper Voltan resolution, arguing that while the General Assembly could set up committees of limited membership, it could not establish a committee open automatically to all Member Nations such as UNCTAD, and then exclude one or more of them from activity.[31] There was no doubt that the adoption of the resolution plunged the United Nations into the most serious constitutional crisis since its founding in 1945. The Western and Western-oriented nations thought that abhorrence of South Africa's racial policies could not justify singling out a State Member for unequal treatment in respect of the benefits of membership in the world body. The suspension of South Africa from UNCTAD, they argued, violated a fundamental concept underlying the United Nations and endangered all other rights of membership guaranteed by the Charter. They recalled Article 6 of the Charter, which lays down clear principles governing the suspension or expulsion of States Members and decried the move against South Africa as an arbitrary act that offended legality and was contemptuous of the law. Those who supported the suspension of South Africa from UNCTAD defended the right of the General Assembly to determine the membership of any committee or body created by it, and the action against South Africa as a proper exercise of authority in defense of human rights and fundamental freedoms. The Soviet Union and the other members of the Communist bloc opposed the adoption of the Upper Voltan resolution for reasons which had nothing to do with the substance of the debate.[32]

What further exacerbated the debate was the insistence by the representative of Ghana in the Second Committee that the resolution, already rushed to a vote by the Committee even before it had an opportunity to hear the opinion of the Legal Counsel, be submitted without delay for final action by the General Assembly meeting in plenary, even though the item within whose context the debate on South Africa had been carried on had not yet been completed. This prompted the representative of Belgium to note that "the manner in which the Committee had adopted the draft resolution had been irresponsible and had constituted an infringement of the Charter. They sought to stampede everybody into line."[33] When the resolution came up for a vote in plenary, the representative of Canada moved the postponement of its consideration, on the ground that the Second Committee's action risked doing harm to the United Nations by institutionalizing the suspension of Members' rights by resolution of the General Assembly and circumventing provisions of the Charter. The Upper Voltan resolution, he added, also risked creating a precedent of dangerous proportions especially harmful to minorities and the smaller countries, and he pleaded for time to allow for serious consideration of the issues raised by the Legal Counsel and their implications.[34] The Canadian motion was lost by a roll-call vote of 52 to 47, with 23 abstentions.[35] The roll call was requested by the representative of Tanzania in order to distinguish "between the supporters of human dignity and South Africa."[36]

Clearly, at issue was the question of whether or not the General Assembly was the ultimate authority to interpret the Charter concerning its own powers and functions. If the resolution were adopted, the United States representative warned, the world would be told that "in the United Nations General Assembly there is no law, no provision in the Charter, no guarantee of the legal rights of any nation that may not be overridden if it obstructs the majority will."[37] The representative of Malawi looked deep into the future when he said:

> The resolution, if adopted, would set a dangerous precedent, for it would serve as an active encouragement for any given group of States having significant voting power to employ it to push through draft resolutions curtailing the membership rights and privileges of other countries with whose policies that group might happen to disagree. We could well be confronted with the hair-raising prospect of having the General Assembly continually subjected to a kind of procedural blackmail in which normal business is completely subverted by voting bargains being struck just for this purpose. And if that possibility seems to representatives to be far-fetched, I would remind them that in the Second Committee one of the sponsors of the draft resolution saw fit gleefully to anticipate the time when similar drafts might be introduced to debar other nations from participating in UNCTAD.[38]

But for the abstentions of the Soviet Union and the other members of the Communist bloc on the ground that the resolution in question implied confirmation of a previous resolution barring East Germany, Korea and Vietnam from UNCTAD while permitting the participation of the Federal Republic of Germany,[39] the Upper Voltan resolution would have won the day. The abstentions provided the necessary margin for sustaining a Presidential ruling that the importance of the issue called for a two-thirds majority and leading to the defeat of the resolution by a vote of 55 to 33, with 28 abstentions.[40]

It did not take long before the majority in the General Assembly aimed another blow at South Africa, this time by excluding the Pretoria regime from its own midst. It came in the form of a challenge to South Africa's credentials at the Assembly's twenty-fifth anniversary session in 1970. According to the rules of procedure, the specific duties of the Credentials Committee of the General Assembly are to examine the credentials of delegates as to whether they have been duly issued by the Head of State or Government, or by the Foreign Minister of a State Member of the United Nations. In an opinion rendered on 11 November 1970, the United Nations Legal Counsel defined credentials for the General Assembly

> as a document issued by the Head of State or Government, or by the Minister for Foreign Affairs of a State Member of the United Nations submitted to the Secretary-General designating the persons entitled to represent that Member at a given session of the General Assembly. Unlike the acceptance of credentials in bilateral relations the question of recognition of a Government of a Member State is not involved, and substantive issues concerning the status of Governments does not arise.[41]

The Counsel's opinion was occasioned by a motion made on 23 October 1970 in the General Assembly by the representative of Somalia that the Credentials Committee be requested

> to consider as a matter of urgency the credentials of the delegation currently occupying the seat of South Africa and to make a special report on the matter.[42]

In support of the Somalian motion, the Nigerian representative said:

The Government of Pretoria represents less than 20 percent of the population of South Africa. In particular, the 15 million Africans have no rights whatsoever and are not represented in any of its organs. The exclusion from the political process of their country is all the more abominable because it is based wholly and solely on racial discrimination and considerations. I do not consider that this is the occasion to go into details of the atrocities being committed against our people by the racist regime in South Africa, but we have the right to know who the representatives of the racist regime of South Africa are and how they have come to participate in the deliberation of our respected Organization. Who do they speak for? What about the 15 million Africans and the other nonwhite communities in South Africa? It is therefore appropriate, and my delegation wholeheartedly supports the proposals made by the Ambassador of Somalia, that we should thoroughly scrutinize the credentials of the *apartheid* regime.[43]

The two delegations, which spoke on behalf of the African Group, served notice that their aim was to unseat the South African delegation. Theirs was the first challenge that sought to exclude a State Member from participating in the work of the General Assembly—a measure the Legal Counsel regarded as tantamount to expulsion from the international Organization. While the Counsel's opinion that only the authenticity of the credentials, not the legitimacy of the issuing State, could be challenged may have carried weight in the Credentials Committee, which rejected the Somalian proposal, it did not prevail on the General Assembly. On 13 November 1970, the Assembly approved

the first report of the Credentials Committee, except with regard to the credentials of the representatives of the Government of South Africa.[44]

Had the General Assembly pressed its disapproval of South Africa's credentials to its logical conclusions, it surely would have precipitated the crisis which enveloped its twenty-ninth session four years later. But it did lay the groundwork for South Africa's expulsion from the General Assembly in 1974. For the next two years the General Assembly followed the formula adopted in 1970[45] of withholding approval of South Africa's credentials and leaving it to the Assembly's President to interpret the action as a solemn warning to the South African Government to mend its ways. In 1973, the General Assembly went one step further when, by a vote of 72 to 37, with 13 abstentions, it rejected South Africa's credentials outright.[46] The change in language had an immediate impact on the deliberations of the Special Political Committee, which concluded its debate on South Africa with a resolution which denied the right of the Pretoria regime to represent the people of South Africa and declared the liberation movements recognized by the Organization of African Unity as its authentic representatives.[47] Adopted on 14 December 1973, by a vote of 88 to 7, with 28 abstentions, the resolution only raised the curtain for things to come. In 1974 it was the Credentials Committee itself that rejected South Africa's credentials,[48] paving the way for the resolution of 30 September 1974, in which the General Assembly called upon the Security Council to review the relationship between the United Nations and South Africa. Within one month the Security Council was ready to vote on a draft resolution which called for the immediate expulsion of the South African Republic from the United Nations. The draft resolution was vetoed by the United States, the United Kingdom and France, which were united in their rejection of expulsion as a means of inducing change and of compelling compliance with United Nations prescriptions.[49] This, however, did not deter the General Assembly from pursuing the same or similar end by procedural means.

Immediately upon being notified of the Security Council's inability to take action on its resolution of September 30, the General Assembly called for a Presidential ruling on the status of South Africa's delegation in the light of the decision of 30 September 1974 to reject its credentials. President Bouteflika ruled on 12 November 1974, that the absence of a decision by the Security Council in no way affected the General Assembly's refusal to recognize the credentials of the South Africa delegation and that while it left open the question of South Africa's membership in the United Nations, the decision that South Africa could not participate in the work of the Assembly was unaffected.[50] The ruling was upheld by a vote of 91 to 22, with 19 abstentions, after it was challenged by the representative of the United States. Thus the efforts begun in 1962, when the General

Assembly requested the Security Council to consider South Africa's expulsion from the United Nations among the measures to compel Pretoria's compliance with their respective resolutions,[51] were brought nearer to fruition.

Having driven the South African Republic from its midst there was little the General Assembly could do which was not anticlimactic. Hence the mounting pressure in the ensuing years for mandatory sanctions against South Africa. On 4 November 1977 the Security Council, which for decades had resisted pronouncing itself on the South African situation in terms which would have entitled it to invoke Chapter VII of the Charter, voted unanimously to impose a mandatory embargo on arms to South Africa. Sponsored by Canada and the Federal Republic of Germany, Security Council resolution 418 (1977) was hailed as a milestone in the history of the United Nations struggle against *apartheid* and encouraged the hope that other mandatory sanctions against South Africa were in the offing. As the year 1978 drew to a close the drive for mandatory economic sanctions was gaining momentum. In a resolution adopted by a vote of 105 to 6, with 16 abstentions, the General Assembly requested the Security Council to consider urgently a mandatory embargo on the supply of petroleum and petroleum products to South Africa under Chapter VII of the Charter of the United Nations.[52]

NOTES

1. For example, reporting to the 31st session of the General Assembly in 1976 on The Soweto Massacre and its Aftermath, the Special Committee on Apartheid stated:

> There can be no solution to the grave situation in South Africa without the replacement of the minority racist regime by a Government based on the principle of equality and the exercise of the right of self-determination of all the people of South Africa. . . .
>
> All those opposed to *apartheid* should abandon their vain efforts to persuade the criminal regime to abandon racism and should take firm action to isolate the racist regime and assist the oppressed people and their liberation movements in the struggle for the total eradication of *apartheid* and the exercise of the right of self-determination (A/31/22/Add.1, p. 9).

2. United States Mission to the United Nations, Press Release USUN-151(70), p. 9.

3. S/PV.1796–1808, passim.

4. The reaction of the People's Revolutionary Government of Equatorial Guinea to a decision taken by the Commission on Human Rights at its 35th session in 1979 to appoint a Special Rapporteur to make a thorough study of the human rights situation in the country in accordance with Economic and Social Council resolution 1235 (XLII) of 6 June 1967 governing situations which reveal a consistent pattern of violation of human rights, is very instructive. Since the situation in Guinea leading up to the Commission's action was discussed in camera, the records of the debate and the statement made by the representative of Equatorial Guinea, if any, have not been made public. But in May 1979 the Permanent Representative of Equatorial Guinea sent a letter of protest to the President of the Economic and Social Council in which he took exception to the Council's approval of the Commission's action by acceding to the latter's recommendation to appeal to the Government of Equatorial Guinea to extend its cooperation to the Commission and enable it to make the investigation. In his letter dated 11 May 1979, the representative of the People's Revolutionary Government stated:

> ... The Permanent Representative of the Republic of Equatorial Guinea would not wish to pass judgement on the Commission on Human Rights and its subcommissions, whose recommendations formed the basis of the decision of the Economic and Social Council. Its observations will be concerned with the biased and, of course, unjust procedure of the Commission on Human Rights.
>
> The Economic and Social Council and its organs were not established to breed contempt for the sovereignty, independence, dignity and all other attributes and rights recognized as belonging to peoples and Governments. The established norms which lay down the procedure and operation of the Commission ... have never been respected in the case of Equatorial Guinea, and the Commission has always ignored the highly political motivations of the authors of the communications which gave rise to the proceedings in question, who pursue very different objectives from those of the United Nations. Moreover, the Sub-Commission concerned with human rights questions has allowed persons to participate in its work who are members of terrorist organizations supported by colonial and neo-colonial powers which are plotting to overthrow the legally constituted Government, despite the official protests of the Government of the Republic of Equatorial Guinea to the Sub-Commission.
>
> This attitude, which sets an undesirable precedent, will by no means improve the relations of Governments with United Nations bodies, and the Government of Equatorial Guinea strongly condemns it.
>
> The Government of the Republic of Equatorial Guinea has, on a number of occasions, explained its position on this alleged violation of human

rights. The United Nations cannot become involved in problems of this kind, which can diminish its effectiveness in relation to a question as important as that of respect for human rights. The revolution of Equatorial Guinea cannot associate itself with the vested interests of the colonialists and neo-colonialists; all that Equatorial Guinea stands for is bound up with this policy.

Even from the procedural point of view, the Government of the Republic of Equatorial Guinea considers that, based on the foregoing, the recommendations of the Economic and Social Council are unfounded and unacceptable. Moreover, this decision is in violation of the provisions of the United Nations Charter itself regarding the implementation of decisions. Furthermore, the recommendation is unconstitutional from the standpoint of the laws of the Republic of Equatorial Guinea, particularly since on various occasions the Government has confirmed that no human rights problem exists in Equatorial Guinea. No State or world Organization can coerce the people or Government of the Republic of Equatorial Guinea against their will. The United Nations is called upon to consider other questions of vital importance for the peoples of the world.

For the text of the Commission's resolution 15(XXXV) adopted on 13 March 1979 by 20 votes to 2, with 9 abstentions, see Report of the Commission on Human Rights on the work of its 35th session (E/1979/36, p. 122); For the decision of the Economic and Social Council, see Resolutions and Decisions of the Economic and Social Council, E/1979/79, p. 47.

For the text of the letter of the Permanent Representative of Equatorial Guinea to the President of the Economic and Social Council, dated 11 May 1979, see E/1979/57, p. 19.

5. A/31/PV.45, pp. 44–47.

6. Ibid., p. 63.

7. Department of Public Information, Press Release P/M.2420, 12 November 1952.

8. For the most part the Western nations took a negative attitude in the question of the Committee's competence to deal with domestic problems of States Members.

9. Department of Public Information, Press Release PM/2380, p. 2–3.

10. General Assembly, Seventh Session, ad hoc Political Committee, 8th Meeting, 3 November 1952, p. 29.

11. Ibid., 21st Meeting, 20 November 1952, p. 34.

12. S/PV.1990, p. 23.

13. Resolution 31/6(I). It was adopted by 134 votes to 0, with one abstention.

14. From a statement by Ambassador Leslie O. Harriman of Nigeria, as Chairman of the Special Committee against *Apartheid*, A/31/PV.42, 26 October 1976, pp. 33–35.

15. Economic Club Dinner in New York, 13 November 1973. United States Mission to the United Nations, USUN 110(73), p. 5.

16. See, for example, G. M. Theal's classic *History of South Africa*, first

published in Capetown in 1900. Reprinted in Capetown in 1964; see also *Cambridge History of South Africa*, Cambridge University Press, 1963.

17. Statement by Ambassador Botha to the Security Council on 24 October 1974 (S/PV.1800, pp. 38–40).

18. Statement by the Representatives of the Blacks in South Africa. For text see *The New York Times*, 22 August 1976.

19. Text furnished by the South African Mission to the United Nations. Press Release dated 20 June 1977, pp. 21–22.

20. Statement by the Permanent Representative of Lebanon in the General Assembly on 14 October 1976, A/31/PV.32, p. 43–44.

21. General Assembly, Second Part of the First Session, Joint Committee of the First and Second Committee, 4th Meeting, 1946.

22. The General Assembly had twice rejected the motion of the South African Government for a pronouncement by the International Court of Justice on whether or not the issue of race relations in South Africa was essentially a matter of domestic jurisdiction of States in the sense of Article 2(7). Similar attempts by other States Members on other occasions were likewise frustrated.

23. See, for example, A/Res./33/74 entitled Non-Interference in the Internal Affairs of States adopted by the General Assembly 15 December 1978. The resolution urges all States

> to abide by the provisions of resolutions 31/91 and 32/153 in which the General Assembly denounced any form of interference in the internal or external affairs of States . . .

and reaffirms that

> a declaration on noninterference in the internal affairs of States would be an important contribution to the further elaboration of the principles for strengthening equitable cooperation and friendly relations among States, based on sovereign equality and mutual respect.

24. Office of Public Information Press Release SG/SM/2291, 9 January 1976, pp. 10–11.

25. American Journal of International Law 71(1) January, 1977, p. 65; p. 74; pp. 82–83.

26. When, for example, the ad hoc Political Committee in 1952 rejected South Africa's challenge to discuss the domestic situation of a Member State, the main argument put forward in reply was that the General Assembly, by adopting a series of resolutions on the treatment of people of Indian origin, had clearly demonstrated that it did not consider the question as being entirely within the domestic jurisdiction of South Africa. Whereupon the Belgian representative suggested that to maintain that the question of competence had long been settled because the General Assembly had adopted several resolutions and taken a stand on substance was to beg the question. Either the Assembly was competent or it was not competent. If it was not, it could not correct that initial defect by

taking decisions, however numerous, which assumed its competence (ad hoc Political Committee, 11th Meeting, 7 November 1952, p. 6).

27. *Fifth Report on State Responsibility*, International Law Commission, 28th Session 1976 (A/CN.4/291, Add.2, pp. 40–41.

28. ECOSOC Resolution 974 D(XXXVI), 23 July 1963.

29. A/C.2/L.1022. The draft resolution also endorsed UNCTAD's resolution 26(II) suspending South Africa. For text see Proceedings of UNCTAD, second session, vol. I, annex I, p. 56.

30. A/C.2/SR.1240, p. 106.

31. For text see A/C.2/L.1030, 2 December 1968.

32. For a summary of the proceedings see A/C.2/SR.1238–1242.

33. A/C.2/SR.1242 p. 8.

34. A/PV.1740, pp. 1–9.

35. Ibid., p. 43.

36. Ibid., p. 30.

37. A/PV.

38. A/PV.1740, p. 109.

39. Ibid.

40. Ibid. The President's ruling was sustained by 56 votes to 48, with 13 abstentions.

41. A/8160, p. 3.

42. A/PV.1882, pp. 111–115.

43. Ibid., p. 116.

44. A/Resolution 2636(XXV).

45. A/Resolution 2862(XXVI); 2948(XXVII).

46. Amendment to First Report of the Credentials Committee, A/L.700. For Report see A/9179.

40. A/Resolution 3151(XXVIII) G 311.

48. Report of the Credentials Committee, A/9779.

49. See S/PV.1808, passim.

50. A/PV.2281, pp. 72–76. The ruling reads:

> On the basis of the consistency with which the General Assembly has regularly refused to accept the credentials of the delegation of South Africa, one may legitimately infer that the General Assembly would in the same way reject the credentials of any other delegation authorized by the Government of the Republic of South Africa to represent it, which is tantamount to saying in explicit terms that the General Assembly refuses to allow the delegation of South Africa to participate in its work (A/PV.2281, p. 86).

51. A/Resolution 1761(XVII) of 16 November 1962.

52. A/Resolution 33/183 G of 24 January 1979.

Chapter IV

THE CHILEAN ENCOUNTER

Chile's disastrous encounter with Marxism and its resonance in the United Nations is another striking example of the successful harnessing of the most lofty sentiments in the service of objectives that offer no framework for universal commitment. Coups d'état are a common occurrence and most of them come and go unheralded and unnoticed. Not so the coup d'état in Chile of 11 September 1973, which became a cause célèbre high on the agenda of the United Nations and a subject of heated debate and public and private inquiry. This may be accounted for not so much by the fact that the coup d'état constituted a sharp break with Chile's century-old traditions of civic life and democratic order, as by the reaction of the Third World and of the Communist camp. The Third World saw, in the overthrow of the Allende regime that cost the President his life, an assault on a new experiment which, in the words of the Mexican Foreign Minister, "sought to achieve profound structural changes in the life of the Chilean nation heading towards socialism," and which "the whole world followed with great interest and many with deep-rooted hope."[1] This was echoed in even more forceful language by Foreign Minister Bouteflika of Algeria, who told the General Assembly on 11 October 1973 that the overthrow of the Government of President Allende

> constituted an open challenge to all the countries of the Third World, assuming thus its true significance. . . . The Chilean people at present are living a tragic trial which calls into question not only their own freedom and threatens the results so painfully acquired by their social and economic revolution, but constitutes also a danger to the freedom and independence of all our peoples.[2]

To the Soviet Union and the other members of the so-called socialist camp, the Chilean experience was more than a confrontation between the forces of "progress" and "reaction", and more than an attempt by international imperialism" to deny victory to the struggle of peoples for national and social liberation; the coup d'état of 11 September 1973 was a fatal blow to the geopolitical policies of the Soviet Union and meant the loss of a strategic outpost in the ideological war of the Communist creed. Thus it was only natural that the Communist countries should have shouldered the burden of initiating and sustaining the campaign against Chile's military regime and of setting its tone and direction. What began at the twenty-eighth session of the United Nations General Assembly in the fall of 1973 as a modest campaign for the lives and safety of Luis Corvalan, Secretary-General of the Communist Party in Chile, and other prominent members of President Allende's Popular Unity Government, ended up as a frontal attack against the bleakly, totally anti-Communist Pinochet Government and as a crusade against a "fascist" regime. Under the guise of concern over reported gross violations of human rights and fundamental freedoms by the military junta in Chile, the Soviet Union succeeded in enlisting wide support in the United Nations for its vendetta against an ideological foe.

With the exception of Algeria, Mexico, the Netherlands, Norway, Pakistan and Tanzania, which variously expressed regret at the events in Chile in their statements in the general debate at the twenty-eighth General Assembly which opened in the wake of the overthrow of the Allende regime, the Communist countries were the only ones to raise their voices in protest against the coup d'état in Santiago. The Foreign Minister of Mongolia spoke for all, when he said:

> . . . The forces of reaction do not hesitate to prevent the introduction of democratic, social and economic changes in various countries, or to divert peoples from their chosen path of progressive development. This is evident from the military "putch" in Chile, which was carried out with the support of foreign imperialist forces. The Mongolian people resolutely condemn the overthrow of the legitimate Government of Popular Unity elected as a result of the will of the Chilean people, the treacherous murder of an outstanding statesman and politician, President Salvador Allende, and the

bloody reprisals against the progressive forces of the country. We express our heartfelt solidarity with the working people of Chile and demand an immediate end to the terror and repression against the progressive forces in the country, and respect for the will and aspirations of the Chilean people.[3]

All but Romania and China of the Communist countries broke off diplomatic relations with President Allende's successor Government. The overthrow of the Allende regime was originally treated by them as a politico-ideological event and neither the Soviet Union nor any member of the Soviet bloc perceived the situation in Chile in the context of human rights. What they asked for, besides hoping for the condemnation of the coup d'état by the General Assembly, was the use by the President of the General Assembly and by the Secretary-General of their good offices to secure humane treatment for persons who were prominent in the Government of Popular Unity and exposed to reprisals by the ruling military junta. It was the Norwegian Foreign Minister who first expressed concern over reports of maltreatment and persecution in Chile and asserted the right of the international community to expect respect for human rights and the immediate release of all political prisoners.[4] The Foreign Minister of the Netherlands, who was especially concerned over reports of torture and inhumane treatment of such prisoners, called for an impartial inquiry to ascertain the facts.[5] These two different perceptions of the events in Chile persisted to the very end; neither the ambience or venue in which the Chilean situation was considered, nor the auspices under which the debates had taken place, were able to break down those differences. What stood out was the ease with which an issue of human rights lent itself, even in the light of day, to exploitation for patently political and propaganda purposes.

As a politicoideological issue, the situation in Chile offered limited opportunities for such exploitation; coups d'état are not outlawed and there is no international code for ousting a government. But if there exists no code of political behavior for States, there is agreement on standards of human rights and their violation is clearly a matter of international concern. Thus, unless the developments in Chile could be reduced to an issue of human rights, there was no other way in which they could have been brought into international focus and remain for years on the active agenda of United Nations bodies. This helps explain why the Soviet Union, in spite of the obvious risks it involved, decided to raise the Chilean issue in the Commission on Human Rights and set in motion a process which at the end of five years had far from run its course;[6] the General Assembly, the Economic and Social Council, the Commission on Human Rights and the Sub-Commission on the Prevention of Discrimination and Protection of Minorities have each debated the situation in Chile at their annual meetings, heard reports from an ad hoc committee of inquiry set up for the purpose, and expressed their views in formal resolutions and decisions.

In raising the Chilean situation in the Commission on Human Rights the Soviet Union risked compromising a basic tenet of its foreign policy not to concede to the United Nations or any other international body the right to inferfere in the internal affairs of States. Indeed, the Soviet Union was variously challenged to explain why international attention was focussed on the situation in Chile while similar situations elsewhere were completely ignored. This goes far to account for the Soviet Union's hesitancy to go beyond condemnation as the proper action of the United Nations and its reluctant acceptance of the idea of an ad hoc working group to inquire into the facts. To the Marxist countries the debate on Chile in the United Nations was but part, and not necessarily the most important part, of a world-wide campaign to isolate the Pinochet Government politically and morally and hasten its downfall. Their concern with human rights and fundamental freedoms was at best incidental; as time went on, their interventions in the debates on Chile came to bear an increasingly politicoideological character in which human rights and fundamental freedoms gave way to Marxist rhetoric.

That the Soviet Union and its allies succeeded so well in exploiting the United Nations forum for patently political purposes and engaging the world Organization in the campaign against the military junta in Chile was due in no small measure to the broadmindedness of Western nations and their desire to be accommodating, if only to postpone the moment of truth. The Soviet initiative in enlisting the United Nations in the war against the "counterrevolutionary" Government of Chile posed a dilemma for the Western nations and perhaps for all others concerned with human rights. They could not pass over in silence the obvious misdeeds of the junta and ignore the torment that had been visited upon Chile without violating their traditional stance and posture. Yet to intervene meant to abet in the promotion of partisan objectives under a spurious wrapping of respectability. To some this may have seemed a small price to pay for the Soviet Union's precedent-setting involvement in the processes of the United Nations for dealing with gross violations of human rights and fundamental freedoms. Others may have acted in the spirit of received left-wing opinion which has always dictated that only tyranny of the right was destructive of the free and good life. The overwhelming majority of the States Members of the United Nations chose to keep their own counsel. While the Soviet bloc and most of the Western Powers were united in their denunciation of the military junta, however different their approach, and the majority of the Latin American countries protested against the strident voices of condemnation and the selective view of violations of human rights, the nonaligned world was guided by the political declaration of the Fourth Conference of Nonaligned Countries of 1973, and supplied the majorities behind the resolutions against the Pinochet Government. In 1973, the Nonaligned Conference, which had adjourned two days before the coup d'état of 11 September, hailed the Allende Government and the people of Chile for their struggle to consolidate their independence and build a new society and expressed solidarity with their efforts to achieve the economic and social transformation already started, to avoid civil war and preserve national unity.[7]

It was obvious from the very beginning that the Soviet Union was determined to extract the last ounce of propaganda value from the tragic events in Chile and to turn righteous indignation into unprincipled interest. On 19 February 1974, the representatives of Bulgaria, Byelorussian SSR, Cuba, Czechoslovakia, Hungary, Mongolia, Poland, Ukrainian SSR and the Union of Socialist Soviet Republics, addressed an urgent appeal to the Chairman of the Commission on Human Rights, which had convened on 4 February for its thirtieth session in New York, to intervene with the Chilean authorities

> to remove the mortal danger threatening Luis Corvalan and other members of the Popular Unity [Government] who consistently struggled for the rights of the Chilean people, who adhered to democratic principles and came out in favor of observance of law, and ensure that the Chilean authorities do not hinder the departure of these persons from the country if they so wish.[8]

They recalled that when in October 1973 the lives of Communist Party Secretary-General Corvalan and his associates in the Popular Unity Party were in danger from physical reprisal, voices were raised in the General Assembly in their defense and the President of the Assembly, as well as the Secretary-General, addressed corresponding appeals to the Chilean Government. The ten representatives expressed the hope that the intervention of the nations they asked for would have a like effect and bring relief to the victims of the junta. A letter of similar content was sent by the permanent representative of Yugoslavia.[9]

The letters were addressed on the eve of the Commission's scheduled annual debate on the item on its agenda which dealt with gross violations of human rights and fundamental freedoms and at once achieved effects of great emotional power. By design or accident, it fell to the widow of President Allende to open the debate when the representatives of the Soviet Union, Bulgaria, the German Democratic Republic, Yugoslavia, Czechoslovakia, Poland and Byelorussia yielded the floor to Mrs. Allende, who spoke for the Women's International Democratic Federation, a nongovernmental organization in consultative status with the Economic and Social Council and as such entitled to address the Commission at the invitation of the Chairman. The staging of Mrs. Allende's appearance and her hour-long statement[10] in which she bore witness to a soul-searching drama heightened the dramatic impact of her indictment of the military junta and created an emotional atmosphere in which representatives of governments could give passionate, even violent, testimony to their sense of grievance.

The debate in the Commission was dominated by the interventions of the Soviet bloc, whose theme was the fascist nature of the coup d'état in Chile and the duty of the United Nations to condemn and denounce the military junta.[11] In line with their letter to the Commission's Chairman of 19 February 1974, the action the signatory States sought was in the form of a telegram to the Chilean Government deploring the violations of human rights and insisting upon the safety of persons exposed to special danger and their freedom to seek asylum abroad. A proposal by the representative of the Netherlands for an ad hoc inquiry group,[12] first suggested by his Foreign Minister on 26 September 1973 in the General Assembly,[13] and a similar proposal made by Mrs. Allende in a letter of 30 December 1973 to Secretary-General Kurt Waldheim,[14] elicited no comment from them. On 1 March 1974, the Commission agreed on the text of a telegram to the Chilean Government, in which it stated that it had

> considered with deep concern numerous reports from a wide variety of sources relating to gross and massive violations of human rights in Chile in contradiction with the Universal Declaration of Human Rights and other relevant international instruments ratified by a great number of countries, including Chile,

and called upon the Government for the

> immediate cessation of any kind of violations of human rights committed contrary to the principles of the United Nations Charter and other international instruments, including the International Covenants on Human Rights.

In addition, the Commission expressed

> particular concern for the protection of persons whose lives are reported to be in imminent danger. These include such outstanding political, social and cultural figures as former ministers, senators and heads and professors of universities, among others, Clodomiro Almeida, Luis Corvalan, Enrique Kirberg, Pedro Felipe Ramires and Anselmo Dule, whose names have been cited as presently in the greatest danger for reasons of health or the conditions of their detention,

and insisted that the

> abovementioned persons and other Chilean citizens and foreigners in similar situations should not be prevented from leaving the country if they wish to do so.

The Chilean authorities were further requested to inform the Chairman of the Commission on Human Rights

> as a matter of urgency about the measures undertaken in pursuance of this telegram and about the fate and welfare of the abovementioned and other persons being reported in dangerous conditions.[15]

The wording of the telegram to the Chilean Government represented a compromise between the Soviet Union and its allies and the Western and Western-oriented nations. The Soviet Union insisted upon representing the situation in Chile in terms of a counterrevolutionary effort to suppress the forward march of socialism, in which more than the violation of individual rights was involved. In fact, the undisguised determination of the Soviet bloc to use the United Nations platform to aim at the "counter-revolutionary" Pinochet Government prompted the representative of the Netherlands to remark at the 1272nd meeting of the Commission in 25 February 1974, that

> the words and deeds of members of the Commission showed that they tended to look at human rights in the perspective of the direct interests of their governments, which does not always coincide with the interests of persons and peoples the Commission was supposed to defend.[16]

The Western Powers could see no other ground for appealing to the Chilean Government than concern over the reported gross violations of human rights. While the Soviet Union obtained partial satisfaction when the Commission agreed to breaking a long-established precedent by mentioning in the telegram the names of the leading members of the Popular Unity Party for whose safety it had expressed special concern, there is no doubt that by taking the initiative in the first place and agreeing to the wording of the telegram to the Chilean Government, the Soviet Union appeared to give grudging recognition to the assertion by the Commission of Human Rights of the right to call governments to account for gross violations of human rights and fundamental freedoms. As we shall see later on, the Soviet Union tried to fortify itself against the assault of such spurious novelty, while the West staked too much on an isolated experience which provided no continuity of attitude or a reference for judgment.

When the Economic and Social Council convened for its fifty-sixth session in the spring of 1974, the initiative was seized by Western Powers which sought to keep the Chilean issue within the context of human rights. On 14 May 1974, the Social Committee of the Council adopted by a vote of 41 to none, with 2 abstentions, a resolution sponsored by the Netherlands, Sweden and the United Kingdom, which endorsed the dispatch by the Commission on Human Rights two months earlier of the telegram to the Chilean Government and called upon that Government

> to take all necessary steps to restore and safeguard basic human rights and fundamental freedoms in Chile particularly in those cases involving a threat to human life and liberty.[17]

As in the Commission on Human Rights, so in the Economic and Social Council, the divergence in perception of the Chilean situation between the Soviet bloc and the West was unmistakable.[18] While the latter laid stress on the importance of safeguarding human rights, the Soviet Union and its allies emphasized the struggle of the Chilean people for "democracy" and "true independence", and appealed for the full support of the Chilean "patriots" by the "progressive" peoples all over the world—code words which have a special meaning of their own. Several representatives invoked the urgent need of achieving international solidarity in restoring the exercise of human rights in Chile by comparing that country to Germany under Nazi rule and therefore characterizing it as an international outlaw. "The United Nations", the representative of the German Democratic Republic concluded,

> had come into being in reaction against the fascism of Hitler, which had been characterized by its violation of human rights, and the Organization had the duty to demand that the fascist terror in Chile should cease.[19]

The two perceptions of the Chilean situation continued to coexist in relatively easy counterpoint through the twenty-seventh session of the Sub-Commission on Prevention of Discrimination and Protection of Minorities in August 1974. The Sub-Commission was under pressure from the Soviet expert to act "as swiftly as possible to save from execution four persons who were threatened with death", and to take "all possible steps" to put an end to the reign of arbitrary rule and injustice in Chile.[20] This time, however, the Soviet Union was constrained to make rather far-reaching concessions to the West, by agreeing to cosponsor a resolution which invoked indirectly a procedure established by the Economic and Social Council in resolution 1503(XLVIII) of 27 May 1970, conceding to the United Nations an authority in the field of implementing human rights that, theoretically, might be regarded as radical and has been anathema to proponents of the principle of nonintervention in the internal affairs of States. The principal features of the procedure are the reliance upon information from nongovernmental sources to activate it; the authority of the Sub-Commission on Prevention of Discrimination and Protection of Minorities to evaluate that information for purposes of making recommendations to the Commission on Human Rights for further action, and the authority of the Commission to make inquiries into the facts, with the express consent of the State concerned, and to make appropriate recommendations. The text of the resolution of the Sub-Commission, cosponsored by the experts from France, Italy, Mexico, Pakistan, Sudan, Tunisia, the Soviet Union and Yugoslavia, and adopted on 21 August 1974 by a vote of 17 to none, with 4 abstentions, reads:

> *The Sub-Commission on Prevention of Discrimination and Protection of Minorities,*
>
> *Noting* that the General Assembly, in its resolution 3059(XXVIII), expressed its grave concern that torture and other forms of cruel, inhuman or degrading treatment or punishment are still practiced,
>
> *Noting* the serious concern expressed by the Commission on Human Rights about gross and mass violations of human rights in Chile, particularly those involving a threat to human life and liberty,
>
> *Deeply concerned* about reports of gross violations of human rights and fundamental freedoms in Chile including arbitrary arrest, torture, cruel and inhuman treatment of the prisoners and detainees in gaols and concentration camps,
>
> *Considering* that, notwithstanding the actions of the Commission on Human Rights and of the Economic and Social Council, and notwithstanding the General Assembly's specific rejection of all forms of torture and other cruel, inhuman or degrading treatment or punishment, numerous grave allegations continued to be made charging a consistent pattern of such flagrant violation of human rights,
>
> 1. *Makes an urgent appeal* to the Government of Chile to respect the Universal Declaration of Human Rights and to comply with the International Covenants on Human Rights, signed and ratified by the Government of Chile, and to take all necessary steps to restore and

safeguard basic human rights and fundamental freedoms in Chile, particularly those involving a threat to human life and liberty;

2. *Recommends* that the Commission on Human Rights at its thirty-first session study the reported violations of human rights in Chile, with particular reference to torture and other cruel, inhuman or degrading treatment or punishment;

3. *Requests* the specialized agencies, other intergovernmental organizations, as well as nongovernmental organizations in consultative status concerned to submit to the Secretary-General for reference to the Commission on Human Rights recent and reliable information on torture and other cruel, inhuman or degrading treatment or punishment in Chile;

4. *Requests* the Secretary-General to bring the present resolution to the attention of the Chilean authorities.[21]

In reality, however, the Soviet Union had little interest in the recommendations of the Sub-Commission. These were completely ignored by the Foreign Ministers of the Soviet bloc nations in their statements in the general debate at the twenty-ninth General Assembly in 1974, as their references to Chile continued in a polemical vein. A new note was introduced by the Foreign Minister of the German Democratic Republic, who warned that the acts of the military junta in Chile against "upright patriots" was creating a dangerous source of tension in Latin America and challenged international public opinion as a whole.[22] The Foreign Minister of Mongolia said that the people of his country resolutely demanded that the "savage" repression against "Communists and other representatives of democratic and progressive forces" in Chile be halted.[23] And the Foreign Minister of Czechoslovakia spoke approvingly of the world-wide solidarity with the Chilean people which was reflected in the United Nations and urged the world body to continue to take steps against the mass violations of human rights in Chile and for the release of Luis Corvalan and other patriots.[24]

Moreover, in October 1974, Algeria, Cuba, Democratic Yemen, German Democratic Republic, Guinea Bissau, Mali, Mongolia, Senegal and Yugoslavia, later joined by Gabon, Poland and Gambia, tabled a draft resolution in the Third Committee of the General Assembly which, while it recalled in the preamble the urgent appeal to the Chilean authorities made by the Sub-Commission in its resolution of 21 August 1974, it omitted all reference to the Sub-Commission's recommendations for a study of the situation in Chile to be made by its parent body, the Commission on Human Rights. The joint resolution was purely admonitory, designed to denounce the Chilean junta rather than to suggest remedies. It called upon the Chilean authorities

> to respect fully the principles of the Universal Declaration of Human Rights, to restore basic human rights and fundamental freedoms immediately, to put an end to the judicial proceedings instituted against persons detained or imprisoned because of their political convictions, including outstanding personalities in the political, trade union and cultural fields, to order their immediate release and to grant safe conduct to anyone desiring it;

and requested the President of the twenty-ninth General Assembly and the Secretary-General

> to take any appropriate measures, in the light of paragraph 3 above, which may help to reestablish basic human rights and fundamental freedoms.[25]

The West's reaction to the attempt to evade the commitment made by the Soviet expert in the Sub-Commission was foreseeable. That same day, the representative of the Netherlands introduced in the Third Committee a draft resolution cosponsored by Australia, Denmark, Finland, New Zealand and Sweden, and subsequently also by Belgium and Norway, entitled Protection of Human Rights in Chile, which was aimed principally at endorsing the recommendation of the Sub-Commission for a Study by the Commission on Human Rights of the reported violations of human rights in Chile.[26] To prevent any deviation from the purposes of the draft resolution, the human rights addressed were qualified by the statement "with particular reference to torture and cruel, inhuman or degrading treatment or punishment." The resolution also appealed to the Government of Chile "to heed the widely-expressed concern and to respect the basic rights enshrined in the Universal Declaration of Human Rights."

In the end, to avoid confrontation, a balance was struck between the protagonists of analysis and polemics, when the two draft resolutions were withdrawn in favor of a compromise text moved by the sponsors of the original drafts and cosponsored by the United Kingdom, Bulgaria, Byelorussian SSR, the Congo,

Czechoslovakia, the Ukrainian SSR and the Soviet Union. Concessions were made by each of the groups in question, and they were reflected in the sharper language addressed to the Chilean Government and in the endorsement of the Sub-Commission's recommendation for a study by the Commission on Human Rights of the reported violations in Chile.[27] The resolution was adopted on 22 October 1974, by a roll call vote of 83 in favor to 9 against, with 21 abstentions. Voting against the resolution were Argentina, Bolivia, Brazil, Chile, Colombia, Guatemala, Nicaragua, Paraguay and Uruguay, Barbados, Costa Rica, Dominican Republic, Egypt, El Salvador, Ethiopia, Fiji, Grenada, Honduras, India, Indonesia, Jordan, Malawi, Malaysia, Philippines, Singapore, Spain, Thailand, Togo, United States and Venezuela.[28]

With the adoption of the resolution the situation in Chile became a fixed feature on the agenda of the United Nations, with a guaranteed annual review by the United Nations bodies directly concerned. More than a safe international platform from which to harass the military junta in Chile, the passage of the resolution created a framework of self-justification for the politico-ideological intentions of the Soviet Union; it freed the Soviet Union's initiative from the uncertainties which inhibited the full flowering of the campaign against the Chilean Government. By cosponsoring a text which promised an orderly procedure for ascertaining the facts and rendering judgment they sapped the will of the West to suffer reality.

As already suggested, the Soviet Union and its allies carefully avoided any reference to existing United Nations procedures for dealing with gross violations of human rights and sought nothing from the world body other than denunciation of the Chilean Government and freedom and safety for certain persons who were closely associated with the Allende regime. The initiatives of the West for further action may have embarrassed them, but they served the purpose of ensuring the Chilean issue a permanent place on the agenda of the United Nations and providing the Soviet Union with a convenient platform from which to aim at the Pinochet Government. When the Commission on Human Rights convened for its thirty-first session in February 1975, it had before it massive documentation on the situation in Chile, generously supplied by governments and nongovernmental organizations in compliance with the request made by the Sub-Commission on Prevention of Discrimination and Protection of Minorities in its resolution of 21 August 1974 "to submit to the Secretary-General for reference to the Commission on Human Rights recent and reliable information on torture and other cruel, inhuman or degrading treatment or punishment in Chile;" the ILO, UNESCO and the Organization of American States were joined by at least ten nongovernmental organizations in consultative status in submitting the required information.[29] Members of the Commission came amply supplied with dossiers of their own and the Soviet Union and others also spoke approvingly of the "world-wide solidarity" with the Chilean people which was reflected in the United Nations and abroad.

A remark made by the representative of the German Federal Republic at the opening of the debate on Chile on 23 February 1975, to the effect that the Commission on Human Rights was not an organ for promoting ideological crusades,[30] was the first public acknowledgment by the West of the Soviet Union's efforts to bend the Commission to its own purposes. While the West argued that any action taken by the Commission must serve the ends of justice and the cause of human rights, the Soviet Union and its allies were anxious to rush to judgment. They produced a draft resolution[31] which would unceremoniously have condemned the "constant and flagrant violation of basic human rights and fundamental freedoms in Chile" and urged the Chilean Government to implement immediately all General Assembly and other resolutions calling for the restoration of human rights, put an end to arbitrary arrest, torture and forced mass exile, and release all political prisoners. To the argument that more could be achieved by endeavoring to cooperate with States than by condemning them, and that a deeper investigation by the Commission into the facts, in cooperation with the Government concerned, was more likely to foster the restoration of human rights in Chile, the answer was given that everything there was to know was known and that an independent investigation by the Commission, as proposed by the West, would only give the junta more time to carry its "monstrous and barbaric acts" further. The Soviet bloc representatives were in agreement that the Pinochet Government was a tool for "restoring the influence of the capitalist Powers and enabling them to continue the exploitation of the Chilean people." They shared the Soviet Union's conviction that "one day the people of Chile would sweep their oppressors away, as the peoples of Greece and Portugal had recently done."

In the end, as could have been foreseen, the Soviet bloc and the West agreed on a compromise resolution which combined the harsh language of the socialist States with the Western proposal for an ad hoc inquiry group. Among other things, all references which were contained in the Western draft resolution co-sponsored by The Netherlands, Nicaragua and the United Kingdom and which gave the junta the benefit of doubt by recalling the cooperation it had extended to the United Nations High Commissioner for Refugees, the ILO, the International Committee of the Red Cross and the Organization "in their respective fields of competence relating to the protection of human rights in Chile"[32] were omitted in the compromise text. In return, the Soviet Union consented to the appointment by the Commission of a three-member ad hoc working group "to inquire into the present situation of human rights in Chile on the basis of a visit to the country and of oral and written evidence to be gathered from all relevant sources."[33]

With the appointment of the ad hoc working group the factors which for two years seduced the Soviet Union and the West into postures that were inappropriate to their characters had all but disappeared; there was no longer any occasion for compromise to keep the Chilean situation on the agenda of the world body or to enable the United Nations to acquit itself of its responsibilities in the face of gross violations of human rights. But whereas the Soviet Union retained full freedom to prosecute its campaign against Chile as circumstances dictated, the West could not turn its back on its own words spoken against the Chilean Government without offending their constituencies. Unless the Government came forward with convincing proof attesting to the amelioration of the human rights situation in the country, the Western nations could not but continue to address more of the same admonitions to the military junta and engage in more of the same denunciations so consumately desired by the Soviet Union. The withdrawal by the Pinochet regime of its consent to allow entry into Chile of the ad hoc Working Group of Inquiry appointed by the Commission on Human Rights had a disorienting effect.[34] Thus when the Sub-Commission on Prevention of Discrimination and Protection of Minorities convened in Geneva for its twenty-eighth session in August 1975, the West came with divided counsel. While the Soviet Union pressured the Sub-Commission to address itself with speed and vigor to the Chilean situation, even if it meant giving it priority over the items on *apartheid* and the Middle East,[35] at least some experts from the West were not certain whether they did the right thing in concentrating on Chile. The expert from Italy, for example, suggested that the United Nations was acting inconsistently by showering its attention on some situations involving human rights and ignoring others, which only confirmed that the degree of attention given to various cases was governed by political interests. Nevertheless, he argued, intervention in the Chilean human rights situation was necessary, or the world would be guilty of complicity.[36] Others, like the expert from Egypt, wondered whether the Sub-Commission acted properly in getting involved in controversial issues at critical junctures and in passing judgment.[37] The expert from Ecuador, which was one of the few Latin American countries to endorse the intervention of the United Nations in the Chilean situation, regretted that the Sub-Commission was being diverted from its true vocation and engaging in political condemnations which were not within its province. He criticized the Sub-Commission for ignoring the procedures for dealing with violations of human rights and instead of confining itself to determining whether apparent cases of a consistent pattern of violations of human rights should be referred to the Commission on Human Rights as the organ competent to take appropriate decisions, the Sub-Commission was drawing conclusions without evidence and without giving Governments concerned the opportunity to present their views. The expert from Ecuador thought that the Sub-Commission's draft resolution which expressed concern over the reported continued violations of human rights in Chile was ill-conceived and gratuitous.[38] And the United States expert rebuked the experts from the Soviet Union and the Netherlands for their rebuttal of the Chilean observer's statement on the situation in his country as harmful polemics.[39]

Clearly, the Chilean issue had settled down to a war of attrition. But if the incessant drumbeat of criticism levelled against Chile was understandable, and even logical, within the Soviet Union's terms, the position staked out in the debate by the West was devoid of ideological and practical guidance. As already noted, the Soviet Union was engaged in a deliberate campaign against an ideological foe with the hope of bringing down a regime that intruded into its long-range political plans; the West, on the other hand, protested concern over an internal situation which offended its sensibilities and was confronted more with the agony of judgment than with the certainty of truth. Surely the action of the United Nations against Chile was the work of many hands, not all of them pious, and the product of mixed motives, not all of them worthy; but it was the connotative value of a slogan, or a word, or a name, that aided and abetted the meaning of that action. Under Soviet pressure, language was forced to surrender much of its ability to describe reality, and the proceedings in the several organs of the world body became increasingly more tendentious than topically correct. Different criteria went into the making of judgment against Chile and sooner or later they were bound to come into abrupt and painful collision. There was no way out for the West but to reassess its role in the anti-Chilean campaign. Barring that, and following the pattern already well-established in other areas, the West chose to follow the lead given by the Soviet Union and its allies. For there are certain things which work only in basically liberal societies, where the ruling power itself is governed by moral absolutes and is thus guilt-ridden. Such guilt has often proven to be a disabling affliction that led to absurd and dangerous consequences; the West has chosen to exert moral pressure on the Chilean authorities, even when the cause they served was already lost.

Cuba's Foreign Minister set forth in clear and unequivocal

language the Soviet bloc's true perception of the situation in Chile when he spoke in the general debate at the thirtieth session of the General Assembly in 1975. Said the Foreign Minister of Cuba:

> The General Assembly must give highest priority to consideration of the situation in Chile. It is no longer merely a question of claiming human rights and alleviating the drama that torments the people of Chile. The institution of fascism in Chile, as we have said from the very beginning and as events bear out today, is part of an offensive by the most retrograde forces directed not only against the peoples of Latin America but also their brothers in Africa and Asia which are fighting against imperialism, colonialism and racism.
>
> Latin American fascism is the natural ally of racism and colonialism. It is in fact in their service. It seeks to act as a wedge that will break the necessary solidarity between the peoples of the three continents. The struggle against it, therefore, becomes of primary importance for all the peoples of Africa, Asia and Latin America. Were there no such colonial fascism, Mr. Vorster could not travel around South America; the South African Davis Cup team could not compete unconcernedly in Santiago; nor could the partisans and supporters of *apartheid* indulge in wild propaganda in favor of their hateful policy from a number of capitals in the southern tip of South America. Therefore the Foreign Ministers of the nonaligned countries, meeting in Lima last August, rightly declared:
>
> > The Conference took note with concern of the recent visit of the head of the racist regime of South Africa to Uruguay and Paraguay, as well as of the increasing relations of other Governments of Latin America, particularly the Chilean Government, with the South African regime (NAC/FM/CONF.5/para. 37).
>
> The case of Chile is still the subject of unanimous concern. Engendered by the most repugnant treason and violence and conceived as a means of reversing the democratic and liberating process undertaken by the Government of President Allende, the fascist regime makes a mockery of all humanitarian principles, continues its crimes and outrages against the Chilean people and challenges the voices of protest that are raised in all sectors of democratic world opinion. Not a single international conference of note has been held in the past year that has failed to express its most categorical repudiation of the atrocities committed by the Pinochet junta or that has not called for the termination of his hateful policy of repression and the betrayal of national interests. To bear those out, we have the agreements of the ILO, the Dakar Conference of the developing countries, the World Conference of the International Women's Year, the Fifth Ministerial Conference of the Nonaligned Countries, the recent meeting of the Governing Board of UNESCO and many other gatherings of a governmental or nongovernmental character.

Last year the General Assembly gave its President and the Secretary-General a mandate. The efforts deployed by both—which we appreciate—have proved fruitless. The Commission on Human Rights set up an Ad Hoc Working Group to submit a report and visit Chile. Initially the fascist authorities supported the decision of the Commission and declared, like demagogues, that they would welcome the members of the Working Group. At the eleventh hour, when its members were about to board a plane for Santiago, they cancelled the authorization for the journey. By refusing the visit of the Working Group, the fascist junta gave proof of what it was uselessly attempting to deny and it did so, moreover, with the shamefacedness and contempt for the international community which have become a rule of conduct of a regime which today represents, to a degree only matched by its South African allies and mentors, a stigma of our time.

It is now up to the General Assembly at its current session to give the insolence of the Pinochet regime the response it deserves. Solidarity with the antifascist resistance of the Chilean people must be expanded and strengthened until we can put a stop to the activities of the clique which now oppresses them. We are convinced that the General Assembly will know how to do its duty.[40]

The Cuban Foreign Minister's statement was in large measure a preview of the debate on Chile which took place in the Third Committee later on in the session of the General Assembly.[41] In the center of the debate was the first progress report of the Ad Hoc Working Group appointed by the Commission on Human Rights and its recommendations.[42] These included prosecution of the head of the Secret Police for crimes against humanity; immediate termination of the state of siege proclaimed by General Pinochet upon assumption of power; abolition of military courts and review of their judgments by civil tribunals; repeal of all laws passed after the coup d'état of 11 September 1973 which were "contrary" to the Constitution of 1925; restoration of Chilean nationality to all exiles and their freedom to return to their country; restoration of freedom of association and trade union rights; and the reestablishment of an atmosphere of intellectual freedom in schools, colleges and universities and their freedom from military control. Participating in the debate were all the members of the Soviet bloc, most of the Latin American countries, a handful of Western European nations, Australia and New Zealand.

It was Cuba which opened the debate and its representative

restated the thesis that the Pinochet Government was a regime of "murderers imposed through foreign intervention whose only objective was to destroy the achievements of the former Government and to reduce Chile to a mere bastion of imperialism, colonialism and racism." He said that the sequence of events in Chile was of profound significance for all the peoples of Africa, Asia and Latin America, as well as for "democratic circles" throughout the world. The Allende Government, he added, had attracted tremendous interest and had given millions of people reason to hope that an unjust social order could be changed by peaceful means and because of his absolute fidelity to his principles, President Allende himself became a universally recognized symbol of socialism and freedom. He compared Chile under the military junta to South Africa and classed them both as countries whose sovereignty had been usurped by imperialist interests and therefore were without the attributes normal to Members of the United Nations.[43]

The interventions of the other members of the Soviet bloc were but variations on the same theme. A new note was introduced by the representative of Mongolia, who also attacked the economic policies of the Chilean regime. The rights and interests of the population in the economic and social spheres, he said, were constantly being violated in Chile. The junta had put into effect a whole range of measures in the economic sphere which virtually eliminated the gains made by the Chilean people under the leadership of the government of National Unity. Those actions of the junta, the Mongolian representative went on to say, were carried out in order to please foreign and national monopolies and were not only a flagrant betrayal of the basic interests of Chile, but had brought the country to the verge of bankruptcy. Despite the very high rate of inflation and unemployment, he concluded, the junta was taking no measures to prevent the impending economic catastrophe, but was continuing to maintain an atmosphere of terror and violence and to allocate enormous resources to armaments.[44]

Clearly, what the Soviet bloc nations asked of the General Assembly was that it pronounce itself not on the reported violations of human rights in Chile, but on whether the Chilean political system was just or unacceptable and its Government legal or an usurper. The answer to those questions, the representative of Portugal declared, depended upon the convictions held by the various speakers; he himself found sufficient evidence in the Progress Report of the Working Group of violations of human rights by the Pinochet regime to warrant universal condemnation.[45] The representative of Denmark remarked that while in some cases expressions of concern for human rights might not have been unmixed with political considerations, the position of the United Nations was on the whole based on sincere concern. Denmark, he said, felt a moral obligation to speak up whenever human rights were violated, whether in Chile or elsewhere, regardless of the political or social system of the Government concerned.[46] The Norwegian representative stated bluntly that his country would not agree to the misuse of human rights issues for ideological purposes, and warned that there was no place for political opportunism in that context or the credibility of the United Nations in its task of promoting human rights for all would be gravely undermined. There was danger, he added, that as a consequence of the attitudes expressed in the Committee, the Chilean Government would arrive at the conclusion that from its standpoint and under the conditions which prevailed in Chile, a further stiffening of its internal and external attitudes was the only alternative open to it.[47] The United Kingdom representative declared that his Government had no interest in conducting a vendetta against the Chilean Government and that while it felt that the United Nations had an obligation to speak out in the present circumstances, the world Organization could not prejudge the outcome of the procedures of investigation or fail to take account of whatever hopeful signs of improvement in the human rights situation in Chile. To do so, he added, would only destroy the credibility and authority of the United Nations.[48] The representatives of Australia[49] and New Zealand[50] spoke in a similar vein, suggesting that specific instances of violations of human rights could not be overlooked just because similar violations were suspected to occur in other countries.

Those doubts and reservations concerning the fairness of the debate on Chile were completely absent in the statement of the representative of Sweden. The Swedish representative insisted upon the justice of the United Nations in calling Chile to account, but only after he had launched into an attack upon the then incumbent Government in Spain and appealed for international support of the Spanish democratic opposition in its efforts to "restore freedom to the people of Spain and respect for human rights and fundamental freedoms".[51] The Swedish statement provoked protest from the representative of Spain who called it intemperate and an example of the kind of distortion "not uncommon in the United Nations" which consisted of confusing political motivations with the moral and humanitarian objectives of the Charter. He accused the Swedish representative of lack of prudence, which he said was responsible for the prevailing selective morality at the United Nations and which chose its victims in accordance with whether expediency or political intrigues were focussed on one side or the other of the spectrum of social and economic systems in the international community.[52]

The radicalization and polarization of the Chilean issue was unmistakable; and so was its divisiveness. Only the Chilean people could set themselves up as judges of the junta in their country, said the representative of Bolivia, as he expressed surprise that countries which traditionally had been indifferent to events in Latin America and to Latin American aspirations, frustrations and misfortunes, were now showing an unusual interest in its affairs and presuming to tell Chile what kind of government it should have. He recalled that his country, too, had experienced a social revolution, and that in the name of that revolution concentration camps were set up, men, women and children were tortured and the country impoverished; but because those iniquities were committed in the name of social progress and the opposition was denounced as reactionary or fascist, little concern was shown for the persecuted, and the complaints lodged with the Commission on Human Rights were buried in the files of international bureaucracy never to see the light of day. With the passage of time, the Bolivian representative continued, his country had come to regard the world's indifference as a blessing in disguise, since it enabled the people of

Bolivia to solve their own problems without foreign interference. Chile, too, he concluded, could well take care of its own problem and he counselled the "self-appointed champions of human rights" to set their own houses in order and stop interfering in other people's affairs.[53]

Bolivia's sentiments were shared by Argentina, Brazil, Uruguay and seven other Latin American nations that voted against the resolution on Chile, which followed largely the recommendations contained in the report of the Ad Hoc Working Group. But even Costa Rica, which along with Honduras and Venezuela abstained in the voting, both in the Committee and in plenary, was deeply troubled by the proceedings. Speaking in explanation of its vote, the representative of Costa Rica said:

> Costa Rica had always held that the protection of human rights must have a universal character, which must be maintained if the defect of partiality which would deprive the United Nations of all credibility was to be avoided. A trend which was extremely dangerous for the Organization could currently be observed: violations of human rights seemed to be increasing throughout the world, but the efforts to combat them were focussed exclusively on certain situations, while others involving equally serious and persistent violations were ignored. The refusal to view the problem in a universal context demonstrated tolerance, not to say complicity, with regard to certain countries.
>
> So much was being made of the case of a country that was going through a special and transitory phase, for it was well known that Chile had never been noted for defending violations of human rights. While acknowledging the sincerity of the concern of some of the sponsors of resolution 3219(XXIX) of 1974, Costa Rica questioned whether that resolution had been inspired by purely humanitarian objectives or by a genuine concern for human rights in Chile. The 1975 debate undoubtedly showed that the treatment of the question of human rights in Chile had been influenced by political publicity aimed at well-defined political goals.[54]

Others, too, expressed strong reservations regarding the propriety of United Nations action against Chile, even while they voted in favor of the resolution. The United States representative, for example, declared that while his delegation would vote for the resolution, it was not done without reservations. In the first place, he said, the approach was questionable: Chile now was in a particular situation and that could easily give rise to the argument of interference in the domestic affairs of a State. Secondly, some of the circumstances existing in Chile with respect to human rights were also found elsewhere, in particular in certain countries whose representatives had spoken out most strongly against events in Chile. That was pure hypocrisy, he added, and the United States condemned that attitude and did not wish to associate its vote with it. It would have been desirable and more honest to word the draft resolution in more general terms, the United States representative concluded.[55] Similarly, the representative of Trinidad and Tobago stated that he had voted in favor of the resolution with a heavy heart. His country, he said, was persuaded that human rights should be regarded as a principle and that violations of that principle should be treated as impartially as possible and condemned with equal vigor so far as possible. Unfortunately, two observable trends diminished the strength of that principle and these were, first, the attachment to certain political ideals, which defined violations in accordance with the angle from which they were viewed; second, the tendency of certain countries, usually Western European, to oppose violations of human rights only, or largely, when they occurred in certain other countries, generally other Western European countries or countries with populations of European origin, like Chile today and Spain, Greece and Brazil at other times. The confluence and occasional overlapping of those two trends, the representative of Trinidad and Tobago went on to say, produced a strange coalition which expressed unhappiness over the undoubted violations of human rights in Chile and created the impression of performing a role of accusatory selectivity. That, he concluded, was not what was wanted in the United Nations, as violations of human rights everywhere is and ought to be the concern of all nations.[56]

After two years of public debate, the basic issues which had led to placing the Chilean situation on the agenda of the United Nations were so blurred by the banality of the rhetoric they produced, that it was impossible to distinguish between judgment of fact and judgment of value. The Chilean question had been turned into an unremitting campaign of international class war in which the so-called socialist States had the upper hand, thanks largely to the concessions made to the wayward pieties of the

Soviet bloc nations. The Soviet Union and its allies urged the condemnation of evil and avoided any plausible suggestion of how to escape it, because that offered an instantaneous solution to what could not patently be instantly changed and fitted into their design against Chile.

Thus, when the Ad Hoc Working Group submitted its report[57] to the Commission on Human Rights at its thirty-second session in February 1976, the socialist States did not hesitate for a moment to accept it as offering categorical statements of truth and as confirming their analysis of the "fascistization" of life in Chile. The Cuban representative, for example, concluded from a reading of the report that the international community was duty-bound to rescue the people of Chile from the claws of fascism and urged the Commission to extend the mandate of the Ad Hoc Working Group so that it could continue to inform international public opinion of the true situation in Chile.[58] The Byelorussian representative found in the report confirmation "beyond any doubt" of the institutionalization of terror as a method of government in Chile, and asked the Commission to add its voice to the condemnation expressed by all "democratic" peoples of the world.[59]

Most of the Western representatives were satisfied that the report contained, if not evidence, at least grave presumptions of serious violations of human rights in Chile.[60] But they could not overlook the fact that the report was prepared without benefit of on-the-spot investigation and perhaps more importantly, that it touched all vital bases of Chilean public life and national policy, including the constitutionality of certain junta decrees, the justification of the state of siege, the discretionary power exercised by the specialized organs of State security, the limitations on human rights imposed by constitutional and legislative provisions enacted by the Pinochet Government, and the institutionalization of torture and degrading and inhuman treatment of prisoners and detainees. In the face of such a bill of indictment and intimate probing into Chile's internal affairs the Commission, many felt,[61] had to summon up an objectivity scarcely attainable by mortals, or at least the ability to assess the situation with a humanely balanced judgment. Hence, for reasons already explained, the debate on Chile in the United Nations had from the very beginning followed a set pattern which was characterized by reaction to rhetoric rather than to issues, confirming the observation of Trollope that politics did not need issues, only competition. Sooner or later, the United Nations should have stopped to inquire whether it commanded the moral authority and the resources to deal equitably with the Chilean and other Chilean-like situations. It did not do so as if compelled by a driving need to go on record in denouncing Chile as an initiation rite to redemption.[62]

The particular vision that moved the Soviet Union and its allies to inveigh against the Pinochet regime did not necessarily outrage the rest of the Members of the United Nations, even though they often voted together on resolutions denouncing the military junta; there was rarely a psychological unity between the conscious purposes which guided the different nations in their attitude toward Chile. Thus the strength behind the anti-Chilean campaign was not the strength of hopeful combatants, nor the strength that comes from a desperately brave belief in human solidarity; it was the strength or weakness that derives from a fortuitous coalition of political or ideological interests and the companionship it offers to States Members for public rehearsal of their humanity. It was not easy to sustain the campaign, as shown by the monotonous repetition of facts and opinions and restatement of old positions in successive years. If there was anything new at the sixtieth session of the Economic and Social Council, which convened soon after the close of the thirty-second session of the Commission on Human Rights, it was the apprehension among Soviet bloc members that the campaign against the military regime in Chile might, after all, establish an unwanted precedent or point of reference in the future. This explains why the representative of the German Democratic Republic found it necessary to couple his endorsement of the Commission on Human Rights' resolution on Chile with the following explanation:

> In conformity with Articles 55 and 56 of the Charter, it was the task of the United Nations to promote cooperation between States in ensuring respect for and observance of human rights and fundamental freedoms with a view

> to the creation of the conditions necessary for peaceful and friendly relations among nations based on respect for the principle of equal rights and self-determination of peoples. However, the obligation to cooperate in that endeavor was based on the assumption that the safeguarding of human rights was within the domestic jurisdiction of every State and was implemented in every country in accordance with its social system and its national and cultural traditions. Because the safeguarding of human rights was an obligation of all Member States, it had become an object of international cooperation, as indicated in Chapter IX of the Charter. The various human rights conventions, the Convention on the Elimination of All Forms of Racial Discrimination and also the Human Rights Covenants had been drafted accordingly. But they did not provide for rights of the individual which might be implemented by the United Nations against the citizen's State.
>
> The competence of the United Nations and the legitimacy of international concern were quite different in such cases as South Africa, Chile and the territories occupied by Israel, where the gross and systematic violation of human rights created a situation likely to impair friendly relations between nations or endanger peace. It should be noted in that connection that Economic and Social Council resolutions 1235(XLII) and 1503(XLVIII) were not concerned with single cases of violations of human rights but rather provided for investigation of situations revealing a consistent pattern of violation such as South Africa and Southern Rhodesia. That did not mean that there was no racial discrimination in other countries, but obviously it made a difference in terms of international concern. A State could, if it wished, authorize an international body to investigate individual cases under the procedure set forth in the various human rights instruments, but it could not be forced to submit to such procedures by a majority decision, especially if the majority was not a majority of the contracting parties. . . . Attempts to distract the attention of the Commission on Human Rights from systematic mass violations of human rights and fundamental freedoms which were likely to impair the general welfare or friendly relations among nations could only have the effect of preventing attention from being focussed on *apartheid*, racism, racial discrimination and colonialism. . . .
>
> Friendly cooperation of States as provided for in the Charter should not be replaced by a confrontation in the field of human rights.[63]

The representative of the German Democratic Republic only restated the position first enunciated by the Soviet Union in the early years of the United Nations to justify the world body's intervention against the policies of racial discrimination in South Africa.[64] The timing may have been influenced by the expressions of disappointment voiced by Western representatives on the

Economic and Social Council at the state of human rights in the world and at the tendency of the United Nations to be selective in its choice of targets for condemnation of violations of human rights. Thus, for example, the representative of Denmark was severely critical of the Commission on Human Rights and called upon it to

> pursue universal and not selective aims. The Commission had received numerous complaints of violations of human rights in many countries, in particular those lodged in pursuance of Economic and Social Council resolution 1503, and while it might be difficult to redress the alleged grievances even where they proved well-founded, those complaints should still be discussed—confidentially—with a view to finding solutions to them. . . . It was depressing to note that the Human Rights Commission, which should be the principal organ for the protection of human rights, seemed not to be playing the role assigned to it as a general, impartial, nonselective and unbiased defender of human rights.[65]

Indeed, several months after the close of the sixtieth session of the Economic and Social Council, the Sub-Commission on Prevention of Discrimination and Protection of Minorities, meeting at its twenty-ninth session in August 1976, recommended to its parent body, the Commission on Human Rights, that it make a thorough study of the human rights situation in Uganda,[66] and also expressed concern over reported violations of human rights in Argentina and expressed the hope that "international standards of human rights will be respected for the benefit of all now deprived of their human rights and fundamental freedoms."[67]

Whether or not the Sub-Commission's decision on Uganda compelled a significant reassessment of the role of the United Nations in the field of human rights, the fact that the Chilean situation figured for the fourth consecutive time on the active agenda of the General Assembly was an embarrassment to the Soviet Union. The Soviet Union had to battle away to keep life and purpose in the campaign against the Pinochet regime and yet all it could offer were wishes rather than concrete recommendations; political realities foreclosed any recommendations that could have materially altered the situation in Chile. But this did not deter nations that had been less inhibited in their advocacy of United Nations intervention in behalf of human rights to use the failure of the world body to bring about desired changes in Chile to argue the need for more radical international action in situations involving gross violations of human rights. Unless the Soviet Union was able to come forward with substantial recommendations of how to deal with the recalcitrant military junta, or join in the chorus of advocacy of greater authority for the United Nations in enforcing international standards of human rights, its credibility was bound to suffer. The choice, as may be seen, was in the direction indicated by the representative of the German Democratic Republic in the Social Committee of the Economic and Social Council.

Thus, speaking in the general debate on 8 October 1976, at the thirty-first session of the General Assembly, the Foreign Minister of the Ukrainian Soviet Socialist Republic declared:

> ... All honorable people on earth must condemn the inhumane, bloody junta in Chile. The United Nations must demand the cessation of the flagrant violation of human rights and freedom in Chile and the cruel treatment of the Chilean patriots, and must call for the immediate freeing of Luis Corvalan and other democrats languishing in the junta's gaols.
>
> It is the struggle against the most gross violations of human rights in Chile, in South Africa and in the Arab lands occupied by Israel, that constitutes a fundamental means of deepening the cooperation among States in the promotion of respect for and observance of human rights. Peoples of the world should do their utmost to provide for everyone, everywhere, an opportunity to live without poverty and unemployment, so that everyone can enjoy the right to work, education, freedom from exploitation, racial discrimination and oppression; as well as an opportunity to benefit from the scientific and technical revolution and progress.
>
> We, in the Ukrainian SSR, where all the activities of the Communist Party and the State show concern for promoting well-being and the free comprehensive development of all the members of our society, fully appreciate and understand the efforts of those States which are always striving genuinely to ensure human rights and to participate in international cooperation in this field.
>
> However, we cannot but denounce the attempt of certain circles in Western countries to use the noble slogans of the protection of human rights to camouflage flagrant and continuous violations of these rights in their own countries and to slander socialism, to interfere in the internal affairs of other countries, to undermine the national liberation movements of people and to discredit the policy of peaceful coexistence and detente.

> Such a speculation on the problem of safeguarding human rights is utterly unacceptable and should be ruled out in the United Nations.[68]

Five days later, the Foreign Minister of the Byelorussian SSR took a similar line when he stated:

> .... Our people have been raised in the spirit of proletarian internationalism, and they express their wholehearted solidarity with the struggle of the African peoples against racism and *apartheid*. They demand the cessation of atrocities of the fascist junta in Chile and the immediate release of that ardent champion of freedom, Luis Corvalan, and other Chilean democrats. The Soviet people are fighting actively for respect for human rights throughout the world; they resolutely oppose interference in the internal affairs of other countries and, naturally, they will not permit anyone to interfere in their affairs.
>
> As we know, there are still people to be found in the West who are fond of mischief making, of looking for violations of human rights where none exist. They are inclined not to notice the most flagrant mass violations of human rights in Chile, in the occupied Arab territories, in Southern Rhodesia and South Africa ...[69]

While these statements struck no new note, they anticipated the debate in the Third Committee. As already suggested, the Chilean situation had been too long on the agenda of the United Nations and too much politicized to maintain a responsible forward course; what had previously been persuasive became ominously insistent. The only way in which the campaign for human rights in Chile could expand into a genuine universal human rights issue was by expressing authentic international interests and concerns. They called for satisfactory answers to such questions as whether the year-long debate on the human rights situation in Chile expressed real or simulated rage; whether the United Nations avoided or practiced moral selectivity and double standards, and whether the world body acted in a truly humanitarian spirit. The bulk of the statements made on the item in the Third Committee touched precisely on those questions and betrayed a wide groping for the proper answers.

Thus the representative of Fiji, without specific reference to Chile, expressed fear that by singling out States in which there were gross violations of human rights, while remaining silent about those which, discreetly but deliberately, denied the rights of their own citizens, the United Nations was jeopardizing its credibility as an impartial, consistent and objective international body.[70] The representative of Italy thought that the question of human rights in Chile could not be considered in isolation from similar situations in other countries, but within the broader context of the world situation of human rights and of the role of the United Nations in their protection.[71] The representative of the German Federal Republic warned against the continuous politicization of the debate on Chile and declared that unless the United Nations strictly avoided any selectivity so that what was expected from Chile was also expected from others in similar situation, the moral authority of the world body was put in jeopardy.[72] Similar sentiments were expressed by the representatives of the United Kingdom,[73] France,[74] Ireland[75] and other Western representatives. The representative of Belgium argued that the Chilean case was of universal interest and that unless it was properly handled, it could harm the cause of human rights everywhere.[76] It was clear that whatever words were used they added up to a confession of uneasiness over the singular partnership between East and West in the defense of human rights in Chile.

Similarly, the total silence maintained by the Soviet bloc in respect to the issue of United Nations jurisdiction in the field of human rights raised by the Ukrainian SSR and Byelorussian SSR Foreign Ministers in the general debate, attested to the net of contradictions in which it was caught up. To have pressed the point would not only have confirmed the accusations of moral selectivity and double standards practiced by the United Nations, but would have also ranged the Soviet Union and its allies behind the arguments of most of the Latin American countries that the world body had overreached itself in its "zealous" defense of human rights in Chile to the point of gross impropriety.[77] As was suggested by the representative of France by way of general comment, when a nation had been so profoundly divided as Chile, it was impossible for the unity of the country to be achieved overnight. The Committee, he said, should not take positions on questions which were outside its competence, but express its convictions that the adoption of broad and generous measures by the Chilean authorities would help facilitate the national reconciliation which was necessary if the difficulties confronting the country were to be overcome.

On 23 November 1976 the Third Committee, after a series of separate votes on several paragraphs, approved by a recorded vote of 98 to 14, with 18 abstentions, a resolution which

> 1. *Expresses its profound indignation* that constant and flagrant violations of human rights have taken place and continue to take place in Chile, in particular the institutionalized practice of torture, cruel, inhuman and degrading treatment and punishment, the disappearance of persons for political reasons, arbitrary arrest, detention, exile and cases of deprivation of Chilean nationality;
>
> 2. *Calls once more upon* the Chilean authorities to restore and safeguard, without delay, basic human rights and fundamental freedoms and fully to respect provisions of the international instruments to which Chile is a party, and, to this end:
>
> (a) To cease using the state of siege or emergency for the purpose of violating human rights and fundamental freedoms and, having regard to the observations by the Ad Hoc Working Group on the Situation of Human Rights in Chile, to reexamine the basis on which the state of siege or emergency is applied with a view to its termination;
>
> (b) To put an end to the practice of torture and other forms of cruel, inhuman or degrading treatment or punishment by Chilean State agencies, particularly the Dirección de Inteligencia Nacionál, and to prosecute and punish those who are responsible;
>
> (c) To clarify forthwith the status of individuals whose disappearance is attributable to political reasons;
>
> (d) To release immediately those who have been arbitrarily arrested or detained without charge and those who are in prison solely for political reasons;
>
> (e) To release, furthermore, those who are detained or imprisoned on account of acts of commission or omissions which did not constitute a criminal offense at the time they were committed;
>
> (f) To guarantee fully the right of *habeus corpus* (amparo);
>
> (g) To cease the arbitrary deprivation of Chilean nationality and to restore it to those who have been so deprived;
>
> (h) To respect the right of everyone to freedom of association with others, including the right to form and join trade unions for the protection of his interests;
>
> (i) To guarantee the right to intellectual freedom.
>
> 3. Deplores the fact, despite previous assurances to the contrary, the Chilean authorities persistently refuse to allow the Ad Hoc Working Group to visit the country in accordance with its mandate;
>
> 4. Invites Member States, United Nations agencies and international

organizations to take steps which they may consider appropriate as a contribution to the restoration and safeguarding of human rights and fundamental freedoms in Chile, in accordance with the purposes and principles of the Charter of the United Nations, and welcomes the steps already taken to this end;

5. Invites the Commission on Human Rights to extend the mandate of the Ad Hoc Working Group, as presently constituted, so as to enable it to report to the General Assembly at its thirty-second session, and to the Commission, at its thirty-fourth session, with such additional information as may be necessary;

(b) To formulate recommendations on possible humanitarian, legal and financial aid to those arbitrarily arrested or imprisoned, to those forced to leave the country and to their relatives;

(c) To consider the consequences of the various forms of aid extended to the Chilean authorities.[78]

Voting for the resolution were all European nations with the exception of France, Spain and the Federal Republic of Germany, which abstained. Also abstaining were Indonesia, Israel, Ivory Coast, Malawi, Malaysia, Morocco, Nepal, Niger, Peru, Philippines, Saudi Arabia, Surinam, Thailand, Uganda and the United States. Voting against the resolution were Grenada, Guatemala, Haiti, Honduras, Nicaragua, Panama, Paraguay, Uruguay, Argentina, Bolivia, Brazil, Chile, Costa Rica and the Dominican Republic.[79]

The next two years saw much of the same, and more, with the General Assembly, the Commission on Human Rights and the Sub-Commission on the Prevention of Discrimination and the Protection of Minorities amassing resolutions reiterating their indignation at the state of affairs in Chile and summoning the Pinochet Government to turn from its wayward ways. Among other things the Commission on Human Rights, at the recommendation of the General Assembly, appointed a Special Rapporteur on the situation of human rights in Chile, in lieu of the Ad Hoc Working Group but along the lines of its mandate, and two companion experts to study, in cooperation with the Special Rapporteur, the question of missing and disappeared persons in Chile.[80] The Sub-Commission, on its part, acting on the request of the Commission on Human Rights, undertook a study on the consequences of the various forms of aid extended to the Chilean authorities, and appointed Professor Antonio

Cassese of Italy as Special Rapporteur to analyze the volume, origins, development and significance of the assistance given to the present regime in Chile, and to study whether a quantitative or qualitative change in the aid now being given might contribute to restoring respect for human rights in Chile.[81] The Sub-Commission also recommended, in response to the concern expressed in the General Assembly, the Economic and Social Council and the Commission on Human Rights, for the situation of persons detained or imprisoned in Chile under the state of siege and other emergency legislation, those who have disappeared and the families and dependents of such persons,

> that a voluntary fund administered under the authority of an independent board of trustees should be established to receive contributions and distribute humanitarian, legal and financial aid to those detained or imprisoned in Chile under the state of siege and other emergency legislation, to those forced to leave the country and to their relatives.[82]

And the General Assembly itself, rounding out five years of close attention to events in Chile, called once more upon the Chilean authorities to restore and safeguard, without delay, basic human rights and fundamental freedoms, and urged these authorities, in particular

> To cease the state of emergency, under which continued violations of human rights and fundamental freedoms are permitted;
> To restore the democratic institutions and constitutional safeguards formerly enjoyed by the Chilean people;
> To ensure an immediate end to torture and other forms of inhuman or degrading treatment and to prosecute and punish those responsible for such practices;
> To take urgent and effective measures in response to the profound international concern at the fate of persons reported to have disappeared for political reasons, and in particular to investigate and clarify the fate of these persons;
> To cease arbitrary arrest and detention and to release immediately those who are imprisoned for political reasons;
> To restore fully the right of *habeas corpus*;
> To restore Chilean nationality to those who have been deprived of it for political reasons;
> To allow those who have been forced to leave the country for political reasons to return home and take appropriate measures to assist their resettlement;

To remove restrictions on political activities and reestablish the full enjoyment of the freedom of association;
To guarantee the standards of labor protection called for by international instruments and fully restore previously established trade union rights;
To fully guarantee freedom of expression;
To safeguard the human rights of the Mapucho Indians and other indigenous minorities, taking into account their particular cultural characteristics.[83]

NOTES

1. A/PV.2139, pp. 2–4.
2. A/PV.2150, pp. 63–64.
3. A/PV.2129.
4. A/PV.2125, p. 26.
5. A/PV.2128, p. 132.
6. Cf. pp. 106–107.
7. Political Declaration of the Fourth Conference of Nonaligned Countries, Algiers, 5–9 September 1973 (A/9330, No. 56). In 1977, the Colombo Conference of the Nonaligned Countries condemned the "imperialist intervention" and the establishment in Chile of an antinational regime to undo the achievements of the Popular Unity regime of President Allende.
8. For text see E/CN.4/1149.
9. For text see E/CN.4/1150.
10. E/CN.4/SR.1271, pp. 6–11.
11. For summaries of statements see E/CN.4/SR.1271–1279.
12. E/CN.4/SR.1272, p. 10.
13. See above, note A/PV.2128, No. 171.
14. Office of Public Information, NV/263, 19 February 1974.
15. For text see Commission on Human Rights, Report on the thirtieth session, 1974, E/5464, pp. 56–57.
16. E/CN.4/SR.1272.
17. For text see E/AC.7/L.672.
18. For a summary of the debate see E/A.C.7/SR.7.
19. E/AC.7/SR.745, p. 113.
20. See, for example, E/CN.4/Sub.2/SR.688, p. 5; SR.691, p. 6; SR.692, p. 3; SR.707, p. 11.
21. See text of resolution 8(XXVII) entitled The Question of Human Rights of Persons subjected to any Form of Detention or Imprisonment adopted by the Sub-Commission on 21 August 1974 (Report of the Sub-Commission on its Twenty-Seventh Session, E/CN.4/Sub.2/354, p. 53).
22. A/PV.2243, pp. 61–62.

23. A/PV.2245, p. 7.

24. A/PV.2250, p. 43.

25. For text see A/9829, pp. 7–8.

26. For text see ibid., pp. 8–9.

27. For text see ibid., p. 16.

28. Ibid., p. 10.

29. Commission on Human Rights, Report on the Thirty-First Session. 1975, E/5635, p. 23.

30. For a summary of the debate see E/CN.4/SR.1318–1323.

31. For text see E/CN.4/L.1302.

32. For text see E/CN.4/L.1301/Rev.1.

33. For text see Commission on Human Rights, Report on the Thirty-First Session, op. cit., pp. 66–67.

34. In a communication dated 7 July 1975 (NV/448, 11 July 1975) to Secretary-General Kurt Waldheim, the Permanent Representative of Chile to the United Nations transmitted a note from his Government which read as follows:

Sir,

I have the honour to communicate to you the text of the official statement by my Government concerning the visit to Chile of the Ad Hoc Working Group of the United Nations Commission on Human Rights. The statement reads as follows:

"The Government of Chile, in a gesture such as none of its international detractors has made, agreed in February last that a Working Group of the United Nations Commission on Human Rights should visit us in order to inform itself of the present situation concerning human rights in Chile. The Government gave its collaboration to the Group from the outset and was making preparations to receive it and to provide it with all necessary facilities for the performance of its mission.

"Subsequently, it has been found that the campaign of lies which, for exclusively political reasons, has been plotted against Chile is not only continuing but intensifying, especially in United Nations forums. For instance, the International Labour Conference and the Conference of the International Women's Year, displaying their contempt for the investigation which the Working Group would be making, and without any basis other than slanderous allegations, have recently prejudged the situation by condemning Chile for supposed violations of human rights.

"This shows that the campaign of defamation is misleading world public opinion, which is not yet in a position to appreciate the sincerity of the Government of Chile. It also shows that there exists in international circles no serious disposition to verify and accept the truth of the situation in Chile and that, on the contrary, the prevailing mystification would not hesitate at this time likewise to distort any report produced by the Working Group.

"It should also be noted that the Working Group, exceeding its mandate, which is to investigate 'the present situation' concerning human rights in Chile, has accepted in Europe and America the testimony of exiles and fugitives from Chilean justice who have been away from the country for more than a year, so that they cannot speak about the present situation. In addition, it has been ascertained that, for the purpose of making their statements in New York, these people were rounded up by the Ambassador of Cuba.

"Moreover, on the eve of the arrival of the Working Group, there has been discovered within the country a subversive plan aimed at ensuring that the Group would be received in an atmosphere of domestic commotion. This movement, encouraged and guided by Soviet radio stations, was designed to fill the foreign embassies with spurious victims of political persecution, to promote agitation in the streets and to unleash a guerrilla struggle. Its obvious purpose was to create public alarm, to provoke the security measures that would have been necessary and to give the Working Group a distorted impression of the actual fact that human rights are respected in Chile.

"The above-mentioned circumstances have convinced the Government that, at this time, the Working Group would be unable properly to carry out its assignment and to ascertain the true situation in Chile, and that its imminent arrival was the decisive reason for the subversive plan which has been discovered.

"It is for this reason that, pending restoration of the necessary conditions of objectivity, and in accordance with his prime duty of preserving internal peace, the President of the Republic has been obliged, very much to his regret, to suspend the visit of the Working Group of the United Nations Commission on Human Rights until a more propitious occasion.

"Santiago, 7 July 1975."

I shall be most grateful if you will have this communication circulated to the representatives of Member States as an official United Nations document.

Accept, Sir, the assurances of my highest consideration.

(*Signed*) Ismael HUERTA
Vice-Admiral
Ambassador, Permanent Representative

35. E/CN.4/Sub.2/SR.729, pp. 141–143.
36. E/CN.4/Sub.2/SR.731, pp. 163–164.
37. E/CN.4/Sub.2/SR.738, p. 222.
38. E/CN.4/Sub.2/SR.738, p. 221. For text of resolution, adopted by 18 votes to none, with 5 abstentions, see Report of the Sub-Commission on Prevention of Discrimination and Protection of Minorities, Twenty-Eighth Session 1975, E/CN.4/1180, pp. 57–58.
39. E/CN.4/Sub.2/SR.731, p. 170; For the U.S.S.R.'s rebuttal, see ibid., p. 170; for the statement of the Member from the Netherlands, see ibid., p. 169.
40. A/PV.2380, pp. 53–57.
41. See A/C.3/SR.2144–2155.

42. For text of the Introduction by the Chairman of the Ad Hoc Working Group, see A/C.3/640.
43. A/C.3/SR.2144, pp. 17–21.
44. A/C.3/SR.2150, pp. 7–11.
45. A/C.3/SR.2146, pp. 3–4.
46. Ibid., p. 10.
47. A/C.3/SR.2147, pp. 5–10.
48. A/C.3/SR.2148, p. 7.
49. A/C.3/SR.2150, p. 19.
50. A/C.3/SR.2150, p. 16.
51. A/C.3/SR.2149, p. 25.
52. A/C.3/SR.2151, p. 15.
53. A/C.3/SR.2148, pp. 8–10.
54. A/C.3/SR.2155, pp. 20–21.
55. Ibid., p. 17.
56. Ibid., p. 22.
57. E/CN.4/1188.
58. E/CN.4/SR.1354, p. 4.
59. E/CN.4/SR.1355, p. 7.
60. See, for example, the statements by the representatives of France and Italy, E/CN.4/SR.1358, pp. 2–3.
61. See, for example, the statement by the representative of the German Federal Republic, E/CN.4/SR.1357, pp. 2–5, g.
62. See resolution 3(XXXII) adopted by the Commission on Human Rights on 19 February 1976 by 26 votes to 2, with 4 abstentions. Report of the Commission on Human Rights on the Thirty-Second Session, pp. 57–59.
63. E/AC.7/SR.780, pp. 2–3.
64. See Moses Moskowitz, *Human Rights and World Order*, Oceana Publications, New York, 1958, Chapter IV.
65. E/AC.7/SR.777, pp. 2–3.
66. For text of the resolution see Report of the Sub-Commission on Prevention of Discrimination and Protection of Minorities on its Twenty-Ninth Session, E/CN.4/1218, p. 4.
67. Ibid.
68. A/31/PV.15, p. 17.
69. A/31/PV.24, p. 53.
70. A/3/31/SR.48, p. 5.
71. A/3/31/SR.48, p. 9.
72. A/3/31/SR.47, pp. 3–4.
73. A/3/31/SR.48, p. 14.
74. A/3/31/SR.54, p. 12.
75. A/3/31/SR.56, p. 10.
76. A/3/31/SR.48, p. 12.
77. A/3/31/SR.56, pp. 2–4.
78. Resolution 3124(XXXI).

79. A/3/31/SR.50, p. 14.

80. Resolution 11(XXXV) of 6 March 1979. Commission on Human Rights, Report on the Thirty-Fifth Session, E/1979/36, pp. 115–118.

81. Resolution 11(XXX) I of 31 August 1977. Report of the Sub-Commission on its Thirtieth Session, E/CN.4/Sub.2/399, p. 49.

82. Ibid., II, p. 50.

83. Resolution 33/175 adopted on 20 December 1978 by 96 votes to 2, with 38 abstentions.

Chapter V

MIDDLE EAST RATIONALIZATIONS AND ASSUMPTIONS

Perhaps no other area of United Nations concern abounds in more rationalizations of unstudied assumptions than the conflict in the Middle East between the Arabs and Israel. It is an area where causes are taken for consequences, institutions for fashions, secondary effects for world historical convulsions, and prejudice for natural law. The situation in the Middle East has created outrageous contradictions where proffered solutions—products of locked patterns of thought that have changed little since the origins of the conflict—themselves become part of the problem. It is a struggle that has many fronts, all but few poorly defined and all laden with notions and sentiments so entrenched and unconsidered that they would not either be challenged or examined. The passions aroused by events in the Middle East have encouraged variations on profoundly unacceptable themes and all the mountains of exegesis have done little to clarify the situation; one can no longer see the view for all the signposts that may point to it.

How to produce concerted action on a problem when the parties involved have differing goals and respond to varying motivations defies an answer. Israel's stake in the conflict is its own physical survival and national identity and the future of the whole of Jewry; that of the Arabs is to erase the basic slur on Arab potency which the creation of Israel holds for them. The hope that time will yield a common goal of peace broad enough to embrace the aspirations of the parties to the conflict and accommodate their contradictions has yet to materialize; indignation has continued to prevail over insight, polemics over profundity, and anger over analysis. Reasons of policy, insistently urged, can harden into reasons of principle and take on the shape of truths whose sanctity condones all violations of sense and language. Relationships have become so elusive and complicated that they resist the most determined scrutiny, while the whole Middle East situation, clearly manipulated rather than developed and constantly subjected to exploitation, by opportunism, refuses to lend itself to clear formulation or answer.

Throughout, the role of the United Nations in the conflict has been such that instead of narrowing the gap between the opposing sides it has only widened the breach. Not that the world body could be expected to undo what has been done and offer a firm clue, if not a final answer; the operative reality of the United Nations has militated against its role as a dynamic instrumentality capable of energetic initiative and strong action to alleviate, moderate or resolve conflicts. It is the fact that the United Nations has permitted itself to be drawn into the corrupting vortex of diplomatic maneuvering by running with the wind instead of tacking into it; it has been at its most transparent when positive action was needed most.

In the Middle East conflict one party seems to have no faults and the other no virtues. Rarely, if ever, since its creation in 1948 has there been a break in the constant repetition of accusations against Israel verging on incantation, nor in its censure which has invariably followed with the inevitability of a categorical imperative. Far from being the prophet in command of the truth, the United Nations has for the most part of thirty-odd years acted as a coefficient of equivocation and ambiguity, predilection and preference. The tone of embattled integrity that bristles through the myriad of Security Council, General Assembly, Human Rights Commission and other resolutions of United Nations bodies cannot disguise the masquerade of patently political interests as high moral principles. Partisan peeves and motives, entrenched attitudes and violent animosities and hatreds have all too often found their way into those resolutions which, in the view of the majority, argue their own validity by virtue of the large number of votes in support of the Arab position.[1] Adopted with breathtaking disregard for the niceties of critical discourse and without reference to equity or consequence, the resolutions only serve to provoke old passions of history and to perpetuate strange and dangerous illusions. The United Nations has chosen, consciously or unconsciously, to become a party to a dispute between the Arabs and Israel and has taken on a role in a desperate play divorced from clear principle or belief and in total disregard of the Charter and the international values for which it stands.

Increasingly the Arab–Israel conflict has been dealt with by the United Nations more rhetorically than analytically. The overwhelming support which the Arab cause has enjoyed in the international body by virtue of the sheer numbers arrayed on the side of one party dispensed with the need of placing the conflict on the level of civilized dialogue between opponents rather than a cacophony of mutual anathema. The rest of the world, for reasons of its own, did little to try to redress the balance between the ambiguous and contradictory forces behind the Middle East dispute and sought refuge in a political and intellectual neutrality which only encouraged the propensity of nations to censure the conduct of others rather than improve their own defects. The cant and mystification that so often pass for objectivity abetted the substitution of easy rhetoric of accusation and condemnation for the struggle to understand. Rarely, if ever, did the United Nations follow the high notes of principled indignation with the low notes of political accommodation. Instead, it contributed to the freezing of a situation in which there were only knights who never told a lie and knaves who never spoke the truth.

Moreover, the erosion of the impartiality of the United Nations as a place where a party to an international dispute could expect and receive a fair hearing in an atmosphere of sincerity and decorum had set in almost at the beginnings of the international Organization; the more critically-minded throughout the world had long ago found it progressively more difficult to address themselves with respect to United Nations actions and decisions. But when the world body decided, consciously or unconsciously, to center its attention on certain select issues, including the Middle East conflict, to the virtual exclusion of other issues of equal or greater gravity and consequence, its moral right to sit in judgment over third parties was severely undermined. As time went on, this concentration on so-called pet issues played havoc with United Nations perspectives of international trends and events and encouraged the growth of practices and procedures that often took on proportions of Orwellian cynicism.[2] A careful reading of the records shows, for example, that whenever the United Nations voted to inquire into allegations of misdeeds by Israel and to create fact-finding bodies to examine the facts and verify the conditions, Israel always stood condemned by the very resolution which ordered the inquiry; the issues were almost always prejudged, the allegations set forth as proven facts, and the members of the fact-finding bodies blithely appointed even though their bias was universal knowledge.[3] In one case, a fact-finding body included a country at war with Israel. In these circumstances the United Nations could not rise with dignity to the level of events.

The invitation extended on 14 October 1974, to the Palestine Liberation Organization (PLO) to participate in the deliberations of the General Assembly on the question of Palestine in plenary meetings and its subsequent admission to observer status with the United Nations inevitably ranged the world body more formally than ever before on the Arab side of the Middle East conflict and transformed an international dispute between States into one between the organized international community and one of its Members. By these acts the United Nations gave hostage to fortune and affirmed resort to force as an acceptable means to induce change in the Middle East situation. Acting as if propelled to radical measures in pursuit of moral certainties, the majority of the States Members of the United Nations elevated the fallacy to the status of a principle. They sought to deny to Israel the rights which have become axiomatic and sacred to themselves, and struck attitudes which at home they would not or could not sustain; they demanded of Israel a token of its dedication to the United Nations by accepting its own tragic sacrifice.

There is no doubt that the invitation to the PLO was part of a grand design to confer international legitimacy on the organization and to alter the terms of the debate on the Middle East in the United Nations and other international forums. The idea originated formally with the Council of the League of Arab States, which early in September 1974 decided to call for the inclusion of an item in the agenda of the twenty-ninth session of the General Assembly entitled "Question of Palestine", and recommended the "recognition and reaffirmation of Palestine's right to national independence and of the Palestinians' right to return to their homes."[4] In the explanatory memorandum which accompanied their letter of 11 September 1974 requesting the inclusion of the "Palestine question" in the General Assembly's agenda the forty-three signatories, whose number subsequently increased to more than seventy, stated as follows:

> 1. The General Assembly has been continuously seized with the problem of Palestine since April 1947. In consequence of some of the early resolutions of the General Assembly regarding this issue, a great number of Palestinians have been displaced and forced to endure the status of refugees, and the Palestinian people have been prevented from exercising their inalienable rights, including the right to self-determination, in accordance with the Charter of the United Nations and the recognized norms of international law.
>
> 2. Nevertheless, for more than 20 years, the question of Palestine as such and the question of the status and fate of the people of Palestine as such have not appeared on the agenda of any session of the General Assembly, even though the Assembly and other organs of the United Nations have dealt with various aspects, ramifications or consequences of the Palestine problem throughout this period.
>
> 3. Since 1948, however, the General Assembly has recognized and reaffirmed the right of the Palestine refugees to repatriation and, since 1970, has recognized and reaffirmed the inalienable rights of the people of Palestine, including its right to self-determination. In addition, the international community outside the framework of the United Nations has, in recent years, recognized these rights through various forums.
>
> 4. As the United Nations has borne since its inception an historic, political and juridical responsibility regarding the problem of Palestine, it is, therefore, incumbent upon the General Assembly to consider the question of Palestine in its true nature and proper form, and to inscribe an item entitled "Question of Palestine" as a separate item on the agenda of its twenty-ninth session.[5]

The item was placed on the agenda over the sole objection of the representative of Israel, who warned the General Committee at its meeting on 19 September 1974 that the item and its "foregone conclusions" would only introduce new elements and new considerations into the Middle East situation and further hamper, delay and possibly undermine the entire Middle East peace-making effort. "Those acquainted with the handling of the Israeli–Arab conflict by the deliberative bodies of the United Nations", Ambassador Tekoah added, "knew that it would not be the first time that the General Assembly, with its built-in majority, would be creating obstacles to a peaceful understanding and agreement in the Middle East.[6] On 14 October 1974, Syria introduced draft resolution A/L.736 which was sponsored by seventy-one countries and which asked that the PLO, as "the representative of the Palestinian people" and "principal party to the question of Palestine" be invited to participate in the deliberations of the General Assembly on the question of Palestine in plenary meetings where it was to be discussed without prior reference to any major Committee.[7] Before the day was over, the draft resolution was adopted by a roll-call vote of 105 to 4, with 20 abstentions.[8]

It was a risky rationale that led to the adoption of the draft resolution. By the support given the PLO, the United Nations may indeed have made a solution of the Middle East conflict more difficult than ever by reinforcing the extemists and weakening the prospects of realistic moderation. It may also have determined, wittingly or unwittingly, an inter-Arab controversy in favor of militant extremism. Certainly, draft resolution A/L.736 contravened a long-established United Nations practice which limited participation in debates in plenary to Member States; the shattering of such a time-hallowed precedent could not but serve partisan interests in the Middle East conflict.

Ironically, several weeks before the General Assembly voted to invite the representatives of the PLO to participate in the debate in plenary on the question of Palestine, it rejected a request by Turkey for similar participation by representatives of the Turkish population in Cyprus when the Cyprus question was discussed by the General Assembly, also in plenary meetings. The Turkish request was overwhelmingly rejected, on the ground that it violated a well-established practice which regarded the plenary meetings of the General Assembly the exclusive preserve of governmental representatives.[9] To enable the representatives of the Turkish and Greek populations of Cyprus to present their views, agreement was reached to convene the Special Political

Committee in a special meeting for that purpose. As announced by the President of the General Assembly at the opening of the debate on Cyprus on 28 October 1974, the agreement was reached on 21 September 1974, and was recorded as follows:

> At this morning's meeting it was decided that the item entitled "Question of Cyprus" should be allocated to the plenary Assembly. However, an understanding has been reached that the General Assembly, when it considers that item, will invite the Special Political Committee to meet for the purpose of affording representatives of the Cypriote communities an opportunity to take the floor in the Committee in order to expresss their views. The General Assembly will then resume its consideration of the item, taking into account the report of the Special Political Committee.[10]

No less risky was the substantive debate which, given the general tenor of most of the statements and of the final resolution that emerged from it, could only fan the fires of radicalism in the Arab world and thicken the clouds of anger and hostility that darkened the skies over the Middle East. The way the Arab States and their allies posed the questions permitted no conclusion other than their own contention. The central theme of their interventions[11] was the duty of the international community to redress the "wrong done to the people of Palestine" when the United Nations voted in 1947 to partition the land without consulting the people who lived on it; they called for the restoration of the "legitimate national rights" of the Arab people of Palestine without defining the term and without referring to obligations and correlative duties, and for their exercise of the right to self-determination without alluding to the principles generally accepted as governing that right. The most far-reaching political arguments were built on the basis of dubious or disputed facts and judgments were made without regard to the existence of another side to the dispute and another set of claims.

How those "wrongs" were to be redressed was answered long ago in the Palestinian National Covenant of 1964, as amended in 1968.[12] That document, which defines the position of the PLO in the Middle East conflict, stubbornly rejects the existence of Israel even as a negotiating premise. Article 19 of the Covenant declares:

> The partitioning of Palestine in 1947 and the establishment of Israel is fundamentally null and void, whatever time has elapsed, because it was

> contrary to the wish of the people of Palestine and its natural right to its homeland, and contradicts the principles embodied in the Charter of the United Nations, the first of which is the right of self-determination.

According to Article 20,

> The Balfour Declaration, the Mandate document, and what has been based upon them are considered null and void. The claim of an historical or spiritual tie between Jews and Palestine does not tally with historical realities nor with the constituents of statehood in their true sense. Judaism, in its character as a religion of revelation, is not a nationality with an independent existence. Likewise, the Jews are not one people with an independent personality. They are rather citizens of the States to which they belong.

And in Article 21,

> The Palestinian Arab people, in expressing itself through the armed Palestinian revolution, rejects every solution that is a substitute for a complete liberation of Palestine, and rejects all plans that aim at the settlement of the Palestine issue or its internationalization.

The Covenant was reaffirmed by PLO leader Yasser Arafat in his statement on 13 November 1974 opening the debate on the Palestine question,[13] when he called for the creation of a secular, democratic Palestinian State which would leave Israel only the sea; Israel was to be the chrysalis from which the Palestinian State was to rise. He called for peace, but no peace has ever been made except when each of the parties recognized the right of the other to exist. Commenting on the statement made by Mr. Arafat and others who had followed him, the representative of Israel said:

> The speakers who opened today's debate have confirmed its real purpose—to undermine Israel's rights, to question the inalienable rights of the Jewish people to its homeland, to strengthen and encourage the PLO in its activities directed against the life of Israel and of its people, to establish a PLO springboard from which the murder organization can continue its efforts to destroy the Jewish people. This is what justice means to the PLO. This is what the PLO's olive branch is.[14]

In fact, no attempt was made throughout the debate to move toward a more realistic position and to develop a framework for negotiation; the fears that the debate would only add a false legitimacy to the barrage of twisted propaganda and provide new conveniently troubled waters for meddlers to fish in were more than justified. Instead of patient, prescriptive analysis demonstrating the possibility of practical change, the world was treated to polemical tracts filled with fiery rhetoric devoid of practical guidance. Words tumbled down in undisciplined profusion and were repeated with solemn, mindless circularity. How easily the passion for absolutes turned into a thirst for vengeance! The deliberate omission in the resolution which emerged from the debate of any reference to the existence of the State of Israel, or to Security Council Resolutions 242 and 338 on the settlement of the conflict, left no doubt as to the true aim and purpose of the exercise staged in the General Assembly.

It is often painful to try to arrive at workable explanations of the behavior pattern of the United Nations and to account for actions which are patently contrary to all the rules of propriety. The debate on the question of Palestine brought out the infinite variety of ways in which the Middle East conflict is perceived and the willingness of the majority in the General Assembly to commit the United Nations to an absolute morality to the point of extinction of a Member State and in total disregard of all rules of international conduct and conscience. The unperturbed invitation extended to a nongovernmental organization to participate in a General Assembly debate in plenary was followed by the unprecedented reception given PLO leader Yasser Arafat by the Assembly's President when he arrived on 13 November 1974 to open the debate—a reception normally reserved to heads of State. On the second day of the debate President Bouteflika issued a ruling in which he invoked rule 72 of the provisional rules of procedure to limit interventions in the debate to one statement per State Member.[15] Protesting the ruling of the President as an attempt to bar even a semblance of balanced debate and a denial of a fair and equitable hearing to his country, Israeli Ambassador Yosef Tekoah said:

> Your proposal is an expression of the bias that you have regretfully displayed against Israel and its rights since the beginning of the present session. This has been reflected, among other instances, in the manner in which yesterday morning's meeting was set and conducted, and in the totally illegal arrangements you made, on your own initiative, for the appearance at that meeting of the head of a murder organization bent on

> the destruction of a Member State of the United Nations and on indiscriminate killing of its citizens.
>
> I should like to place these facts on record and to record my delegation's strongest protest.[16]

In the end, the ruling was upheld by 75 votes to 23, with 18 abstentions.[17] The brief explanation of the vote by the representative of Bolivia drove home the point when he said:

> My delegation voted against the proposal because we consider that by adopting it we would be violating two principles: the right of all States to defend themselves and the right to dialogue, which has been respected since the beginning of this debate. If the dialogue itself was uneven with 20 delegations against one, the debate is being converted today into an uninterrupted monologue without any defense by one of the parties.[18]

Rounding out the symmetric procession of events was the introduction and circulation of two draft resolutions at the end of the debate and their submission to a vote on the same day. The first draft resolution, A/L.741, dealt with the substance of Palestinian rights and read as follows:

> *The General Assembly*,
>
> *Having considered* the question of Palestine,
>
> *Having heard* the statement of the Palestine Liberation Organization, the representative of the Palestinian people,
>
> *Having also heard* the statements made during the debate,
>
> *Deeply concerned* that no just solution to the problem of Palestine has yet been achieved and recognizing that the problem of Palestine continues to endanger international peace and security.
>
> *Recognizing* that the Palestinian people is entitled to self-determination in accordance with the Charter of the United Nations,
>
> *Expressing its grave concern* that the Palestinian people has been prevented from enjoying its inalienable rights, in particular its right to self-determination,
>
> *Guided* by the purposes and principles of the Charter,
>
> *Recalling* its relevant resolutions which affirm the right of the Palestinian people to self-determination,
>
> 1. *Reaffirms* the inalienable rights of the Palestinian people in Palestine, including:
>
> (a) The right to self-determination without external interference;
>
> (b) The right to national independence and sovereignty;
>
> 2. *Reaffirms* also the inalienable right of the Palestinians to return to their homes and property from which they have been displaced and uprooted, and calls for their return;

3. *Emphasizes* that the full respect for and the realization of these inalienable rights of the Palestinian people are indispensable for the solution of the question of Palestine;

4. *Recognizes* that the Palestinian people is a principal party in the establishment of a just and durable peace in the Middle East;

5. *Further recognizes* the right of the Palestinian people to regain its rights by all means in accordance with the purposes and principles of the Charter of the United Nations;

6. *Appeals* to all States and international organizations to extend their support to the Palestinian people in its struggle to restore its rights, in accordance with the Charter;

7. *Requests* the Secretary-General to establish contacts with the Palestine Liberation Organization on all matters concerning the question of Palestine;

8. *Requests* the Secretary-General to report to the General Assembly at its thirteenth session on the implementation of the present resolution;

9. *Decides* to include the item entitled "Question of Palestine" in the provisional agenda of its thirteenth session.[19]

The second draft resolution, A/L.742, recommended the admission of the PLO to observer status with the United Nations as follows:

The General Assembly,

Having considered the question of Palestine,

Taking into consideration the universality of the United Nations prescribed in the Charter,

Recalling its resolution 3102(XXVIII) of 12 December 1973,

Taking into account Economic and Social Council resolutions 1835(LVI) of 14 May 1974 and 1840(LVI) of 15 May 1974,

Noting that the Diplomatic Conference on the Reaffirmation and Development of International Humanitarian Law Applicable in Armed Conflicts, the World Population Conference and the World Food Conference have in effect invited the Palestine Liberation Organization to participate in their respective deliberations,

Noting also that the Third United Nations Conference on the Law of the Sea has invited the Palestine Liberation Organization to participate in its deliberations as an observer,

1. *Invites* the Palestine Liberation Organization to participate in the sessions and the work of the General Assembly in the capacity of observer;

2. *Invites* the Palestine Liberation Organization to participate in the sessions and in the work of all international conferences convened under the auspices of the General Assembly in the capacity of observer;

3. *Considers* that the Palestine Liberation Organization is entitled to participate as an observer in the sessions and the work of all international

conferences convened under the auspices of other organs of the United Nations;

4. *Requests* the Secretary-General to take the necessary steps for the implementation of the present resolution.[20]

That resolutions dealing with such sensitive issues had been kept under wrap until they were sprung upon the General Assembly at the last moment is highly suggestive. A number of delegations deplored that fact and abstained on that account in the voting. Others resented what they regarded as deception or highly irregular procedure as outright misleading. It prompted, for example, the representative of Australia to note in reference to resolution A/L.742, the following:

> As regards the draft resolution in document A/L.742, my delegation, even though we had had some forecast of its possible content a few days ago, had been given to expect until late last evening that it was unlikely to be presented to the General Assembly and brought to a vote. In the short time that we have been able to consider it and discuss it with our authorities in Canberra we have only been able to conclude that it would have the Assembly give the Palestine Liberation Organization (PLO) status and privileges as an observer that exceed those accorded to fully independent States that are not Members of the United Nations but have long been recognized as observers, and this we would regard as unwarranted. I say this without prejudice to the intention of the Australian Government to take account in the future of the unanimous decision of the Heads of Governments of Arab States at Rabat that the PLO should speak for the Palestinians and the view of the majority in this General Assembly that the PLO should be associated in appropriate ways with United Nations activities.[21]

Resolution A/L.741 was adopted by 89 votes in favor to 8 against, with 37 abstentions; A/L.742 was adopted by a vote of 95 to 17, with 19 abstentions. As already suggested, the way the majority posed the question permitted no conclusion other than its own contention. To that extent the vote accurately reflects the political pieties that prevail in the United Nations and the unquestioning acceptance of slogans and indoctrinating phrases which blunt the mind and keep the world Organization in thrall to grudges and grievances it has helped to nurse. As the final speaker in the debate, the representative of the PLO declared that the Palestinian people considered the invitation to the PLO to participate in the debate "a sign of encouragement which restores our confidence in this international institution and in its capacity to shoulder its responsibilities in enforcing right, justice and peace . . ."[22] The PLO, he continued,

> the only legitimate representative of the Palestinian people, proclaims from this rostrum that it has come here with all the determination required to give the United Nations a historic opportunity to prove to all the peoples of the world that it is still able to play a role in strengthening peace and justice. That fact has been confirmed here today . . .
>
> We did not come here to seek reconciliation with the Zionist terrorists and usurpers. We came here to bear witness to the historic difference between us and the Zionists. We regard diplomatic activities as a complement to our activities on the battlefield. We know that our revolutionary practices and our accomplishments towards restoring peace and freedom are in conformity with the positive position of the international community with respect to our rights. That is why we consider that the increased support for our cause is primarily support for our struggle and encouragement to us to continue that just struggle.
>
> The Palestine Liberation Organization, like our Palestinian people, is happy to see the United Nations at its side today, supporting its cause, reaffirming its right to self-determination and independence on the soil of its forefathers.[23]

But whether or not the resolutions are the voice of international conscience, as its protagonists claim, or no more than a marginal note to history as so many other resolutions adopted by the General Assembly over the years, the language in which they are couched has only added to the confusion which has always surrounded the Middle East issue. For example, for many years the central issue in the conflict was thought to be the coexistence of Israelis and Arabs in a narrow space, the clash of their hopes and aspirations, and the concatenation of their fears. Resolution A/3236(XXIX) on the question of Palestine recognizes only one party to the conflict and only one problem—the vindication of the rights and interests of what it regards as the rightful inheritors of the land of Palestine against foreign intruders and the annihilation of a "rootless creation of horrid imperialism". As has already been noted, there is in the resolution not even a remote allusion to the existence of Israel, to the confrontation of ineluctable realities, to the neeed of a negotiated and peaceful solution that will reconcile all legitimate aspirations, and to the efforts proposed or underway to create a promising framework for such negotiations. The resolution is but another attempt to rewrite history in order to meet selective arguments and serve openly partisan objectives. In the words of the representative of Denmark in explanation of his negative vote,

> . . . the text presented to us today did not meet the criteria of balance and equity so carefully worked out by the Security Council, but even tended to disturb that balance. In our view, the text does not take due account of the complexities of the problem and fails to recognize the mutual rights and obligations of the parties. It fails to mention Security Council resolution 242(1967) and, in particular, to recognize the right of every State in the area, including that of the State of Israel, a full and equal Member of this Organization, to live in peace within secure and recognized boundaries.
>
> Without going into further details regarding the text, I wish more generally to emphasize that the United Nations in essence is to us a world Organization committed to maintaining international peace and security and that its primary tools in the exercise of that duty are negotiation, mediation and conciliation. To us, it is important to strengthen the Organization in the applications of such peaceful means. We continue to believe that it is by such means that the United Nations can lend its original and essential contribution to breaking the vicious circle of violence.[24]

Alas, instead of seeking to improve its capacity for negotiation, mediation and conciliation, the United Nations has been stumbling, without conviction, from one contrivance to the next and has rarely gained command of events. There has never been in the United Nations an independent pole of political authority to express authentic international interests, when governments were bent upon subordinating those interests to narrow national objectives. Surely the General Assembly, as Ambassador Waldron-Ramsey of Barbados noted on the eve of the voting on the Palestine resolution,

> is not a forum suitable for the settlement of disputes. For one thing, it is too big, too open, too parliamentary and perhaps too pregnant with the combative views of contending parties, each seeking to excel the other in verbosity and the winning of debating points . . . I make bold to assert that nowhere in the history of recorded international relations, indeed nowhere in the history of human conflict, was a peace treaty elaborated and signed as a result of a vote taken by the parties involved or their allies. The proper role of this Assembly is to create an atmosphere that would be congenial for the parties . . . to sit down together and work out for themselves an agreement and a treaty of peace that would be just and fair to both sides.[25]

Indeed, it is strikingly preposterous to try to deal with issues so pregnant with consequences, such as the Middle East conflict, through a contest of votes in the General Assembly where a shift in the votes of the smallest and least directly concerned nations can change the balance and from which there is no appeal. The proper role of the Assembly, as Ambassador Waldron-Ramsey suggested, is to create an atmosphere for the parties to negotiate. The enhanced status bestowed upon the PLO so gratuitously by the General Assembly without even a token attempt to inquire into its willingness and ability to rise above its background to accept the burdens and restraints of political responsibility—a procedure normally followed in the admission of States to membership in the United Nations—treated the world to the most astounding offense against international civility; it left the principles of international order without effective recourse. The admsission of the PLO to observer status in the full knowledge of the consequences, showed how an amorphous but controlling bloc of votes in the General Assembly, armed with an authority invoked by a presiding officer willing to bend the Charter and the rules of procedure, can impose, or attempt to impose, the emotional prejudices of that bloc on the international community and make the United Nations function with uninhibited bias. The status accorded the PLO was nothing less than a wilful act of extremism. On that point the representative of the United Kingdom expressed a widely shared sentiment when he said:

> ... That question, as we see it, turns in essence on the nature of the United Nations itself. This Organization was originally conceived, and up till now has always been regarded, as an Organization of sovereign, independent States. Only States may be Members of the United Nations.
>
> Consistently with that position, the status of permanent observers has also hitherto been confined to non-Member States such as Switzerland or the Vatican, and to regional organizations of States, such as the Organization of African Unity and, most recently, the European Economic Community and the Council for Mutual Economic Assistance.
>
> The draft resolution which we are now going to vote on will, as we see it, alter all that. If adopted, it would give to the Palestinian Liberation Organization what is in effect the status of a permanent observer here. The PLO, whatever view one may take of it, in political terms, is not the

government of an existing State; it has not been recognized by anybody as the government of a State; it does not purport to be one.

Moreover, the draft resolution goes further than this Assembly has ever thought it right to go before, even as regards States and organizations of States. Not merely does it permit the PLO to participate in the proceedings of the General Assembly, but it also gives it the right to take part in the proceedings of all United Nations conferences and indeed virtually instructs the specialized agencies to follow a similar course.

In every respect, therefore, except the right formally to submit proposals and to vote, the PLO is being treated as though it were a Member State of the United Nations.

As I have said, this seems to my delegation to be a fundamental departure from our practice, and to bring into question the nature of the United Nations as it has hitherto been accepted . . .[26]

NOTES

1. Self-reference is one of the glorified virtues in the United Nations. Typical is the remark made by the representative of Kuwait in the General Assembly on 24 October 1974 in response to the statement made by Israeli Ambassador Yosef Tekoah to the effect that Article 9 of the PLO's Charter, affirming that armed struggle was the path to the liberation of Palestine, disqualified that organization from addressing the General Assembly. Said the representative of Kuwait:

> Need I remind this Assembly that in operative paragraph 2 of resolution 3070(XXVIII) this same Assembly
>
> > Also affirms the legitimacy of the peoples' struggle for liberation from colonial and foreign domination and alien subjugation by all available means, including armed struggle (A/PV.2268, p. 37).

2. Commenting on the report of the Special Committee to Investigate Israeli Practices Affecting the Human Rights of the Population of the Occupied Territories to the twenty-fifth session of the General Assembly in 1970, the Permanent Representative of Israel to the United Nations, in a letter to the Secretary-General dated 13 November 1970, wrote:

> The long list of preselected, coached and rehearsed witnesses presented to the Committee produced lurid and often pathological tales of alleged ill-treatment and atrocity.
>
> As an illustration, it is enough to mention the evidence of Mohammed Derbas, who appeared before the Committee in Cairo on 23 April 1970. He described very vividly how, following the 1967 war, he was forced into an

Israeli hospital in Haifa and there castrated by an Israeli doctor, who was assisted by an Israeli nurse. What in fact happened was that for medical reasons Derbas had undergone two operations for the removal of his testicles. These were performed by Arab surgeons, in the Gaza Strip, in 1965 and 1966, respectively (that is, prior to the 1967 hostilities). Already in July 1966, he had arrived in Egypt in an illusory hope of a remedy by transplantation, as recorded in a medical report by an Egyptian professor dated 28 July 1966. The report, signed by Professor Muhamad Safawat, is in this Mission's possession. This episode clearly demonstrates how human misfortune is exploited for cheap propaganda (A/8164, p. 2).

3. A careful reading of General Assembly resolution 2443(XXIII) of 19 December 1968, which created the Special Committee to Investigate Israeli Practices Affecting the Human Rights of the Population of the Occupied Territories, shows unmistakably its prejudgment of the issues the Special Committee was to investigate to the point of dictating its conclusions. The resolution was inspired by the International Conference on Human Rights in 1968 which, in resolution I, expressed "its grave concern at the violation of human rights in Arab territories occupied by Israel"; "drew the attention of the Government of Israel to the grave consequences resulting from the disregard of fundamental freedoms and human rights in occupied territories"; and called upon the Government of Israel . . . "to respect and implement the Universal Declaration of Human Rights and the Geneva Conventions of 12 August 1949 in occupied territories . . ."

The Membership of the Committee, appointed by the President of the General Assembly, consisted of Ceylon, Somalia and Yugoslavia, none of which had diplomatic relations with Israel, while Somalia did not even recognize the right of Israel to independence and sovereignty.

It may be noted that all uncommitted States Members that were approached refused to serve on the Special Committee, giving the one-sided character of resolution 2443(XXIII) as the reason.

4. See A/BUR/SR.219, pp. 19–24.

5. A/9742, p. 4.

6. A/BUR/SR.219, pp. 20–21.

7. See A/PV.2267, pp. 6–7.

8. A/PV.2268, pp. 42–45. For the debate and explanations of vote, see A/PV.2267–2268.

9. See A/BUR/SR.219, p. 30. For the debate in plenary, see A/PV.2236, pp. 37–70.

10. A/PV.2267, p. 2.

11. For the verbatim record of the debate see A/PV.2282–2296.

12. For text see S/11932, 14 January 1976.

13. A/PV.2282, pp. 47–51.

14. A/PV.2283, p. 31.

15. A/PV.2285, pp. 22–25.

16. A/PV.2285, p. 26.
17. A/V.2285, p. 34.
18. A/PV.2285, p. 37–40.
19. The resolution was adopted on 22 November 1974 by 89 votes to 8, with 37 abstentions. It bears the symbol 3236(XXIX).
20. It was adopted on the same day as 3237(XXIX) by 95 votes to 17, with 19 abstentions.
21. A/PV.2296, p. 78–80.
22. A/PV.2296, p. 111.
23. A/PV.2296, pp. 117–118.
24. A/PV.2296, pp. 66–67.
25. A/PV.2295, p. 66.
26. A/PV.2296, pp. 22–25.

Chapter VI

THE RACIAL EQUATION

There is no limit to the ways in which the Middle East conflict is perceived. To some it is purely and simply a question of colonialism. Thus, for example, in his statement in support of the participation of the Palestine Liberation Organization in the General Assembly's debate on the question of Palestine, the representative of Dahomey said:

> The fundamental cause of the Palestinian problem, consequently, the fundamental cause of the crisis in the Middle East, is a purely colonial situation, to which the international community has a duty to put an end once and for all. This cause is aggravated by expansionist designs the consequences of which must, as a matter of greater urgency than ever before, be eliminated in all their forms.[1]

As a colonial situation, the Middle East conflict suggests its own solution—denial of Israel's legitimacy as a nation-State and withdrawal from it of the protection of the Charter. Colonialism has long since been outlawed by the United Nations and has few defenders, and the deliberate identification of Israel with colonialism has great propaganda value. As will be noted later on, the assertion that the struggle of the Palestinian people is an element in the wider struggle for freedom from alien occupation, colonialism and foreign domination, has become standard reference in virtually all resolutions adopted by the United Nations and its organs and agencies bearing on the Middle East.

More recently, distortions and hyperboles current in the United Nations have put Israel in the company of racists as well. Efforts have been made to erase all political, moral and legal distinctions between Israel and the white-ruled States of southern Africa and to identify Israel with the South African Republic in the consciousness of the world. A sad and dangerous state of mind overtook the nations which in the evening of 10 November 1975 legislated that Zionism was a form of racism and racial discrimination. "Why in the UN's 30th year", asked the *Diplomatic World*[2] in an editorial on 20 October 1975, following approval by the General Assembly's Third Committee of draft resolution A/C.3/L.2159 equating Zionism with racism and racial discrimination,

> did the sponsors press this question of Zionism to a vote in such a bizarre context? One may suppose that the more militant anti-Israel elements, disappointed in their hopes of barring Israel from participation in the Assembly by calmer counsel, found this way of venting their anger and of rubbing Israel and Western noses in the dirt in the bargain.
>
> Whatever the reasons, the price they may have exacted is a weakened U.N. By a single stroke all the brave words about interdependence and conciliation we have been hearing these past weeks were virtually canceled out. The United States and those other Western nations that detected in their own political circles and public opinion a rising current of interest in the U.N. and improved recognition of its potential for usefulness, now will have to go back and explain how something like this could happen in any serious, rational organization with the slightest claim to honesty and integrity. . . . Millions of persons in all parts of the world, including those countries that voted for the resolution, may well wonder whether October 24, U.N. Day, is even worth celebrating.

The resolution is a lineal descendent of countless other resolutions adopted over the years by the General Assembly and other organs of the United Nations that charted a disastrous course for the international Organization. By leaving no choice to Israel other than self-effacement, it posed a direct challenge to the reality of mutual security within the framework of the United Nations Charter and to the ability of the world Organization to speak for the conscience of humanity; it bared the weaknesses inherent in the United Nations decision-making processes and their inadequacy for dealing with the welter of morally complex and politically contentious problems before the international body. Those who voted for the resolution rushed to their dismaying judgment without questioning the authenticity of the premise, mindless of the facts, and heedless of the consequences.

Draft resolution A/C.3/L.2159, henceforth known as resolution 3379(XXX), was adopted by the General Assembly on 10 November 1975 by a roll-call vote of 72 in favor to 35 against, with 32 abstentions. The affirmative votes were cast by the twenty Arab sponsors, the Eastern European countries with the exception of Romania, a substantial number of African and Asian nations, including China, and several Latin American and southern European States. Opposing the adoption of the resolution were the great bulk of Western nations, along with a number of Latin American, African and Asian countries.[3]

Immediately after the voting Secretary-General Kurt Waldheim, abandoning the traditional aloofness of his office from political disagreements, declared that he was "profoundly conscious of the gravity of the situation which has arisen in the General Assembly" as a result of the vote.[4] The following day the President of the General Assembly, Prime Minister Gaston Thorn of Luxembourg, deplored the adoption of the resolution as "the unhappy product of pressures by those who wanted to impose a point of view which is historically and philosophically wrong".[5] Protesting the adoption of the resolution were people from all walks of life from the far corners of the earth, official personages, religious leaders, and groups and organizations of every kind and description.[6]

"The resolution was capriciously introduced and wantonly pursued", said Mr. Ivor Richards of the United Kingdom.[7] It began as a series of amendments to a draft resolution recommended by the Economic and Social Council for adoption by the General Assembly in implementation of the program for the Decade for Action to Combat Racism and Racial Discrimination that was ushered in on Human Rights Day in 1973.[8] Sponsored by Afghanistan, Algeria, Cuba, Democratic Yemen, Guinea, Iraq, Jordan, the Libyan Arab Republic, Morocco, Somalia, the Syrian Arab Republic, the Sudan and the United Arab Emirates, the amendments proposed the addition of a clause branding "Zionism" a form of racism and racial discrimination" and calling for its condemnation along with racism, racial discrimination, *apartheid*, colonialism and alien domination.[9] But these amendments proved unacceptable to the majority of African nations, which regarded them as a gratuitous intrusion into their concerted campaign against racism and racial discrimination and as an attempt to dilute the purposes of the Decade.[10] After two weeks of futile negotiations the amendments were withdrawn, only to be replaced by an independent draft resolution which was ultimately adopted without change.

Procedural obstacles in the way of adoption of the resolution were quickly overcome. According to a decision taken by the Third Committee of the General Assembly on 29 September 1975, the deadline for submission of draft resolutions and amendments relating to the Decade for Action to Combat Racism and Racial Discrimination expired at 1 P.M. on 1 October 1975.[11] Since the new draft resolution on Zionism was submitted on October 15, it was not receivable unless the Committee reversed its decision of September 29, either under rule 123 of the rules of procedure which calls for a two-thirds majority, or under rule 125, which calls for a simple majority. An incipient debate on the applicable rule and on the advisability of inviting the Legal Counsel's opinion, was cut short by an Iraqi move for closure of the debate won by 72 votes to 27, with 26 abstentions.[12] The Committee then voted on the applicable rule of the rules of procedure and decided by 72 votes to 24, with 28 abstentions, in favor of rule 125.[13] This was followed by a vote on the admissibility of the draft resolution; it was declared receivable by 75 votes in favor, 22 against, with 26 abstentions.[14] On October 17, the draft resolution was adopted by 70 votes to 22, with 26 abstentions,[15] but not until the Third Committee, by a vote of 68 to 45, with 16 abstentions, had rejected a proposal by the representative of Sierra Leone to defer consideration of the resolution until the next session of the General Assembly in 1976.[16] As had happened before, the debate on Sierra Leone's proposal was cut short by a Libyan Arab Republic motion for closure. The motion was carried by 66 votes to 29, with 32 abstentions.[17]

What, one is bound to ask, singles out resolution 3379(XXX) from among the many lurid resolutions adopted by the General Assembly and other organs and agencies of the United Nations over the years? "A great evil has been loosened upon the world", United States Ambassador Daniel Patrick Moynihan declared after the vote had been taken. "The abomination of anti-Semitism", he said,

> had been given the appearance of international sanction. The General Assembly today grants symbolic amnesty—and more—to the murderers of 6 million European Jews. . . . The United Nations is solemnly proclaiming that Zionism is a form of Nazism. What we have here is a lie, a political lie of a variety well known to the twentieth century and scarcely exceeded in all that annal of untruth and outrage . . .[18]

"To attempt to equate Zionism with racism is a falsification of history and an attack on the integrity and existence of a people", Ambassador Johann Kaufmann of the Netherlands warned.[19] Father Nunez of Costa Rica termed the resolution "an unbridled invitation to genocide against the Jewish people."[20] He quoted from a letter addressed to the Secretary General of the United Nations by leaders of the Catholic and Protestant Churches meeting in Memphis, Tennessee, on 5 November 1975, that

> To compare Zionism with racism is a calumny against the Jews and a return to the old anti-Semitism that was a scourge of mankind for centuries.[21]

And Israel's Ambassador Haim Herzog warned that the attack on Zionism

> constitutes not only an anti-Semitic attack of the foulest type, but also an attack in this world body on Judaism, one of the oldest-established religions in the world . . .[22]

Surely, the resolution is an unabashed attempt to channel undifferentiated, emotional racial feelings into lasting political gains. Although racism has never been defined, the term has come to summon forth in the minds of people the assertion of superiority of a given group, people or nation on the basis of racial differences having no scientific validity, in support of claims to privilege and dominance. It is identified today almost exclusively with the white race and its colonial past and present, with South Africa as racism incarnate. By equating Zionism with racism and identifying Israel with South Africa,[23] Israel, and the Jewish people at large, are placed outside the pale of the law and the protection of the United Nations Charter. Such is the logic that flows from the evolution of the anti-*apartheid* campaign against South Africa and that gives substance to the belligerent intentions of the resolution's sponsors.[24] An essentially Arab design to further isolate Israel in the United Nations and abroad has been clothed in a noble universal purpose, to function as premise for the wildest hypotheses and the most absurd conclusions.

That the Soviet Union and the entire Communist bloc, excepting Romania which did not participate in the vote, ranged behind the Arab States in their espousal of the resolution, was more than a political act of accommodation. For the Soviet Union has been traditionally hostile to Zionism on ideological grounds deeply rooted in Marxian writ. Political Zionism stands condemned in Marxist-Leninist teaching as a reactionary bourgeois-nationalist ideology riddled with fundamental fallacies. It stands

> at the very opposite pole from the ideology of working-class internationalism, which calls for the unity of workers of all countries against their common class enemy, world monopoly capitalism and on this basis for a common struggle against all forms of national and racial oppression as being divisive and destructive of the interests of workers everywhere. In its extreme nationalism and separatism, in its capitulation to anti-Semitism, in its efforts to divide Jewish workers from other workers, Zionism serves the interests of the exploiters and oppressors of all workers and all peoples.[25]

Marxism-Leninism was never able to live in solid comfort with the idea of Jewish nationalism. Lenin denied that the Jews on a world scale, lacking a common territory, cultural and economic life, could constitute a nation in any generally recognized, let alone Marxist, sense of the term. And the notion that anti-Semitism, which sparked the birth of the political Zionist movement at the end of the nineteenth century, was incurable and eternal, challenged the Marxist-Leninist doctrine that changes in the social order would cure all political, economic and social ills. Lenin, who fought against the autonomous organization of Jewish workers in the Russian Social Democratic Labor Party, conceived of the Jewish problem almost wholly in terms of anti-Semitism which, in his view, was the product of economic conflicts rationalized in terms of religious and national hatreds. He decried any and all attempts to turn the Jews into a nation as the work of "a partisan of the old and cast-like in the

Jewish group, an accomplice of the rabbis and bourgeois." He saw in assimilation the ultimate solution to the Jewish problem.[26]

This remained Lenin's conviction, even though after the Bolshevik Revolution he had to admit that assimilation, especially linguistic assimilation, might take a long time and, to succeed, it had to be voluntary. This helps explain his policy of fostering Yiddish schools and a Yiddish press and cultural institutions, which he believed would help draw the Jewish masses into the vortex of revolutionary changes unleashed by the October Revolution.[27]

Stalin's approach to the Jewish problem was similar. He categorically rejected the conception of the inherent desirability of national existence which, in his opinion, was only "an historical category belonging to a definite epoch, the epoch of rising capitalism," and he denied absolutely the existence of a Jewish nation. "A nation", he wrote,

> is a historically evolved stable community of language, territory, economic life and psychological make-up manifested in a community of culture . . . and it is sufficient for a single of these characteristics to be absent, and the nation ceases to be a nation . . .

The Jews, Stalin said, might possess common national characteristics,

> but they cannot be said to constitute a single nation if they are economically disunited, inhabit different territories, speak different languages, etc.[28]

And, like Lenin, Stalin acknowledged the importance of the Yiddish language in schools and other public institutions as necessary to achieve the ultimate purpose of assimilation. For two decades after the Revolution of 1917, a prosperous system of cultural life flourished in the Soviet Union, with the Yiddish language at the core of a distinct Jewish nationality, which could look forward to an autonomous Jewish regime in Birobidzhan, Siberia. All that came to a brutal and tragic end on the eve of World War II; the price paid by Jews in terms of the total dedication of all cultural activity to the advancement of Communism—a price paid by all nationalities in the Soviet Union[29]—proved unavailing.

The Soviet Union's aversion to Zionism never ceased. Its

surprising support of partition of Palestine in 1947 and its crucial aid to Israel by the delivery of arms early in the war of liberation in 1948, were motivated by Russia's desire to see Great Britain out of an area of traditional rivalry. Once this objective was attained and Israel veered toward the American orbit, the tactical reasons disappeared and the Soviet Union's traditional antipathy toward Zionism reasserted itself.[30] Indeed, the Soviet Union was among the first to seek the "excommunication" of Zionism, by reducing it to a term of opprobrium in the United Nations. During the early 1960s, when the General Assembly and other United Nations organs dealt with questions raised by the so-called Swastika epidemic of 1959–60, the Soviet Union sought the condemnation of Zionism along with colonialism, neocolonialism, imperialism, *apartheid* and racial discrimination, including anti-Semitism. Since neither the condemnation of Zionism, which was a Soviet condition for the condemnation of anti-Semitism, nor the condemnation of anti-Semitism commanded sufficient support to ensure adoption, the question was never put to the vote.[31]

Clearly, the resolution equating Zionism with racism and racial discrimination is not an isolated phenomenon with no roots in the past and with no connection with anything that followed it. Zionism, it is generally agreed, has profoundly transformed the spiritual and material physiology of the Jewish people and it is impossible, all the protestations to the contrary notwithstanding, to separate the two. Neither is it possible to separate Zionism from Judaism and the Jewish religion. After all, Zionism draws much of its spiritual and moral power from an intense past and from a meticulous particularity of human and geographic reference reaching back into the origins of the Jewish people; the faith that the future existence of the Jewish nation was conditioned by its return to the historic homeland is the essence of Jewish messianism from which modern political Zionism derives much of its ideological and more of its emotional appeal.[32] In fact, the universal significance of a Jewish restoration to Palestine is widely acknowledged also in the Christian world, as the prediction of the Prophet Isaiah of the "remnant" which shall "return", reinforced by St. Paul, exerted a powerful influence on pious minds, both Catholic and Protestant.[33]

The intimate connection between Zionism and Judaism has never been lost on Arab and Moslem theologians, whose doctrine of Zionism as an emanation of the "perversity" of Judaism has been widely propagated in the Arab and Moslem world.[34] Thus, for example, in a paper entitled "The Essence of the Palestinean Problem", delivered by Dr. Kamel el Baker, President of Om Dorman Islamic University, at the Fourth Conference of the Academy of Islamic Research at Al Azhar in Cairo in September 1968, we read:

> ... Judaism is a "religion" in which the believers follow a certain creed. Zionism is the same as Judaism but it seeks to achieve the end sought by Judaism but through political action. The document declaring the establishment of the State of Israel asserts this fact, for it does not hide that the State of Israel is but a name for a Jewish State. Zionism, therefore, is the means employed by the Jewish religion for self-realization, and the Jews' method of establishing their unity vis-à-vis others in the area. Who, then, is the other party concerned in the conflict? Resorting to the law of majority as the closest criterion of natural justice emphasizes beyond doubt that the establishment of a Jewish State in Palestine means a confrontation of Islam and Muslims, for the cultural and demographic superiority in the usurped land is for Islam and Muslims.
>
> This, then, is the essence of the Palestinian problem—and religious Jewish State founded by Zionists—even though it may appear in the form of political implications guised by the successors of the Crusaders in modern garb.[35]

The extent to which the Arab–Israeli conflict has been plagued not only by polarized secular ideologies but by an artificially fostered religious animosity, may be gauged from the following paper read at the Conference by Professor Muhammad Taha Yehia, Dean of the Faculty of Theology in Djakarta, Indonesia. Representative of the general tenor of the statements and papers delivered at the Conference and entitled "The Attitude of the Jews towards Islam and the Muslims in the early Days of Islam", it was summarized as follows:

> Reading through the story of the Jews in history books, and comparing it with the statements of the Quran, the Old and New Testaments I gained an insight into their conditions throughout the ages from the time when an apostle was first sent to them, to the time of Jesus and Muhammad and from then up to the present time.

From those studies and comparisons I have come to this decisive conclusion that worldly avarice, obstinate contention, and cruelty are deeply ingrained in the innermost being of the Jews who try to achieve their individual and social ambitions by fair means or foul. They are so obstinate as to reject even the teachings of Allah's prophets and apostles, so cruel as to exact severe retribution for an injury, so aggressive as to flout all positive and religious laws and human feelings. With them, the end justifies the means, for arrogance and evil-doing are inherent qualities of their nature. . . .

Before discussing the attitude of the Jews towards Islam and Muslims in the early days of Islam, it behooves us to refer to the distortion of the Jewish creed that filled the life of Jews with perfidy and evil. . . .

From the very beginning Jews declared their hostility to Islam and even to all the other religions, and have not ceased to do so ever since. . . .

Islamic tolerance is in complete contrast to Jewish intolerance and cruelty. . . .

I should like to say before I conclude that I have thoroughly scrutinized the nature of the Jews. They are avaricious, ruthless, cruel, hypocritical and revengeful. These traits govern their lives. They never change nor are they inclined to change. They always try to seize any opportunity to take revenge on Islam and Muslims. . . .[36]

Like a waterway that drains from many streams, anti-Zionism is fed by many springs, rarely fresh, often muddy and frequently poisonous. The willful distortion, misrepresentation and defamation of the Zionist movement contribute massively to widening the chasm between peoples and nations and deliver hostages to the mean-minded and prejudiced. They not only turn the historical, political, strategic and military debate of the Arab–Israeli conflict on image and emotion rather than on substance and fact, but also disguise a boundless evil which cuts a devastating swath across the political landscape of the world. If it be true that the preliminary identification of a problem can be almost as important as the treatment of it, the recognition that the identification of Zionism with racism and racial discrimination forges a lethal weapon capable of bringing down an avalanche of fire and fury is the command of the hour.

As has already been suggested, the aim of the resolution of 10 November 1975 was to outlaw Zionism and all that it embodies, more concretely, the State of Israel.[37] In reality, however, it is more than an attempt to undermine the legitimacy of the State of Israel and render it easy prey to all political predators; it is also an assault on an ancient people, an ancient religion and an ancient culture and civilization. Only those with a total bias toward self-deception will attempt to draw a line of demarcation separating the people of Israel from the land of Israel and Zionism from Judaism;[38] only those who are lost in the thickets of illusion will undertake to counsel a people to make agonizing choices between deeply-held values and commitments. It is presumptuous to sit in judgment on the inward authority of values, faith and shared purpose that bind and unite people. However divided Jews may be in their interpretation of the meaning and implication of Zionist thought and doctrine, they alone can arbitrate their differences.

Thus, wittingly or unwittingly, resolution 3379(XXX) declaring Zionism a form of racism and racial discrimination is an aggressive extension of the preachings and actions of old which culminated in the Nazi holocaust. For as long as the resolution remains intact on the statute books of the United Nations, it can always be invoked to engender doubtful acts and create tragic situations. It is an unholy weapon which any tyrant, anytime and anywhere, can wield with the blessing of the international community to persecute, uproot and destroy men, women and children in the guise of fighting racism and racial discrimination.

Compounding the enormity of the resolution was the insistence of the sponsors upon turning patently political motivations into authentic history and raising self-reference to the status of valid sources of authority. It will be recalled that before the vote on the resolution was taken, the representative of Sierra Leone proposed its postponement until the following session of the General Assembly in 1976.[39] Supporting the postponement of consideration of the resolution, Ambassador Maina of Kenya said:

> In the Third Committee my delegation supported the postponement of this question in order to allow us and many other delegations time to study the question of Zionism. This was not an idle request or a political maneuver. My delegation cannot recall any time when the question of Zionism has been studied in substance by the United Nations. It is true that we cannot blame others for our ignorance, but it is fair to confess it when it exists and it is also fair to ask for time to eliminate that ignorance. The English dictionary . . . defines "determination" inter alia as: "make up one's mind, decide, fix as known". My question therefore is, on what basis do I arrive

at this proposed definition of Zionism? What has been going on both inside the United Nations and outside is not helpful and confirms my ignorance. More important, the absence of an appropriate authoritative scholarly study before this body on which to base the proposed definition of Zionism raised serious difficulties. Indeed, apart from expressions of anger and sometimes insults or pleasure, depending upon the inclination of speakers, what has been going on sheds little or no light on the subject.

It is common practice for this Organization to request its organs to conduct studies and provide data on difficult issues on which the United Nations has been asked to take decisions. No adequate reasons have been given for rushing this definition through before some of us have had time to benefit from studies, both private and public.

For these reasons my delegation has no option but to abstain from voting either for or against this obviously oversimplified definition of Zionism.[40]

The resolution's sponsors based their "determination" that Zionism was a form of racism and racial discrimination on the Declaration on the Elimination of All Forms of Racial Discrimination of 1963;[41] General Assembly resolution 3151 G (XXVIII) of 1973; the Declaration of Mexico City on the Equality of Women and their Contribution to Development and Peace of 1975;[42] resolution 77(XII) of the Assembly of Heads of State and Government of the Organization of African Unity of 1975;[43] and the Political Declaration and Strategy to Strengthen International Peace and Security Among the Nonaligned Countries, adopted by the Conference of Foreign Ministers in Lima, Peru, in August 1975.[44] But with the exception of the Declaration on the Elimination of All Forms of Racial Discrimination of 1963, which has no bearing on the subject, all the other declarations and resolutions cited in the preamble of resolution 3379(XXX) only confirm that the word Zionism had entered into the vocabulary of infamy of a sizeable number of States Members of the United Nations; they lend no more authority to the proposition that Zionism is a form of racism and racial discrimination than the statement of the representative of Somalia a year later in the Third Committee of the General Assembly on 3 October 1975, that "the single operative paragraph showed beyond question the link between Zionism and racial discrimination".[45] The Somalian representative spoke for the sponsors of the resolution and he referred to the operative paragraph which reads: "Determines that Zionism is a form of racism and racial discrimination".

The Declaration on the Elimination of All Forms of Racial Discrimination, as suggested, has no bearing on the question raised in the resolution on Zionism. It was invoked by the sponsors in the probable belief that mere reference to that 1963 document automatically changed their inference into a palpable fact. The Declaration was recalled, in particular, for its affirmation that

> any doctrine of racial differentiation or superiority is scientifically false, morally condemnable and socially unjust and dangerous,

as well as for its expression of alarm at

> the manifestation of racial discrimination still in existence in some areas in the world, some of which are imposed by certain Governments by means of legislative, administrative or other measures.

Everyone with the courage of his bias can read Zionism and everything else into those paragraphs and achieve verisimilitude by straining the evidence to fit the hypothesis.

Resolution 3151 G (XXVIII) of 1973, the second source of authority invoked, is the last of a six-part resolution of the General Assembly on different aspects of *apartheid*, such as Trade Union action, the program of work of the Special Committee on *apartheid*, dissemination of information and intensification and coordination of United Nations action against *apartheid*, action by national and international organizations, the United Nations Trust Fund for South African refugees, and the situation in South Africa resulting from the policies of *apartheid*. It was in the context of the situation in South Africa that resolution 3151 G (XXVIII) condemned

> the action of those States and Companies which continue to provide to the South African regime military equipment and supplies and assistance for local manufacture of such equipment in violation of the resolutions of the General Assembly and Security Council;

and

> in particular, the unholy alliance between Portuguese colonialism, South Africa racism, Zionism and Israeli imperialism.

However, beyond an assertion in the final preambular paragraph of the existence of a

> collision between Portuguese colonialism, the *apartheid* regime and Zionism, as exemplified by the political, military and financial aid supplied to each other by Portugal, South Africa and Israel,

their is nothing in the records of the debate on the subject in the Special Political Committee which would confer upon resolution 3151 G (XXVIII) the status of an originating source of theory for the formal equation of Zionism with racism and racial discrimination. In fact, the words "Zionism and Israeli imperialism" was inserted by Burundi as the "third partner" in the "unholy alliance", and only carried one step further the Arab campaign against Israel by seeking to establish a common essence of racism, Nazism and Zionism.

Once the mental threshold to an open attack on Zionism was crossed—and it was crossed a long time ago—it was a simple matter to invoke institutional authority to declare Zionism an evil along with racism, *apartheid*, imperialism, colonialism, neocolonialism and the like. And it was precisely in this manner that Zionism was introduced as a word of opprobrium into the Declaration of Mexico on the Equality of Women and their Contribution to Development and Peace, which was adopted by the World Conference of International Women's Year in 1975. The relevant clauses read as follows:

> *Taking* into account the role played by women in the history of humanity, especially in the struggle for national liberation, the strengthening of international peace, and the elimination of imperialism, colonialism, neocolonialism, foreign occupation, Zionism, alien domination, racism and *apartheid*. . . .
>
> *Recognizing* that women of the entire world, whatever differences exist between them, share the painful experience of receiving or having received unequal treatment, and that as their awareness of this phenomenon increases they will become natural allies in the struggle against any form of oppression, such as is practiced under colonialism, neocolonialism, Zionism, racial discrimination and *apartheid*, thereby constituting an enormous revolutionary potential for economic and social change in the world today. . . .
>
> *Decides* to promulgate the following principles:
>
> 24. International cooperation and peace require the achievement of

national liberation and independence, the elimination of colonialism and neocolonialism, foreign occupation, Zionism, *apartheid*, and racial discrimination in all its forms as well as the recognition of the dignity of peoples and their right to self-determination. . . .

26. Women as well as men together should eliminate colonialism, neocolonialism, imperialism, foreign domination and occupation, Zionism, *apartheid*, racial discrimination, the acquisition of land by force and the recognition of such acquisition, since such practices inflict incalculable suffering on women, men and children.

The Declaration is largely the product of the so-called Group of 77, which embraces the developing countries of Asia, Africa and Latin America and which worked on portions of it at smaller conferences in Somalia, Zaire and Venezuela.[46] The Declaration has been characterized by one of its protagonists as a document which "draws a broad picture of the political and economic content of the women's struggle, breaking new ground in this respect by lining up 'Zionism' with *apartheid* and racial discrimination as a malign force."[47] According to the testimony of a member of the Drafting Committee which finalized the text of the Declaration,

> the usual debate over the insertion of Zionism was not new, and I am not aware that this aggravated any tensions among women as women. It did make clear that a large section of the world sees certain political problems in a particular way. They see them as having great potential for international conflict, and we've been saying this in many ways at UN meetings and conferences for years. No doubt we'll continue to say them as long as these areas of tension need to be identified. *Apartheid* is one, Zionism is one, etc. There was nothing new about that area of political difference.[48]

There is no substantial or authoritative record of the debates at any stage of the elaboration of the Declaration, but given the background it is at least doubtful whether there was much discussion about the propriety or implications of inserting the term Zionism in a document of this kind. The intention was clearly to impose the text of the Group of 77 upon the Conference and to discourage debate on it. This explains why the text, for example, was not introduced in the First Committee of the Conference until two days before the close of the Conference, and why it was voted priority over the draft of a declaration sponsored by the United States, the United Kingdom and West Germany[49] and introduced in the First Committee several days earlier. On this subject, Ambassador Barbara White of the United States has this to say:

> From our point of view, the basic problem with the Declaration was that the Group of 77 never negotiated on it. We sought negotiations many times and they basically refused to negotiate. Before and during the Conference we knew they were drafting a declaration and negotiations could have taken place before the Conference here in New York, or at any time during the Conference. We kept indicating that we would like to talk about it, but we never had the opportunity. We felt one of the best ways was to put down what we thought on paper. In the Declaration submitted by the United States, the United Kingdom and West Germany, you can see basic similarities between ours and theirs. There were two problems with the other one that was eventually adopted as the Declaration of Mexico. One was the condemnation of Zionism which we felt had no place in such a document and which we felt could be interpreted as saying that Israel should not exist. The other was some reference to the Charter of Economic Rights and Duties of States and the new international economic order in terms that they knew we had voted against in other forums. Obviously, the U.S. wasn't going to change its position at this Conference on those issues. If they had wanted to, they could easily have referred to them in more acceptable terms. They chose not to, so we had to vote against it. I have no doubt that Israeli women and Arab women feel just as strongly about the issues of Palestine as the men of those countries. One of the primary reasons why the U.S. did not want the Conference to concentrate on these political and economic issues was because there are plenty of other U.N. conferences to discuss these in. We wanted to concentrate this time on the particular problems of women, and I think by and large the Conference did. . . .[50]

By a roll-call vote of 59 to 19, with 25 abstentions, the first Committee decided to retain the word Zionism,[51] the Declaration as a whole was adopted by 89 to 1, with 14 abstentions.[52] The vote in plenary was 61 to 23, with 25 abstentions, for retention of the word Zionism,[53] and 89 to 3, with 18 abstentions, for the adoption of the Declaration.[54]

Resolution 77(XII), the third source of authority invoked in resolution 3379(XXX) as a basis for determining that Zionism was a form of racism and racial discrimination, was adopted at the twelfth ordinary session of the Assembly of Heads of State and Government of the Organization of African Unity held in Kampala from 28 July to 1 August 1975. It states, inter alia, that

> the racist regime in occupied Palestine and the racist regine in Zimbabwe and South Africa have a common imperialist origin, forming a whole and having the same racist structure and being organizationally linked in their policy aimed at repression of the dignity and integrity of the human being,

and is the second of two resolutions on the Middle East which range far and wide over the whole area of conflict, and which seek to mobilize the African nations and "reinforce their struggle against the Zionist aggression." Adopted over the opposition of Zaire and with reservations by Sierra Leone, Senegal and Liberia,[55] resolution 76(XII) calls upon

> all OAU Member States to take the most appropriate measures to intensify pressures exercised against Israel at the U.N. and other Institutions, including the possibility of eventually depriving it of its status as member of these Institutions;

and

> considers Zionism a danger to world peace, and decides to organize an information campaign in which all African information media would participate to unmask the racist aggressive nature of the Zionist entity in a continuous and planned manner, and to confront and refute all Zionist misleading propaganda campaigns aimed at arousing hostility against both the Arab and African Worlds.

Resolution 77(XII) is similar in spirit and language to its sister resolution and calls upon all Member States of the Organization of African Unity

> to support the people of Palestine by every means in its struggle against Zionist racist colonialism to restore their full national rights . . .

and

> to take all appropriate measures to intensify pressure against Israel at the United Nations and the other agencies, including the possibility of eventually depriving it of its status as a member of these agencies.

Like resolution 76(XII) this resolution, too, was adopted over the opposition of Zaire and with reservations by Ghana, Sierra Leone, Senegal and Liberia.

The Political Declaration and Strategy to Strengthen International Peace and Security and to Intensify Solidarity and Mutual Assistance among Nonaligned Countries, the fourth source of authority invoked in support of the determination that

Zionism was a form of racism and racial discrimination, was adopted by the Conference of Ministers for Foreign Affairs on Nonaligned Countries which met in Lima, Peru, toward the end of August 1975. The Declaration, which condemns Zionism "as a threat to world peace and security" and calls upon all countries to oppose "this racist and imperialist ideology", is a lineal descendent of resolutions 76(XII) and 77(XII) of Kampala adopted a month earlier. But the true progenitors of the equation of Zionism with racism and racial discrimination are the Political Declaration, the Declaration on the Struggle for National Liberation and Resolution 2 of the Fourth Conference of Nonaligned Countries, which was held from 5 to 9 September 1973, in Algiers.[56] Paragraph 14 of the Political Declaration notes that,

> While considerable progress has been made towards East-West *detente*, the fact that peoples are in direct confrontation with colonialism, racial discrimination and *apartheid*, alien domination and foreign occupation, neocolonialism, imperialism and Zionism, remains an indisputable reality of our age.

This theme is reiterated in paragraph 3 of the Declaration on the Struggle for National Liberation, which states:

> The confrontation of peoples with colonialism, neocolonialism, Zionism and imperialism, remains a fundamental reality of our area, continually emphasizing the common destiny and the indivisible nature of the struggle of the peoples of the Third World.

It is amplified in subsequent paragraphs as follows:

> *Apartheid* in South Africa is not just a system of racial discrimination; it is above all a form of colonialism based on fascist oppression of the people by a minority of alien settlers who exploit the people and deprive them of their fundamental rights, denying the most elementary human values. In Zimbabwe, Namibia, and the countries under Portuguese domination, the racist minorities are pursuing a systematic policy of settlement and are bent on changing the ethnic composition of the peoples of these countries, destroying their cultural heritage and exploiting the wealth of these countries for their exclusive benefit.
>
> In this connection, the case of Palestine, where Zionist-settler colonialism has taken the form of a systematic uprooting of the Palestinian people from their homeland and represents a very serious threat to their survival as a nation, is exactly the same as the situation in Southern Africa, where racist

segregationist minorities use the same method of colonial domination and exploitation pursuant to the requirements of a single imperialist strategy . . .

. . . The patent reinforcement of the Pretoria-Salisbury-Lisbon axis, now increasingly being extended to Tel Aviv, highlights the identical objectives pursued by these regimes and calls for coherent and appropriate action on the part of the nonaligned countries, the national liberation movements and all the other forces which defend liberty, progress and peace in the world.

The Declaration closes with an affirmation of the resolve of the nonaligned countries

to do everything in their power to isolate colonialist, racist and *apartheid* regimes, inter alia, by:

1) the severance or suspension or freezing of all relations with Portugal, South Africa, Rhodesia and Israel;

2) the denunciation of these regimes in all international political, economic, cultural and social forums;

3) the organization of campaigns to inform world public opinion, especially in the Western countries, and to denounce the support that some of the Governments of these countries provide to Portuguese colonialism and to the regimes in South Africa, Rhodesia and Israel. These Western powers must choose between the friendship of the nonaligned countries and the support they give to colonialist and racist regimes.

Finally, in resolution 2 on the Middle East situation and the Palestine issue, the Fourth Conference of Heads of State and Governments of Nonaligned Countries, after

Reaffirming the legitimacy of the struggle of the Palestinian people against colonialism, Zionism and racism to recover in their entirety their national rights, a struggle which forms an integral part of the liberation movement throughout the world;

Calls upon the nonaligned countries to pledge their support for the Arab people of Palestine in their struggle against Zionist racist and colonialist settlements for their recovery of their full national rights, emphasizes that the recovery of these rights is a fundamental prerequisite for a just and lasting peace, and declares its recognition of the Palestine Liberation Organization as the legitimate representative of the Palestinian people and of their just struggle. . . .

Welcomes the decision of certain member countries to break off relations with Israel, and requests the other member countries to take steps to boycott Israel diplomatically, economically, militarily and culturally, as well as in the field of sea and air transport, in accordance with the provisions of Chapter VII of the United Nations Charter.

NOTES

1. A/PV.2267, p. 16.

2. A publication based in New York and dedicated to serving the United Nations and the international community.

3. For the roll-call vote see A/PV.2400, p. 146.

4. For text see Department of Public Information, Press Release SG/SM/2273.

5. For text see Department of Public Information, Press Release GA/5380.

6. For reaction in the United States, see Sidney Liskofsky, U.N. Resolution on Zionism, *American Jewish Yearbook* 77, 1977, pp. 106–115.

7. A/PV.2400, p. 76.

8. For text, see Report of the Third Committee, Part I, A/10320, pp. 4–7.

9. A/C.3/L.2157.

10. See A/10320 op cit., p. 10; also A/C.3/SR.2130, pp. 3–4.

11. A/C.3/SR.2116, p. 2.

12. A/C.3/SR.2130, pp. 4–5.

13. Ibid., p. 7.

14. Ibid., p. 8.

15. A/C.3/SR.2134, pp. 27–28.

16. Ibid., pp. 6–7.

17. Ibid., pp. 16–17.

18. A/PV.2400, pp. 152–155.

19. Ibid., pp. 83–85.

20. Ibid., pp. 58–60.

21. Ibid., p. 51.

22. Ibid., pp. 28–30.

23. For example, the thirty-first General Assembly in 1976 adopted a resolution in which, after

> *Noting* with grave concern
>
> that some Governments, in pursuing strategic and economic and other interests, continue to collaborate with the racist regime of South Africa and thereby encourage it to persist in its criminal policies;

strongly condemns

> the action of those States and foreign economic and other interests which continue to collaborate with the racist regime of South Africa (Resolution 31/6(H)).

Nevertheless, the General Assembly deemed it necessary to adopt a separate resolution on the relations between Israel and South Africa and to enjoin the Secretary-General to give the resolution the widest publicity. Resolution 31/6(E), after recalling earlier resolutions on the subject dating back to 1973, strongly condemns the continuing and increasing collaboration by Israel with the racist regime of South Africa as a flagrant violation of the resolutions of the United Nations and as an encouragement to the racist regime of South Africa to persist in its criminal policies;

and requests the Secretary-General

to disseminate widely the report of the Special Committee against *Apartheid* in various languages, in order to mobilize public opinion against the collaboration by Israel with the racist regime of South Africa.

24. In resolution 31/6(I) of 9 November 1976, the General Assembly proclaimed that

the racist regime of South Africa is illegitimate and has no right to represent the people of South Africa;

and reaffirms

the legitimacy of the struggle by the oppressed people of South Africa, and their liberation movements, by all possible means, for the seizure of power by the people and the exercise of their inalienable right to self-determination.

25. Hyman Lumer, *Zionism: Its Role in World Politics*, International Publishers, New York, 1973, p. 12.

26. Reuben Ainsztein, "The Fate of Soviet Jewry", *The Midstream Reader*, edited by Shlomo Katz, Thomas Yoseloff, New York, 1958, pp. 45–64. See Walter Laquer, *A History of Zionism*, Holt, Rinehart and Winston, New York, 1972, pp. 416–437; Salo W. Baron, *Modern Nationalism and Religion*, Meridian Books and Jewish Publication Society of America, 1960, Chapter VII.

27. Ibid.

28. Ibid., p. 48.

29. For a general discussion of the Soviet concept of nationalism and nationhood and its application, see G. Starouchenko: *Le Principe de L'Autodétermination des Peoples at des Nations dans la Politique Etrangere de l'Etat Sovietique*, Editions du Progres, Moscow.

30. See Yehoshuah, A. Gilboa, "Soviet Politics on Palestine: Tradition and Change", *International Problems*, The Israeli Institute of International Affairs, Tel Aviv University, Vol. X, Nos. 3–4, December 1971, pp. 11–19.

31. See Moses Moskowitz, "The Narrowing Horizons of United Nations Concern with Racial Discrimination", *Human Rights Journal*, International Institute of Human Rights, Strasbourg, France, Vol. IV, Nos. 2–3, 1971, pp. 278–292.

32. Salo W. Baron, op. cit., contains an excellent introductory summary of messianic and modern political Zionism.

33. Ibid., note 7.

34. See, for example, *Arab Theologians on Jews and Israel: Extracts from the Proceedings of the Fourth Conference of the Academy of Islamic Research*, held at

Al Azhar, Cairo, in September 1968; introduced and edited by D. Green, Editions de l'Avenir, Geneva, 1971.

35. Ibid., p. 53.

36. Ibid., p. 19.

37. It is difficult to select from the mass of facts and statements the ones that best sum up the position of Arabs on the legitimacy of the State of Israel. A clear juridical exposition is to be found in the proceedings of the Seminar on Palestine held by Arab jurists in Algiers at the end of July 1967. They denied the very existence of the Jewish people and stated categorically that the Jews were no more than a religious community which has no common language, history or roots. The Arab jurists also denied emphatically the existence of any historical connection between the Jewish people and the land of Palestine. Quoted by Professor Nathan Feinberg in his work *The Arab–Israel Conflict in International Law: A Critical Analysis of the Colloquium of Arab Jurists in Algiers*, The Hebrew University Press, Jerusalem, 1970, Chapter II.

A most recent statement on Zionism is the Declaration of the International Symposium on Zionism, which was held in Baghdad, Iraq, from 8 to 12 November 1976, by the University of Baghdad. For text see A/31/339 of 22 November 1976.

38. Indeed, the assertion that Zionism is synonymous with Judaism is decried by Arabs as another Zionist plot. For, example, urging the adoption of the resolution on Zionism by the General Assembly in the evening of 10 November 1975, Ambassador Al-Sayegh of Kuwait declared:

> Zionism now makes a unilateral proclamation, saying that Zionism is synonymous with Judaism and therefore opposition to Zionism is synonymous with opposition to Judaism—that is, it is anti-Semitism.
>
> Let me recall that the first objections and opposition to the doctrines of Zionism, to the objective of Zionism, to the program of Zionism were aired by Jews, prominent Jewish intellectuals, prominent Jewish thinkers and prominent Jewish organizations. . . .
>
> We too reject the claim of Zionism that Zionism is synonymous with Judaism. . . . We reject the claim of Zionism to be coextensive with Judaism. We reject the claim that Zionism is coextensive with the Jewish people. And therefore we reject the claim of Zionism that to be anti-Zionist is to be anti-Jewish and anti-Semitic (A/PV.2400, p. 121).

39. See above, p. 134.

40. A/PV.2400, pp. 77–80.

41. General Assembly resolution 1904(XVIII).

42. For text see Report of the World Conference of the International Women's Year, Mexico City, 19 June–2 July 1975, E/CONF.66/34.

43. For text see A/10297, Annex II.

44. For text see A/10217, Annex.

45. A/C.3/SR.2132, pp. 7–8.

46. See *Meeting in Mexico:* The story of the World Conference of the

International Women's Year (Mexico City 19 June–2 July 1975) United Nations, 1975 (not an official document), pp. 25–26.

47. Ibid., p. 25.
48. Ibid., p. 26.
49. Report of the World Conference, op. cit., p. 148.
50. Meeting in Mexico, op. cit., p. 27.
51. Report of the World Conference, op, cit., p. 149.
52. Ibid.
53. Ibid.
54. Ibid.
55. Ibid.
56. For text see A/9330 of 22 November 1973.

Chapter VII

THE USES OF CANT

Resolution 3379(XXX) marked the culmination of a campaign to isolate Israel which the Arab States had waged for many years and which aimed at establishing Israel in the eyes of the world as the "other" pivot of a racist axis formed by South Africa and extending into the Middle East. Nothing like sharing a common enemy was better calculated to enable the Arabs to extract every advantage from their deliberate identification with the plight of the black man in South Africa. By equating Zionism with racism and racial discrimination and tagging it on to the anti-*apartheid* campaign, the Arab countries opened up new propaganda fronts in the United Nations for brandishing indignation and new opportunities for raising the Middle East question regardless of relevance or propriety.

In a very large sense, the resolution was designed to provide an acceptable rationale for the acquiescence of the majority of States Members of the United Nations in the harassment of Israel and to justify the crusade-like campaign against the Jewish State in the Middle East dispute. Arab hatred of Zionism, understandable in itself, could not readily be translated into universal terms to sustain it abroad. As a concept, movement or historical reality, Zionism was too abstract to affect the minds and hearts of people in the larger world and to act out its assigned role in the campaign against Israel, while Israel as a State was too concrete to lend credibility to all the evils which had been attributed to it. To discredit Zionism and to undermine its validity, it was necessary to give it more universal dimensions as an unmitigated disaster recognized by large sections of the world and readily identifiable as such. Hence the insistence on equating Zionism with racism and racial discrimination, which the sponsors of the resolution hoped would eventually transmute a regional political-military problem into a universal issue and make the Arab cause an unquestionable cause of all humanity.

The efforts made by the Arab States to identify the Middle East conflict with the struggle of the blacks in South Africa for freedom and dignity have been facilitated in no small degree by the laxity in definition of terms to the point of intellectual misdemeanor which often obtains in the United Nations. Their insistence upon generalizing an essentially culture-bound phenomenon to embrace other human woes as well, and endowing *apartheid* with a mystique capable of summoning up deep associations for which all objective reasons were lacking, robbed the campaign against South Africa's racial policies of its authenticity and compromised its integrity. By subjecting the anti-*apartheid* campaign to their overarching design against Israel, the Arab countries went far toward destroying the uniqueness of *apartheid* as evil incarnate whose annihilation was the supreme command of the hour. If the stigmatization of Zionism as a form of racism and racial discrimination was enough to identify it with *apartheid*, then any skirmish, however insignificant, could be elevated to the twilight of the gods and confused with it; if the bias of one side in a conflict articulated with liturgical intensity and supported by a conformist chorus of self-approval could be carried to its reduction *ad absurdum*, then the underpinnings of the entire system on which the international campaign against *apartheid* is based are shaken loose. If nations with different motivations and for different reasons can easily tag on to an issue which preoccupies the United Nations in order to gain advantage and advance their own interests and objectives, there is nothing to prevent the anti-*apartheid* campaign or any other morally-compelling issue from being exploited, or used as a facile precedent, against any other State Member which has the misfortune of being in a minority in the General Assembly or Security Council.

Thus it may not be so much the legitimacy and respectability conferred upon it that sustains the United Nations' anti-*apartheid* campaign as the fact that South Africa's racial policies provide a fortuitous but reliable platform for rallying nations to a common cause, however varying in reasons and motivations and in aims and purposes. The reasons advanced over the years for the internationalization of the *apartheid* question have provided justifications to suit every conceivable mood and temper, and have enabled the campaign against the racial policies of South Africa to assimilate contradictory forces and accommodate conflicting interests. This explains the ease with which the World Conference to Combat Racism and Racial Discrimination, which met in Geneva in August 1978 pursuant to General Assembly resolution 32/129, brought itself to include paragraph 19 in the Declaration adopted by the Conference that can best be described as a solemn act of ratification of resolution 3379(XXX) declaring Zionism a form of racism and racial discrimination. Paragraph 19 reads:

> The Conference recalls with deep regret the moral tragedy which befell the Palestinian people thirty years ago and which they continue to endure today—manifested in their being prevented from exercising their right to self-determination on the soil of their homeland, in the dispersal of hundreds of thousands of Palestinians, the prevention of their return to their homes, and the establishment therein of settlers from abroad, and in the practice of diverse forms of racial discrimination against Palestinians affecting all aspects of their lives in a manner which prevents their enjoyment of their elementary human rights on a basis of equality; the Conference expresses its grave concern over this continuing situation and deplores Israel's refusal to comply with the relevant resolutions of the United Nations and it calls for the cessation of all practices of racial discrimination to which the Palestinians, as well as other inhabitants of the Arab territories occupied by Israel, are being subjected; the Conference voices its hope that the Palestinian people will soon have the opportunity to exercise its inalienable right to self-determination in accordance with the relevant resolutions of the United Nations on the question of Palestine, and proclaims its solidarity with the Palestinian people in their struggle for liberation and against racial discrimination.[1]

With an Olympian disdain for facts the Conference also pronounced anathema against the alleged unholy alliance between Israel and South Africa and summoned the world to noble anger and fury at the collusion of the two outcasts. Paragraph 18 of the Declaration reads:

> The conference condemns the existing and increasing relations between the Zionist State of Israel and the racist regime of South Africa, in particular those in the economic and military fields, and deplores and warns against cooperation between them in the nuclear field; it particularly deplores the expansion and intensification of those relations at the time when the international community exerts all its efforts towards the objective of completely isolating the racist regime of South Africa; the Conference views this cooperation as an act of deliberate choice, and a hostile act against the oppressed people of South Africa, as well as a defiance of the resolutions of the United Nations and the efforts of the society of nations to ensure freedom and peace in southern Africa; the Conference also notes with concern the insidious propaganda by the Government of Israel and its Zionist and other supporters against the United Nations organs and against Governments which have advocated firm action against *apartheid*.[2]

The theme of collusion between Israel and South Africa followed logically upon the equation of Zionism with racism and racial discrimination. The resolution of 10 November 1975 was not intended as a theoretical statement, but as a means of widening the propaganda front against Israel. In fact, it did not take long before the condemnation of Israel for its alleged collusion with South Africa became standard operating procedure wherever and whenever South Africa's racial policies were discussed; it turned into as much an object of unassailable piety as the condemnation of *apartheid* itself. The identification of Zionism with racism and racial discrimination which the General Assembly had sanctioned on 10 November 1975 gave rise to a new exegesis that enriched the proceedings of United Nations organs, while the surveillance of the Sub-Committee on the Implementation of United Nations Resolutions and Collaboration with South Africa—an arm of the Special Committee against *Apartheid*—helped stoke the fires of righteous indignation. For example, the elevation in January 1976 of South Africa's Consulate-General in Israel to an Embassy and subsequent visits to Israel of high officials of the South African Government were regarded as highly provocative. The announcement on 4 April 1976 of the scheduled visit later that month of Prime Minister Vorster obliged Ambassador Jeanne Martin Cisse of Guinea, Chairman of the Special Committee, to issue a statement to the press in which she expressed the hope that all Governments and organizations would condemn the actions of the Government of Israel in developing closer relations with the Pretoria regime in defiance of the United Nations resolutions, and exercise their influence to persuade the Government of Israel to desist from its present course.[3]

Ten days later Mme. Cisse reiterated her concern over the further strengthening of relations between the two Governments and wondered whether Israel and South Africa were continuing "their vain efforts to divide Africa". "The Government of Israel", she told the Committee on *Apartheid*,

should be informed in no uncertain terms that Governments and peoples opposed to *apartheid* and racism—that is, most of humanity—cannot condone or ignore its relations with the racist regime in South Africa in flagrant violation of United Nations resolutions.[4]

On 30 April 1976, the Special Committee against *Apartheid*, acting on a proposal of the representative of Sudan, invited the Sub-Committee on the Implementation of United Nations Resolutions and Collaboration with South Africa to make an intensive and detailed study of Israeli–South African relations for submission later that year to the thirty-third session of the General Assembly. The preparation of the report, coinciding as it did with a decision to discuss the South African situation in plenary without prior reference to a Committee, as had been customary theretofore, enlarged the opportunity for dilating on the subject of Israel's relations with South Africa and for attempting a Tolstoyan range of depth. The scope, content and conclusions of the report were summarized in the Introduction as follows:

13. The purpose of the present report is to give an account of the growth in relations between Israel and South Africa. The report contains information on the historical background of collaboration between South Africa and the Zionist movement prior to the formation of the State of Israel. It reviews developments in all areas of collaboration between the two countries between 1948 and the present.

14. The report shows that relations between Israel and South Africa, which have ideological and historical roots, acquired new dimensions and were greatly intensified after the June 1967 war in the Middle East and even more after the October 1973 war. Differences between the two regimes caused by diverging foreign policy objectives towards the Arab and the

African countries were set aside when the African States broke diplomatic relations with Israel. Weakened by the advances of the liberation struggle and forced into increasing isolation by growing Arab–African solidarity and world condemnation of their racist policies, the two regimes have resorted to an ever closer collaboration in all areas, as indicated below:

(a) Politically, the collaboration has aimed at driving a wedge between the African countries and between them and the Arab countries, and at linking southern Africa and the Middle East as common strategic concerns of the Western Powers; South Africa expects substantial political dividends from closer association in undermining the boycott campaign.

(b) In the military sphere, this growing collaboration has provided each country with an additional source of arms supplies and technological know-how, as well as access to classified information on strategies and tactics.

(c) Economically, Israel has benefited from raw materials vital to its economy, while South Africa has derived substantial advantages from its favorable balance of trade with Israel and from the possibility of that country as a springboard both for evading the international boycott and for circumventing high European Economic Community tariffs; investment has increasingly taken the form of joint projects by public corporations drawing on the complementarity of the two economies—South Africa's raw materials and Israel's scientific know-how—to promote industrial expansion schemes of benefit to both countries.

(d) In the cultural field, exchange programs and other activities have promoted closer ideological identification between the two countries and have served to further South African propaganda.[5]

The first to address himself on the subject was the representative of the Soviet who said:

> . . . Nor can we overlook another partner of *apartheid*, and here I am speaking of the mutual relations between Israel and South Africa. Incidentally, the same Vorster calls his racist regime a bastion of the West. As for Israel, it was recently called, in that same West again, a firm bastion of democracy. Let us consider, however, how relations are being developed between these two entities—even if they may be bastions, they are racist bastions. Detailed data on this matter are contained in the report of the Special Committee against *Apartheid*. In regard to relations between Israel and South Africa, the report in particular states that, in political terms, cooperation between the Republic of South Africa and Israel has as its purpose to introduce discord between African and Arab countries. In the military sphere, Israel and the Republic of South Africa are expanding their mutual supply of weapons and technology. In economic relations, Israel receives from the Republic of South Africa its needed raw materials, whereas Africa is using Israel as a subterfuge for the international boycott.

This is the criminal cooperation of these two racist regimes. This is further evidence of the fact that Zionism is a form of racism and racial discrimination.[6]

It may be noted that the Soviet Union, Cuba[7] and Poland[8] were alone in associating themselves with the Arab States at the thirty-first session of the General Assembly in 1976 by commenting on Israel's relations with South Africa. No African State south of the Sahara rose to add its voice of indignation at Israel, while the rest of the States Members preferred to keep their counsel. Indeed, the only African State to join in the denunciation of Israel's relationship with South Africa in three years of General Assembly debate on *apartheid* in plenary was Burundi. In a lengthy statement on 27 November 1978, Burundi's representative sought to explain that what motivated Israel's strengthened relations with South Africa was not the breaking off of diplomatic relations between the African States and Israel during the Yom Kippur war in 1973, but the "similarity between the regimes of Pretoria and Tel Aviv", both of which were "profoundly racist and expansionist".[9] Furthermore, but for a casual reference to the subject by the representatives of the German Democratic Republic[10] and Czechoslovakia[11] and the statement made by the representative of the Pan-African Congress of Azania in the General Assembly debate in 1977,[12] and a similar casual reference by China[13] and the interventions of Afghanistan[14] and of the Chairman of the Special Committee against *Apartheid*[15] in the 1978 debate, the Arab world was virtually isolated in pressing their thesis.

The statements made by the representatives of the Arab States were so many variations on the same theme—the alliance between Israel and the Pretoria regime boded ill for Africa and the world and drew its strength from kindred racist ideologies and mutual interest in suppressing people they ruled. This was perhaps best articulated in the statements by the representatives of Morocco and Tunisia. Said the representative of Morocco:

Several delegations have from this rostrum with unequal talent pointed to a confluence of interests between the policies of South Africa and Israel. We believe that the organic links existing between *apartheid* and Zionism are to be seen through ideologies and methods that are remarkably similar. The

> strengthening of their military ties, their economic and cultural links testify—if there is need to testify—to the striking similarity between those castes which are so convinced of their superiority of race. We could not condemn *apartheid* as an instrument of oppression without condemning Israel for the same reason.[16]

"Among the most zealous supporters and allies of *apartheid*", said the representative of Tunisia,

> we find the State of Israel. That should not, however, unduly surprise us. In the present state of affairs, the alliance between Israel and South Africa is the most natural one that could exist; it is dictated by the very nature of the two regimes, whose ideology is based on the doctrine of racial supremacy. We should not underestimate that alliance, because of the brutal force of arms which it represents, but also because behind it are concealed all those who believe in the same ideology—and they are more numerous than is believed. It is evil, because each of the two regimes finds in the other encouragement to continue in its obstinate denial of all justice to its victims. Having said that, we may add that the alliance nevertheless has a merit, that is, it will enable everyone to grasp the racist nature of the two systems, which in certain countries in all seriousness continue to be qualified as "democratic".[17]

If the Arab thesis failed to impress the black Africans, it was first of all because they resented the intrusion of the Arabs into a domain they considered of vital interest to them—a resentment, it may be recalled, which surfaced at the 1975 session of the General Assembly in connection with the consideration of the Decade for Action to Combat Racism and Racial Discrimination, when the Africans resisted Arab pressure to incorporate in the relevant resolutions a reference to Zionism as a form of racism and racial discrimination.[18] Having failed to overcome the Africans' resistance and their fear that any diversion might diminish the impact of the Decade in the struggle against *apartheid*, the Arabs were compelled to introduce on their own the draft resolution determining that Zionism was a form of racism and racial discrimination.

Secondly, few had taken unbidden and uncoerced to the idea of singling out Israel for special censure for its links with South Africa when similar links of far greater consequence were maintained by nations large and small which traded and did business with the South African Republic. The question put to the

General Assembly by Israeli Ambassador Haim Herzog as to why the Special Committee against *Apartheid* deemed it necessary to produce a special report on his country's relations with South Africa, and not on the relations with that country of each of the countries mentioned in the report on the adverse consequences for the enjoyment of human rights of political, military, economic and other forms of assistance given to colonial and racist regimes, prepared by Ahmed M. Khalifa of Egypt, Special Rapporteur of the Sub-Commission on Prevention of Discrimination and Protection of Minorities, was never answered.[19] "Was it because they were of less consequence?", Ambassador Herzog asked himself. No, he replied, and he went on to say:

> According to the latest available statistics, the foreign trade of South Africa totalled over U.S.$12 billion last year. Of this huge sum Israel's share was less than two-fifths of one percent—I repeat, two-fifths of one percent—infinitely smaller than the share of Arab and many other countries. If two-fifths of one percent warrants such extensive reporting in United Nations documents and speeches, then let the same treatment be accorded to all South Africa's trading partners—without exception—on a proportional basis equal to that accorded Israel.
>
> If trade in the magnitude of two-fifths of one percent warrants a report of twenty-nine pages, then what would you say to the trade of groups represented in this hall with South Africa which dwarf in their scope Israel's share? I am not making unfounded allegations here. Since last year's unwarranted attack on us we have thoroughly researched the subject and discovered a picture of international double-faced hypocrisy which defies all description, and which is mind-boggling. . . .
>
> You are witnessing here one of the most disgusting exhibitions of double-talk, two-faced duplicity and unashamed hypocrisy. If you do not wish to engage in the cynical practice of selectivity and discrimination being practiced here then you must open all the books for all to see, and publish all the trades of all the blocs with every country. The most blatant example of this kind of hypocrisy is the allegation of Israeli arms sales to South Africa. I urge each and everyone of you to open the *Military Balance* published by the London International Institute for Strategic Studies at page 44 and read the list of tanks, artillery, aircraft, destroyers and submarines that comprise the large and modernly equipped armed forces of South Africa. It is quite evident that it is not Israel that supplied them.
>
> . . . Let us receive a full account of all trade, investment, tourism, gold purchases, oil supplies, visits, diplomatic and other relations, overt and covert, before passing judgement. Let us open all the books for all to see and let us publish reports on all trade by every bloc. Let us cease from this ugly

practice of selectivity and discrimination. If this Organization is to have any credibility, this exercise in international hypocrisy must stop.

> Hypocrisy is a boomerang and those who throw it should not be surprised if it returns to haunt them.[20]

In the end, however, a majority of 91 to 20, with 28 abstentions, ranged itself behind the draft resolution introduced by Libya, which strongly condemned

> the continuous and increasing collaboration by Israel with the racist regime of South Africa as a flagrant violation of the resolutions of the United Nations and as an encouragement to the racist regime of South Africa to persist in its criminal policies;

and requested the Secretary-General

> to disseminate widely the report of the Special Committee against *Apartheid*, in various languages, in order to mobilize public opinion against the collaboration by Israel with the racist regime of South Africa.[21]

The Ivory Coast, Malawi and Swaziland were the only African States to abstain in the voting and of these only Malawi took the floor to explain its vote by saying that

> The draft resolution contained in General Assembly document A/31/L.9 refers specifically to the relations between Israel and South Africa, giving the impression that Israel—and Israel alone—trades with South Africa. If this resolution is to have any impact at all, then it should include every country in the world that has similar relations with South Africa. My delegation is aware, for instance, that some palaces and even vaults of central banks of these countries which maintain similar if not greater trade relations with South Africa than Israel are as pregnant with South African gold as South Africa itself is contaminated by the policies of *apartheid*. My delegation is also aware that some of the arms we are talking about here have found their way to South Africa through those countries which these resolutions have not named.[22]

Lesotho, which voted with the majority, entered a reservation to the effect that while it voted for the draft resolution, it would have preferred if all countries with similar relations were listed.[23] But it was the representative of Singapore, who abstained in the vote, who best summed up the situation when he observed:

> The anti-*apartheid* cause is a just and worthy one, but a just cause must still be pursued by just means. We should be doing the anti-*apartheid* cause a disservice if we were to employ tactics which were ethically questionable.

> For example, the levelling of accusations which have not been proved beyond a reasonable doubt would not be worthy of our united cause.[24]

It is often difficult to disentangle design from opportunity, but once an item is placed on the agenda of the General Assembly it tends to perpetuate itself. The thirty-second and thirty-third sessions of the General Assembly, in 1977 and 1978 respectively, followed with little variation the pattern set in 1976, replete with special reports and the adoption of special resolutions singling out Israel for its relations with South Africa. Speaking in the debate on 17 November 1977, Israeli Ambassador Herzog said:

> ... For two years now I have come to the Assembly with one simple demand: apply the same standards to all nations whose representatives are assembled here. . . .
>
> But once again we have witnessed the Special Committee against *Apartheid* applying the most cynical double standards to its proceedings, and engaging in such selective duplicity as to cast very serious doubts on its credentials. I refer of course to the Committee's report in document A/32/22/Add.3 entitled "Relations between Israel and South Africa". If the Committee's purpose and *raison d'etre* is to attack Israel, then it is undoubtedly performing its function. If, however, its purposes is to combat the policies of *apartheid* and to expose all relations with South Africa, then the Committee has betrayed its mandate and failed both the General Assembly and the African world.
>
> Seldom have I encountered a more cynical document than the special report of the Special Committee against *Apartheid* on relations between Israel and South Africa. Its one-sidedness, its transparent hypocrisy and selectivity, make it evident that we have here before us a document that has been inspired by motives that are discriminatory and biased and which bear no relation to the problems of *apartheid.*
>
> Indeed what this document reveals is that the members of that Committee have deliberately avoided the issue in question in order to pursue a partisan private war against Israel, in pursuance presumably to the dictate they received from the Arab delegations. The Committee has thus failed in its duty to this Assembly and should in my humble opinion be censured for a document which is dishonest, biased, discriminatory, and an insult to the intelligence of this Assembly.
>
> If ever a Committee has failed in a task assigned to it, it is the Special Committee against *Apartheid.* Let us consider a few pearls of wisdom it has cast before this Assembly.
>
> The report opens with the alarming statement that "The Special Committee against *Apartheid* has followed with grave concern the continuing and increasing collaboration by the Government of Israel with the

apartheid regime of South Africa . . . in the nuclear field . . ." (A/32/22/Add.3, para. 1).

One turns to the relevant page anticipating the earth-shattering revelations that will be made by this Committee and discovers that "The Committee has received disturbing reports" that Israel's cooperation with South Africa "may have extended to the nuclear sphere". In a rare show of objectivity the Committee then reports that "These reports have been denied by the Government of Israel". We are then informed in the next paragraph that several unnamed observers have expressed concern about developments that "may involve the transfer of nuclear know-how", or that "Israel may be supplying nuclear technology" (ibid., Annex, para. 11).

So on the basis of these tendentious reports, which have no basis whatsoever in fact, and in respect of which no proof is adduced, Israel is to be condemned. The Government of Israel has denied these allegations, and I take this opportunity once again to deny them formally. . . .[25]

As was the case in 1976, so in 1977 a resolution cosponsored by the Byelorussian SSR, Indonesia, Malaysia, Mauritius, Mongolia, Mozambique, Quatar and the United Republic of Cameroon, which condemned Israel strongly again "for its continuing and increasing collaboration with the racist regime of South Africa" and once again demanded that Israel desist from such collaboration and, in particular, terminate all collaboration in the military and nuclear fields",[26] was adopted with virtually the same majority as in the year before. The vote was 89 in favor to 19 against, with 30 abstentions.

The thirty-third session of the General Assembly saw more of the same. Opening the debate, the representative of the Sudan tried to summarize the problem as follows: "Birds of a feather", he said,

flock together, and we wish to draw the attention of the world to the dangers threatening it as a result of cooperation and coordination between the racist regimes of Pretoria and Tel Aviv. The collusion between the Israeli and South African Governments in a number of fields, including the political and military fields, has become alarming for the whole of the international community. In spite of resolutions of the General Assembly during the past two sessions, which condemn the strengthening of cooperation between the Zionist and racist regimes, since this constitutes a grave violation of United Nations resolutions and encourages the fascist regime of South Africa to persist in its policy, that cooperation between the two racist regimes is increasing. Israel is the only country that dared to defy the whole world when it agreed to supply South Africa with weapons and military equipment. We ask that measures and legislation be adopted in order to put an end to that odious racist cooperation.

The cooperation between the Zionist and the racist regimes derives from their similarity in terms of their philosophy, their thinking, their mentality and their concepts. Indeed, their common philosophy is entirely based on discrimination. It is a policy that was condemned by the entire international community more than thirty years ago, following the terrible nightmare of nazism. The similarity of the two regimes is evidenced in more than one area. According to news reaching us from time to time, the violations by South Africa of the territorial integrity of Zambia, Angola and Mozambique constitute for Israel just so many means of justifying their own aggression against the Lebanon and other Arab countries which, in fact, is carried out on such pretexts as territorial security and the fight against revolutionaries.[27]

Replying to the Sudanese and other statements, Ambassador Yehuda Blum of Israel accused the Arabs of turning the deliberations on *apartheid* into a charade and ritualistic incantation and of "subverting every forum and debate in their frenzied campaign to accumulate as many anti-Israel resolutions as they could. "Nobody", he said,

could fail to discern the tendentious misstatements in the making of the case against Israel. . . .

That a country which accounts for a minuscule fraction of South Africa's trade merits a special report on relations with South Africa, while other countries with an infinitely larger share of that trade are not singled out, and that such a report is then based on newspaper speculations without any attempt at independent verification, would be sufficient for any independent judiciary to throw the case out of court. . . .

But we have this year been treated to deception of a new kind. Section III of the Report entitled "Military and Nuclear Collaboration". I confess that I read that section no less than four times, searching for some mention of nuclear collaboration. There is not one word about it, for the simple reason that such collaboration does not exist. It exists only in the title and in the table of contents of the Committee's report, presumably because the Committee no longer expects anyone to read the report or take it seriously.[28]

Following the pattern of the past, Afghanistan, Algeria, Bangladesh, Benin, Congo, Cuba, Egypt, Ethiopia, Jordan, Laos People's Democratic Republic, Lybian Arab Jamahiriya, Senegal, Sierra Leone, Sri Lanka, Syrian Arab Republic, Uganda, United

Republic of Tanzania, Viet Nam and Zambia, cosponsored a draft resolution which expressed grave concern over the

> persistence of Israel in escalating its collaboration and strengthening its relations with the racist regime of South Africa in defiance of the resolutions of the General Assembly and of world public opinion;

reaffirmed that

> collaboration by Israel has constituted an encouragement to the *apartheid* regime in South Africa to persist in its criminal policy of *apartheid* and is a hostile act against the oppressed people of South Africa and the entire African continent;

again strongly condemned

> Israel's continuing and increasing collaboration with the racist regime of South Africa;

demanded that

> Israel desist from and terminate all forms of collaboration with South Africa and abide scrupulously by the relevant resolutions of the General Assembly and the Security Council,

and requested the Special Committee against *Apartheid*

> to keep the matter under constant review and report to the General Assembly and the Security Council as appropriate.[29]

The resolution was adopted on 24 January 1979 by a vote of 82 to 18, with 28 abstentions.

Ultimately the adoption of resolution 3379(XXX) aimed at engaging the whole apparatus of the United Nations in an active campaign against Israel and to commit the States Members, if only in a quietly persuasive rather than belligerently coercive way, to combat Zionism as a form of racism and racial discrimination as they were committed to combat *apartheid*, and to mete out to Israel a fate similar to that held out for South Africa. Indeed, shortly before the General Assembly adopted resolution 3379(XXX), it had decided to establish a Committee on the Exercise of the Inalienable Rights of the Palestinian People composed of twenty Member States appointed by the Assembly and charged it to,

> consider and recommend to the General Assembly a program of implementation, designed to enable the Palestinian people to exercise the rights

recognized in paragraphs 1 and 2 of Assembly resolution 3236(XXIX), and to take into account, in the formulation of its recommendations for the implementation of that program, all the powers conferred by the Charter upon the principal organs of the United Nations;

authorized the Committee,

in the fulfilment of its mandate, to establish contact with, and to receive and consider suggestions and proposals from any State and intergovernmental regional organization and the Palestine Liberation Organization;

and requested the Secretary-General to

provide the Committee with all the necessary facilities for the performance of its task.[30]

One of the Committee's first recommendations called for the establishment within the Secretariat of the United Nations of a Special Unit on Palestinian Rights,[31] which bears a close resemblance in spirit and purpose to the Centre Against *Apartheid*. Approved by the General Assembly at its thirty-second session in 1977, the functions of the Special Unit were set forth as follows:

(a) Prepare, under the guidance of the Committee on the Exercise of the Inalienable Rights of the Palestinian People, studies and publications relating to:

1) The inalienable rights of the Palestinian people;

2) Relevant resolutions of the General Assembly and other organs of the United Nations;

3) The activities of the Committee and other United Nations organs, in order to promote the attainment of those rights;

(b) Promote maximum publicity for such studies and publications through all appropriate means.

The Secretary-General was requested

to insure the full cooperation of the Office of Public Information and other units of the Secretariat in enabling the Special Unit on Palestinian Rights to perform its task.[32]

These developments were not unanticipated. This, for example, is the sense of the question put by a correspondent to Secretary-General Kurt Waldheim at a press conference in New York on 9 January 1976 as follows:

Mr. Secretary-General, the General Assembly has passed a resolution condemning Zionism as a form of racism and racial discrimination. It has also passed numerous resolutions calling upon you and the Secretariat and the specialized agencies to promote the elimination of all forms of racial discrimination. What are you doing, what will you do, what will you order your staff to do to promote the elimination of Zionism?

To which the Secretary-General replied:

As you know, I made a statement immediately after the adoption of that resolution, and I consider that statement as a clear expression of my position and attitude in this regard. I therefore do not feel that I have to add anything to what I have said in that statement, referring especially to the split in the membership, and the difficulties arising from that confrontation.

As far as the implementation is concerned, I can only tell you that we have to look into the different resolutions. These will be studied and the necessary steps will be taken in the light of the results of our examination. You mentioned one resolution, but they added others. You will certainly understand that this is a most delicate subject which has to be studied very carefully.[33]

NOTES

1. For the text see Report of the World Conference to Combat Racism and Racial Discrimination, Geneva, 14–25 August 1978 (A/CONF.92/40, pp. 9–26).

The World Conference goes back to General Assembly resolution 3957(XXVII) of 2 November 1973, which designated the period beginning 10 December 1973—the twenty-fifth anniversary of the Universal Declaration of Human Rights—as the Decade for Action to Combat Racism and Racial Discrimination, with the Conference in mid-decade as the principal event. Paragraph 19 was adopted in Committee by 67 votes to 18, with 18 abstentions; the vote in plenary was 84 to 5, with 8 abstentions. After the vote, the representative of the Federal Republic of Germany, speaking on behalf of the European Economic Community, and the representatives of Australia, Canada and New Zealand, stated that their delegations could no longer associate themselves with the results of the Conference nor participate in the further proceedings of the Conference (ibid., pp. 65–67). The United States, as is known, did not take part in the Conference altogether, in line with its enunciated policy not to participate in activities of the Decade which abetted the resolution equating Zionism with racism and racial discrimination. For reservations and declarations submitted in relation to the Declaration, see ibid., annex VII, pp. 107–132.

2. Ibid. The vote on Paragraph 18 in Committee was 65 to 18, with 20 abstentions; in plenary, the vote was 69 to 5, with 23 abstentions.

3. Office of Public Information, Press Release GA/AP/542, p. 1.
4. Office of Public Information, Press Release GA/AP/593, p. 1.
5. A/31/22/Add.1 to 3, pp. 15–43.
6. A/31/PV.51, p. 6.
7. A/31/PV.49, p. 31.
8. A/31/PV.52, p. 23.
9. A/31/PV.60, pp. 43–47.
10. A/31/PV.58, p. 7.
11. A/32/PV.19, p. 77.
12. A/32/PV.70, p. 24.
13. A/33/PV.55, p. 36.
14. A/33/PV.58, p. 82.
15. A/33/PV.56, p. 31.
16. A/31/PV.51, p. 6.
17. A/31/PV.52, p. 16.
18. A/31/PV.52.
19. For the final text of the report see E/CN.4/Sub.2/383, 1977.
20. A/31/PV.49, pp. 57–65, passim.
21. A/Resolution 31/6 E.
22. A/31/PV.58, p. 66.
23. A/31/PV.59, p. 26.
24. A/31/PV.59, p. 32.
25. A/32/PV.72, pp. 8–11.
26. A/Resolution 51/105 D.
27. A/33/PV.53, pp. 8–20.
28. A/33/PV.58, p. 52.
29. A/Resolution 33/188 D.
30. A/Resolution 3376(XXX).
31. Report of the Special Committee on the Inalienable Rights of the Palestinian People, First Report, A/31/35.
32. A/Resolution 32/40 B.
33. Office of Public Information, Press Release SG/SM/227, 9 January 1976, p. 18.

Chapter VIII

REFORM WITHOUT CHANGE

Clearly, the roots and reaches of United Nations actions and decisions are not necessarily solidly anchored in the principles and purposes of the Charter, nor governed and defined by the objectives of the world Organization. The United Nations seems to be more adept at orchestrating tensions than at calming tempers; more adroit at arousing passions and inflaming prejudice than at achieving accommodation; more artful at acting out real or simulated rage than at resolving disputes. And the world body is never more vulnerable than when called upon to deal with issues that involve moral considerations and moral actualities. Human aggression, violence and destruction are unleashed when nations seek and find sanction to act freely and punitively in the name of humanity's highest ideals.

We have seen how the growing emphasis on the acceleration of national independence and the eradication of colonialism hastened the politicization of the United Nations and made it into a partisan body given to practicing double standards; how the struggle against racism and racial discrimination turned into a vendetta against one State Member and was used as a stick with which to beat another; how international action against Chile ostensibly in defense of human rights and fundamental freedoms often became officious, heavy-handed meddling in its internal affairs; and how the assertion of self-determination for Palestinians ended up in the virtual postulation of Israel's destruction as a principal objective. The practice of recognizing so-called liberation movements on the authority of regional intergovernmental organizations contributed to the further erosion of all sense of objectivity in the United Nations; instead of mediating disputes and resolving conflicts the United Nations all too frequently became a party to them.

No amount of historical interpretation can offer consolation for the defects of the United Nations; they run deep and cut to the very essence of its character. At the heart of all criticism of the world body is its manifest partiality. The United Nations has developed a remarkable capacity for creating stereotypes so pronounced as to compel their own political imperatives, and for examining issues totally divorced from any other social, political or moral concern. South Africa, Israel and perhaps a few other countries have been cast in the role of villains so perfectly suited to their villainous trades that their every act could be made to inspire collective outrage. A stern morality has been exacted from these countries by those who blink at the horrors in their own midst, and abuse heaped upon them in the name of a thesis which often rests more on citation compounded than on analysis rigorously pursued. The web of hatred and calumny weaved around them is not the inevitable consequence of a collision of contrary emphases which have been edging up over the years; it is a calculated design to isolate the adversary in order more easily to destroy him.

There is a surrealist quality to many events taking place in the United Nations which makes it very difficult to believe that they are happening in the real world. Debates held in an atmosphere of invective are hastily followed by the counting of "partisan votes, in many instances pledged in advance and uninformed and unaffected by the facts or merits of the controversy."[1] No procedure has yet been invented that would minimize the possibilities of turning the world Organization into a malevolent hub to strike at the vital interests of Member States. Issues which engage the most vital interests of States are decided not upon their merits but by the ability of that party to a dispute which is able to muster the greatest support by virtue of its political affiliation or alignment. The fate of nations is being delivered into uncertain hands as States Members tend increasingly to draw together in the United Nations in voting blocs on the basis of such affiliation or alignment. As former Permanent Representative Carl W. A. Schurmann of the Netherlands noted:

. . . For the preservation of peace and the peaceful solution of international conflicts we have, of course, the United Nations, and there again a new kind of diplomacy has developed—a diplomacy of speech-making and of lobbying. Nearly all countries in the world are Members of the United Nations and about a hundred questions appear each year on the agenda of the General Assembly. This forces governments to take a stand (if not by making a speech, then, at least, by voting) on a great many questions and conflicts that either do not really concern them or on which they would much have preferred to keep their opinions to themselves. Such isolationism, however, is not possible, since a vote of abstention—which is permitted—is, in that milieu, just as much an expression of opinion as a vote of "yes" or "no" on any draft resolution.[2]

The United Nations cannot hope to thrive and fulfil its purpose until it confronts its own motivations and is able to extract itself from the passions which have been build around it. Either it develops a spirit of fairness and objectivity and fosters an atmosphere of intellectual honesty and integrity in which all Governments and all peoples may place their trust, or the United Nations cannot aspire to public acceptance as a serious factor in shaping the future; unless its integrity rises above suspicion, the world Organization will not be entrusted with the power and authority to bring about peaceful change. Nations refuse to be governed by laws that are no protection and put their trust in organizations that cannot guarantee justice. "The United Nations", Secretary-General Kurt Waldheim pointed out in the Introduction to his annual report for 1977–78,

was intended, among other things, to be the guarantor of justice and peace for all nations, and most especially for defenceless and small countries which would otherwise have no recourse in a world dominated exclusively by power politics. We have to face the fact that at the present time the United Nations is not always in a position to exercise this essential function, and that there are many situations in which military power or political influence are far more significant than the principles of justice and the rights of all nations as expressed in the Charter. In the present political circumstances, the United Nations is seldom, if ever, in a position to enforce its decisions and has little means of making them effective in the face of determined opposition. This fact has tended to downgrade the prestige and effectiveness of the Organization and to detract from its primary purpose as the impartial and respected guarantee of international peace and security. The practical result has been that some small States no longer turn to the United Nations as the protector of their sovereign rights.[3]

Whatever the reparative processes by which the United Nations may hope to recover its lost standing and prestige might be, they do not include Charter review as a viable measure. The debates on the subject in the General Assembly and other organs and agencies of the United Nations lend little encouragement to the hope that a review of the Charter, even if it comes to pass,[4] will necessarily pull back the world Organization from fatuity or save it from ignominy. Charter review is in the tradition of reform without change. Throughout the years, representatives of States Members mounted the podium of the General Assembly to voice their views on the need for improving the structure, functions and procedures of the United Nations, ranging from radical proposals for changing the conceptual framework of the Charter as established at San Francisco, to the preservation of the status quo. But all those views put together hardly add up even to a semblance of a dream of people striving to forge a common destiny; the debates furnish many examples of unilateral pursuit by States Members, whether they belong to the First, Second or Third World, not so much of their own interests as of policies congenial to emotions and sentiments that happen to dominate the international political scene at the moment. Lacking is a deep sense of comity—that basic recognition of differences in values and interests and of the need for reconciling those differences rationally and peacefully; without comity it is impossible to project visions against the demands of the future and to work for a cooperative international society as the natural order of things.

We have already noted the reaction of the major Western Powers to the growing anomalies in the structure and functions of the United Nations in connection with the debate on Charter review at the twenty-ninth session of the General Assembly; they manifested little faith in Charter review as a practical approach to the problems confronting the United Nations.[5] In contrast, most of the nations of the Third World saw in Charter review a practical answer to practical problems, as well as an occasion for redressing wrongs of fate and circumstance which denied them the opportunity to contribute their share to the shaping of the Constitution of the Organization in which they now constituted a majority and to impress their image upon it. Thus, for example, speaking in the general debate in 1974, the Foreign Minister of Guinea said:

> My delegation would like to state once again the need to reforge the United Nations Charter. That need is all the more urgent because our Organization, which had 52 members when it was created, now has 138, of which three fourths are from the Third World. Indeed, the United Nations, conceived as an instrument to serve mankind, must needs take account of the economic, political and social development of mankind and must not remain a frozen, sclerotic institution in a world of perpetual flux. That is why the Republic of Guinea will continue to condemn the well-known veto right, whose continued existence amply demonstrates the lack of democracy that unfortunately still marks our Organization, which is supposed to be democratic and just.[6]

General Siad Barre, President of the Supreme Revolutionary Council of the Somali Democratic Republic, had this to say:

> Speaking on the role and the functioning of the United Nations, it is important to emphasize the need to review the basic structures and institutions set out in the Charter. The United Nations cannot continue as a static Organization. It is imperative that we assess its current structural weaknesses and suggest remedial measures. The scope of its powers should be widened, some of its basic organs should be made more representative, and, above all, it must be vested with more effective authority to satisfy the demands and aspirations of mankind. The role of our Organization in its quest for peace and progress calls for a new approach as well as for a firm dedication in dealing with pressing international problems. What we urgently need is a genuine world body vested with the powers and authority required for the realization of its declared aims and objectives.[7]

Speaking in a similar vein, the representative of Libya said:

> A new world is emerging today. There can be no escape from the formulation of new bases comparable with this new beginning. The United Nations must become an effective instrument for the realization of its Charter. We the majority—and we are proud of being a majority—have the duty to lay new foundations for the course of our Organization. We shall not be intimidated by the stubborn attitude of the old Powers. Our interrelationships will not be affected by any willful mischief. In fact, we are terminating our relations with the old racist Powers in an effort to expel them from the Assembly hall, while we welcome new delegations representing friendly countries. . . .[8]

Similarly, Foreign Minister Bouteflika of Algeria told the General Assembly that,

The United Nations, after almost thirty years of its existence, has now entered a decisive phase in its existence. The action of the United Nations in today's world, in order to safeguard peace and international security, to defend the right of peoples to self-determination and the sovereignty of States, to act in favor of development of multilateral cooperation at the level of humanity, all this is one of the leitmotifs of the profound needs of our civilization, in which it has become an irreplaceable factor. But its solidity, its ability to become rooted in the awareness of this area, undoubtedly increases its responsibilities and militates in favor of even greater effectiveness in the way it carries out its mission. This means that a greater democratization of its structure and its rigorous adaptation to the realities in which we live today not only would be consonant with an imperative need but would open before the Organization new and undoubtedly heartening prospects.[9]

The open revolt by the Third World against the veto was inspired more by the resentment of its use by the Western Powers to "shield" South Africa against the consequences of universal wrath and to "resist the forces of progress", than by its offense against the international democratic order. But there can be no doubt that the Soviet Union's reaction to the challenge of the veto power exercised by the Permanent Members of the Security Council foreclosed for the foreseeable future any possibility of Charter review. Indeed, the Soviet Union opposed the very inscription of the item on Charter review on the agenda of the twenty-ninth session of the General Assembly. Speaking in the General Committee on 19 September 1974, Ambassador Yacov Malik said:

... It was known to all that there were two social systems in the world. The Soviet Delegation had endured the pressures of the capitalist group on the socialist minority in the United Nations throughout the period when the Peoples' Republic of China had been excluded precisely because of those measures. Indeed, it was the effort of the socialist group which had made it possible for China to be present at all. Having for so long endured the tyranny of the capitalist group and its automatic majority, the U.S.S.R. would never allow a similar situation to arise.... Without the veto, the socialist minority would be unable to defend itself, and the United Nations could not exist. Only the veto made it possible for a number of socialist States which had applied for membership in 1946 to become Members in 1957.[10]

Thus, with the exception of Romania, the so-called socialist countries refused solidly to entertain even remotely the idea of Charter review, defending the Charter as the fundamental international document of modern times. The representative of the Ukrainian SSR spoke for all when he said:

> The need to increase the effectiveness of the United Nations has been repeatedly stressed in the course of the general debate at this session. All the experience of the work of this Organization irrefutably shows that its effectiveness can be improved only on the basis of strict observance of the Charter and the implementation of decisions of the Security Council and other United Nations bodies. The United Nations Charter enshrines the most important basic principles of contemporary international relations, principles which throughout the existence of the United Nations have been generally recognized in international law and further confirmed in relations among States. The Charter of the United Nations has stood the test of time and proved its viability under present conditions. At times, critics of the Charter question the principle of unanimity in the Security Council, but anyone who feels that way is either deliberately discarding the idea or in the heat of the debate is forgetting the fact that the United Nations itself is based on the principle of unanimity of the permanent members of the Security Council and the effectiveness of its actions depends precisely on that unanimity. The abolition of that fundamental principle could be used in the United Nations system to serve the narrow interests of individual major States or groups of such States, which would undermine the principle of peaceful coexistence of States with different social systems at the very time when those principles are becoming ever more firmly established in international practice. . . . We therefore resolutely oppose preparing plans for the revision—or what is known as the "correction"—of the United Nations Charter, which is the most outstanding international document of modern times.[11]

The General Assembly had to attempt what needed to be done when it decided on 17 December 1974 by 82 votes to 15, with 36 abstentions, to establish an Ad Hoc Committee on the Charter of the United Nations, consisting of forty-two members, to consider the observations Governments were invited to submit regarding Charter review, and any additional specific proposals they might make with a view to enhancing the ability of the United Nations to achieve its purposes.[12] Revision of the Charter is foreseen in Article 109; that Article goes so far as to enjoin that if a review conference had not been held before the tenth annual session of the General Assembly, a proposal for the convening of such a conference shall be placed on the agenda of that session and the conference held if so decided by a majority vote of the Assembly and by a vote of any seven members of the Security Council. In 1955, the General Assembly established a Committee on Arrangements for a Conference for the Purpose of Reviewing the Charter consisting of all Members of the United Nations.[13] After nine years of desultory activity the Committee on Arrangements finally gave way in 1974 to the Ad Hoc Committee. But neither of these Committees was able to do much to bring a review conference nearer to realization, for the reason that international circumstances were never auspicious for a review of the Charter. The 1974 debate only confirmed the ever-widening gap in the positions of the States Members and the existence of fundamental and irreconcilable divergencies of interest among them. This was explicitly recognized in General Assembly resolution 3349(XXIX) of December 17, which invited Governments to submit to the Ad Hoc Committee, in addition to observations on Charter review, suggestions for the more effective functioning of the United Nations that might not require amendments to the Charter. In 1975, the General Assembly decided to reconvene the Ad Hoc Committee on the Charter of the United Nations as the Special Committee on the Charter of the United Nations and on the Strengthening of the Role of the Organization,[14] amalgamating two approaches to the question of United Nations structure and functions: review of the Charter, proposed by Colombia in 1969, and strengthening the role of the United Nations, proposed by Romania in 1972, without reference to Charter review.

In proposing the item for inclusion in the agenda of the twenty-seventh session of the General Assembly, Romania argued that the changing situation in the world and the immensity of the problems that faced mankind required the United Nations to play an ever greater role in international life and called for prompt measures to increase the world body's capacity for action and the effectiveness of its contribution to the rapprochement among peoples and the elimination of the causes of conflict and tension.[15] Having considered the item, the General Assembly expressed agreement with the notion that it was necessary to strengthen the role of the United Nations so that it might bring an increased contribution to the settlement of international issues, and take its place in international life.[16]

Strengthening the United Nations implies not only structural and functional improvements, but a complete review of the political, economic and social work of the international body. As such it appears no less far-fetched than Charter review and, perhaps, equally irrelevant; both Charter review and strengthening the United Nations involve complicated choices which affect the vital interests of all States Members and which few are willing to stake for the sake of good intentions. The difficulties and frustrations attendant upon most cooperative efforts, even in areas where the interests of nations coincide without question, show how far the world has yet to go before the notion of comity and common interests changes from a place of last resort to one of first choice. The vicissitudes of the Special Committee on Peace-keeping Operations, for example, established by the General Assembly at its nineteenth session in 1965 to undertake a comprehensive review of the whole question of peace-keeping operations in all their aspects, including ways of overcoming the financial difficulties of the United Nations, show that there is no substitute for political will; after more than fifteen years of work, the Special Committee is as far as ever from agreed guidelines for carrying out peace-keeping operations.[17]

Perhaps the reason why the awareness of existing deficiencies and the longing for hoped-for improvements have brought us no nearer to a solution of the structural, functional and procedural problems that have plagued the United Nations for more than three decades lies in the fact that the world Organization is too vast and too complex to be changed in accordance with any other but its own dynamics. The United Nations, as has been noted, is a political, not a jural, order and as such it cannot be seduced into a posture inappropriate to its character. Deliberate acts of change may render a poor service to the international Organization; they must emerge pragmatically from compelling needs and come to fruition when the conjuncture of circumstance is favorable to change, by design or accident. The work of the Ad Hoc Committee on the Restructuring of the Economic and Social Sectors of the United Nations System is a case in point. It was established by the General Assembly at its Seventh Special Session in September 1975

> with a view to initiating the process of restructuring the United Nations system so as to make it more fully capable of dealing with problems of international economic cooperation and development in a comprehensive and effective manner . . . and to make it more responsive to the requirements of the provisions of the Declaration and the Programme of Action on the Establishment of a New International Economic Order as well as those of the Charter of Economic Rights and Duties of States. . . .[18]

Resolution 3362(S-VII) of 16 September 1975 aimed at nothing less than, in the words of Secretary-General Kurt Waldheim, "redirecting international economic activities, redressing structural imbalances and creating a more equitable system for the benefit of the entire world community", and to "serve as the basis and framework for the future work of all the competent bodies and organizations of the United Nations system."[19] The task of the Ad Hoc Committee was to elaborate and recommend the necessary measures for the institutional adjustment and adaptation of the United Nations system in order to implement the actions needed to translate the vision of the New International Economic Order—a vision built on the hope for the progressive removal of the wide economic and social disparities between different sections of mankind—into a living reality. But while the vision of the New International Economic Order was undoubtedly a decisive catalyst, the compelling need for reconstructing the economic and social sectors of the United Nations system was there for everyone to see. For example, the proliferation of programs in the economic and social fields had reached a point where it was impossible for management to keep open the lines of communication, to avoid duplication, to cope with the infinite volume of paper work, and to ensure the integral wholeness of the vast enterprise. Programs never seemed to phase out even after they had shown most disappointing results, and often even after the problems which gave them birth had been solved. Progress almost invariably suffered from lack of coherence; multi-agency programs planned unilaterally did not promote long-range overall planning.[20]

The ineffective responses to the real needs of the larger world only compounded distrust in the United Nations. It needed a combination of vision, enlightened self-interest and the dire warnings of the growing anarchy in the administration and management of international economic and social programs to produce the proper conjuncture of circumstances to make possible a concerted campaign for far-reaching modifications in the structure and functions of a major part of the United Nations system. The first test of the relative success or failure of this venture and its prospects for the future will come in 1980 when, in accordance with its decision of 19 December 1977, the General Assembly will meet in special session "at a high level" to assess the progress made in the various forums of the United Nations system in the establishment of the new international economic order and to take appropriate action for the promotion of the development of developing countries and international economic cooperation, including the adoption of the new international development strategy for the 1980s. The General Assembly also decided to establish a committee of the whole, which would meet during the intersessional periods until the special session in 1980, to assist the Assembly by acting as the focal point in overseeing and monitoring the implementation of decisions and arrangements reached in the negotiations on the establishment of the new international economic order in the appropriate bodies of the United Nations system, providing impetus for resolving difficulties in negotiations and for encouraging the continuing work in those bodies, serving, where appropriate, as a forum for facilitating and expediting agreement on the resolution of outstanding issues.[21]

Meanwhile, acting on the recommendations of the Ad Hoc Committee on Restructuring of the Economic and Social Sectors of the United Nations System, which submitted its final report to the thirty-second session of the General Assembly in 1977,[22] the Assembly invited the Secretary-General

> to appoint, in full consultation with Member States, a Director-General for Development and International Economic Cooperation, at a high level which he determines as commensurate with the functions outlined below, who, acting under the authority of the Secretary-General, would effectively assist him in carrying out his responsibilities as chief administrative officer,

under the Charter of the United Nations, in the economic and social fields. Accordingly, the Director-General, under the direction of the Secretary-General, should be in charge of:

(a) Ensuring the provision of effective leadership to the various components of the United Nations system in the field of development and international economic cooperation and in exercising overall coordination within the system in order to ensure a multidisciplinary approach to the problems of development on a system-wide basis;

(b) Ensuring, within the United Nations, the coherence, coordination and efficient management of all activities in the economic and social fields financed by the regular budget or by extrabudgetary resources.

In addition, the Secretary-General could entrust to the Director-General other tasks in areas of responsibility related to the whole of the economic and social activities of the United Nations. The Director-General should be appointed by the Secretary-General for a period of up to four years. He should be provided with the necessary support and resources.[23]

NOTES

1. Benjamin V. Cohen, "The Quest for Collective Security", an address delivered at the Sixty-third Annual Meeting of the American Society of International Law. *Proceedings*, 1969, p. 65.
2. "Two Kinds of Diplomacy", an address delivered at the Sixty-third Annual Meeting of the American Society of International Law, ibid., pp. 248–249.
3. A/33/1, p. 2.
4. For a summary of the debate concerning Charter review in 1974, see A/C.6/SR.1512 through SR.1521. See also Report of the Special Committee on the Charter of the United Nations and on the Strengthening of the Role of the Organization A/33/33, 1978.
5. See, for example, statements by the representatives of France and the United States, above, pp. 15–16.
6. A/PV.2253, p. 51.
7. A/PV.2262, p. 57.
8. A/PV.2263, p. 17.
9. A/PV.2233, p. 26.
10. A/BUR/SR.218, pp. 8–9.
11. A/PV.2255, p. 78.
12. Res.3349(XXIX).
13. Res.992(X).
14. Res.3349(XXIX).
15. A/8792 (1972).

16. Res.2925(XXVII).

17. Res.33/114.

18. Res.3362(S-VII).

19. Statement opening the first session of the Ad Hoc Committee on Restructuring of the Economic and Social Sectors of the United Nations System. See Report of the Ad Hoc Committee, General Assembly, Official Records, Thirtieth Session, Supplement No. 5, pp. 5–6.

20. Ibid., passim.

21. Res.32/174.

22. A/33/34 and Corr.1 and Add.1.

23. Res.32/197. For the recommendations of the Ad Hoc Committee Annex, Section VII, p. 5.

Chapter IX

BEYOND COMMODIOUS PHRASES

To believe that similar institutional changes can be attempted in the political sector of the United Nations system is, of course, to reason by false analogy. The rationalization and improvement of the economic and social sectors are problems of a pragmatic, not conceptual, character on which all countries can unite over and above any differences in policy or ideology. The differences that divide nations in the political sector, which are more conceptual than pragmatic, are not readily transcended; passions are stronger than reason and convictions are rarely reconcilable. But unless the restructuring of the economic and social sectors of the United Nations system is accompanied by a serious effort to bring order into the moral chaos which penetrates deep into the structure and function of the world Organization, the future will be denied for a near-sighted presence. The dangers of concentrating on economic and social activities at the expense of its moral and political vocation, which all Secretaries-General have warned against, are manifest beyond all arguments. The hand which caresses also strangles and, unless it is steadied by a firm grip on principles and morals beyond commodious phrases, the dominating belligerence of the rage which blows in the halls of the United Nations can wipe out whatever humaneness may be inherent in the striving for international cooperation for the promotion of economic progress in the world.

Given the limits within which institutional change in the political sector of the United Nations system is possible, what is likely to be most effective in raising the moral level of the world Organization to ensure equity and justice to all, energize hope and conviction, and introduce a necessary measure of objectivity in respect to third parties? Short of a self-regulating instrument, or a kind of gyroscope, that would automatically forestall the United Nations from committing inequities and injustices, the key to the salvation of the world body lies in a combination of improved decision-making processes and a conscious political action to make these processes fulfil their purpose. Techniques are no substitute for social policy and procedures cannot take the place of political and moral vision.[1] The crucial issue is to prevent the convergence of hostile forces in monstrous injustice against a Member State. This issue is basic to the survival of the United Nations and must be pressed to a conclusion. It calls for a persistent and consistent effort to develop a spirit of fairness and intellectual honesty and integrity to secure democratic safeguards for all States Members of the United Nations.

It was an awareness of the depth of this problem that had led the Security Council and the General Assembly in the early years of the United Nations to the practice of appointing, almost as a matter of standard operating procedure, committees from among their own members to investigate controversial issues about which they were seized, to proceed, if necessary, to the scene of controversy, and report with recommendations to the parent body. The General Assembly had also availed itself of the services of a panel of mediators to assist it in dealing with controversies in general.[2] But of special interest are the efforts made by the International Labor Organization to arrest the growing tendency on the part of States Members to abuse the forum of the International Labor Conference by airing grievances unrelated to the work of the Organization or to place items on the agenda for patently propaganda purposes. It concerns an old United States initiative, revived in 1976 by the Government of Canada, to amend Article 17 of the Standing Orders of the Conference, the better to prevent the bypassing of established procedures for inquiry by tabling resolutions and pressing them to a vote.

Acting on the suggestion of the Canadian Government, the Governing Body of the International Labor Organization agreed at its 201st session in November 1976 to ask the Committee on Standing Orders and the Application of Conventions and Recommendation to review the proposals made in recent years regarding the procedure for the consideration of resolutions relating to matters not included in an item on the Conference's agenda as laid down in Article 17 of the Standing Orders of the Conference. The Committee's report, together with the recommendations, were considered by the Governing Body at the 202nd session in March 1977 at which, after a lengthy debate, it was decided by 34 votes to 17, with 4 abstentions, to submit the recommendations to the International Labor Conference later that year for final action.[3]

At the heart of the recommendations was a proposed new Article 17, which provided that resolutions may be ruled non-receivable if they condemned Member States on matters not covered by ILO standards, or on matters covered by such standards but without inquiries under established ILO procedures. It provided for the examination of resolutions submitted to the Conference by a panel of independent experts chosen from the Committee of Experts on the Application of Conventions and Recommendations. It also provided for the right to appeal decisions on receivability to the Officers of the International Labor Conference.[4]

The proposed amendments met with fierce opposition on the part of the States Members from the Soviet, Arab and Afro-Asian blocs and from a number of Latin American countries; only the West solidly supported the recommendations. To their opponents the restriction on the submission of draft resolutions to the Conference was totally unacceptable, ostensibly on the ground that the proposed procedure for the preliminary screening of draft resolutions curtailed the right of sovereign independent States and struck at the democratic character of the ILO's institutions and procedures. In reality, of course, the countries concerned refused to surrender their freedom of action and their favored parliamentary position.[5]

Defending the proposed amendments, the representatives of the Western nations argued that the procedure on resolutions should not be used either to hold up a constitutional inquiry or for the purpose of condemning any Member State on unproven charges. A presumption of innocence until guilt is proved was a cardinal principle of due process in international as in municipal law and one that should commend itself to all countries, since today's accusers might be tomorrow's accused. Every Government in the world, they argued, whatever its political persuasion or strength, was entitled to expect the Conference to respect its good name and refrain from condemning it until it had been found guilty under the constitutional procedures of a breach of ILO principles. At present, they said, any delegate to the Conference—not just a Government representative, but an employer or worker as well—could, if the whim took him, find material in the daily press on which to base an attack against many a Member State or even, if he really put his mind to it, against every single one. The proposed procedure afforded the safeguards against an intolerable situation.[6] As Professor Ago of Italy told the Governing Board at its 202nd session,

> The right to submit resolutions was undeniable, but its exercise should be subject to three conditions.
>
> First, the sponsor should be an accredited Conference delegate.
>
> Second, to preserve the orderly pattern of international life and organization, he should respect the limits of ILO competence and not touch on matters mainly of concern to other organizations.
>
> Third, and above all, he should not condemn any country before proper inquiry had been made into the charges against it. Of all human rights, none mattered more than the right to a fair trial by due process of law. Condemning an innocent person was much worse than letting a guilty one go scot-free.[7]

The sixty-third Conference of the International Labor Organization, which opened on 1 June 1977, was deeply divided over the question of whether the proposed amendments were to be referred to the Standing Orders Committee or to the Committee on Structure, with the overwhelming majority in favor of the latter. There was general agreement that the proposed amendments to Article 17 of the Standing Orders was one of the most significant issues ever faced by the ILO; the difference was in the conclusions reached. To the vast majority the proposed amendments, as already indicated, added up to a virtual conspiracy by the West against the rest of the world. To the West, the amendments were designed to strengthen the procedure for the preliminary control of resolutions in order to "ensure that no

State, group or individual was condemned or found guilty without a fair hearing and due process and to curb Conference discussion on matters outside the normal concerns of the ILO". On June 3rd, the Conference voted 132 to 2, with 212 abstentions, to refer the proposed amendments to the Standing Orders Committee. In the absence of a quorum the proposal was not adopted.[8] It was thereupon referred to the Committee on Structure which, after three weeks of intensive debate, was unable to reach agreement and confessed failure.[9]

It may be recalled that the proposed amended Article 17 of the Standing Orders of the Conference was part of a campaign to "depoliticize" the ILO led by the United States in protest against what it regarded as the ideological polarization within the world labor body. On 5 November 1975, Secretary of State Henry Kissinger served formal notice of the intention of the United States to withdraw from the ILO at the expiration of the two-year period, unless major reforms were introduced which guaranteed due process and a single standard for judging national violations of ILO norms.[10] American resentment, which had built up over a number of years and is traceable to a variety of causes, reached a critical point in 1974, when the annual International Labor Conference adopted a resolution criticizing labor conditions in Israel's occupied territories, against the wishes of the Governing Body and with none of the usual documentation of violations, and admitted the Palestine Liberation Organization to observer status with the ILO; these were enough to confirm many members of the United States Delegation in their suspicion that the world labor body had lost its bearing. The strong Communist and Third World opposition to the proposed amendments of the Standing Orders which would have curbed their freedom to harass Member States tipped the scales in favor of United States withdrawal.

If it be true that the preliminary identification of a problem can be almost as important as any treatment of it, then the insistence upon due process, which has been the theme of the campaign in the ILO to modify the Standing Orders of the Conference in order to bar politically-motivated resolutions condemning Member States from reaching the floor of the Conference by a screening process germane to the workings of the world labor body, has identified the core problem in the political sector of the United Nations system. Concern with the question of improper and unconstitutional acts of United Nations bodies, their legal effects and the recourses available to aggrieved Member States has yet to be felt in the public forum, although from time to time scholars and diplomats have called attention to the failure to develop procedures for review of contested acts and decisions by United Nations bodies which would command the respect and confidence of States Members whose national interests and, possibly, very existence were at stake.[11] Thus, for example, in an editorial comment in July 1975, Professor Louis Sohn raised the question of due process in the United Nations and suggested the possibility of contesting "illegal" acts of United Nations bodies by amending the rules of procedure of the General Assembly accordingly.[12]

On the subject of substantive due process, Professor Sohn suggested that the major issue was the certainty that grave objections to the constitutionality or legality of decisions were properly considered and were not disposed of by the same body that was being challenged. If, for example, a group of Member States objected to a proposed decision by the General Assembly, the objection was to be referred by the Assembly to some other body for preliminary decision. As a minimum, the Legal Counsel of the United Nations could be requested to present a statement of relevant precedents and give his views on their applicability to the case in question. Also, wherever possible, matters of this kind were to be referred to the International Court of Justice for an Advisory Opinion and special bodies appointed to expedite decisions in urgent matters.

As to procedural due process, Professor Sohn found the ad hoc character of recent decisions the most undesirable of all features. He objected in particular to the tendency of rushing into decisions without any attempt to consider the matter in question carefully and without any real effort being made to negotiate an agreed solution. It was dangerous, Professor Sohn emphasized,

> to have matters decided on the floor of the Assembly without prior consideration by a committee. Important matters should not be decided on the spot by means of procedural motions and points of order. A chance

should be given to develop maximum consensus through consultations among regional groups and major powers.[13]

In a second editorial comment on the subject later that year,[14] Professor Sohn suggested that in view of the likelihood that the United States might wish to challenge or contest a General Assembly action in the future on the ground that it violated the Charter of the United Nations, the only alternative to withdrawal that presented itself was for the United States to accept the jurisdiction of the International Court of Justice for that purpose. It would enable the United States to bring before the Court a dispute with any other State which similarly accepted the Court's jurisdiction concerning the validity of any General Assembly resolution. The main importance of the proposed procedure, Professor Sohn avers, would be its restraining effect upon the action of other States and provide States Members of the United Nations with a legal weapon to challenge those actions and decisions which they regard as contrary to the Charter, as well as an alternative to withdrawal from the world body or withholding funds from it.

Whatever the merits or practicability of Professor Sohn's suggestions might be, the idea of a restraining hand to curb the extravaganzas of the United Nations cannot be faulted. The need for it is obvious. It may be recalled that the Charter contains no provisions for its interpretation; that basic international constitutional document is forever being interpreted and modified by the actions or inactions of the States Members and the organs and agencies of the United Nations. Although the Charter does provide for its amendment and periodic review, the great changes wrought in it over the years emerged pragmatically from daily practice and application without reference to Articles 108 and 109. This, as we have noted,[15] enabled the United Nations to adapt itself without undergoing traumatic experiences to constantly changing conditions, to expand its activities, and to survive. But it also invited grievous assaults on the integrity of the Charter and amendments to the point of altering its long-term direction and purposes and objectives. In fact, as time went on, the line between interpretation of the Charter and its modification grew ever thinner until it could be crossed without even as much as a second thought.[16] There has never been any serious attempt to strike a balance between the extreme positions of loose and strict interpretation and little thought has been given to the question of protecting the States Members against the creation, by changing majorities, of new obligations without their consent. The arbitrary interpretation of the principle of self-determination to fit particular situations; the patently arbitrary application of the domestic jurisdiction clause to effect specific consequences, and the acceptance of the doctrine of wars of liberation in open contravention to the international law of peace prescribed by the Charter, have shown up the United Nations as not being above inventing scenarios to suit particular circumstances.

And it may also be recalled that the Charter provides few possibilities for judicial or political review for the determination of the constitutionality of any United Nations action or decision. The only judicial review available to the international organization is the right to request an Advisory Opinion from the International Court of Justice that is binding neither on the requesting organ, nor on the parties immediately involved in the controversy, nor on the States Members in general.[17] As to political review, an act or decision by any United Nations organ can be reviewed only if the organ in question is subsidiary to the reviewing body[18]—a condition which does not affect the Security Council and the General Assembly. Thus, to the extent that their resolutions and decisions crystallize elements of a new international legitimacy, interpret the law, set standards of State behavior and bind States Members to certain courses of action, the Security Council and the General Assembly reign supreme and are accountable to no one. That this represents more psychological than real power is immaterial; the principle is the same.

We have already noted that at the heart of all criticism directed at the United Nations is its manifest partiality. Perhaps no other single posturing conveys a more despairing image of the world body than its fact-finding activities. Professor Felix Ermacora of the University of Vienna and long-time Austrian representative on the United Nations Commission on Human Rights and several of its fact-finding working groups, has long ago raised the question of the partiality or impartiality of ad hoc fact-finding bodies set up by United Nations organs.[19] He noted, for example, that such bodies normally were established after a thorough debate, within the establishing organ, of the issues which provoked the occasion for fact-finding; that the political terrain for specific fact-finding missions were invariably well-prepared, and that such missions were generally carried out against the background of settled United Nations policies, such as opposition to *apartheid* in South Africa and to the occupation by Israel of occupied territories.

Professor Ermacora distinguishes between fact-finding bodies composed of States Members and those composed of individuals acting in their personal capacities, considering the former as pregnant with deep political implications. "A State", he writes, "engaged in a fact-finding mission in regard to another State, leads to the conclusion that the equality of States is under question because one State looks upon another State's behaviour and exercises control over this other State".[20] But he is not at all sure that fact-finding bodies composed of individuals acting in their personal capacities can be impartial, for the reasons suggested above and for several other reasons. Professor Ermacora pointed out that the same persons who served on ad hoc fact-finding bodies in their individual capacities simultaneously served as representatives of their governments and freely expressed their views on issues under inquiry in one or another organ of the United Nations. He also suggested that fact-finding in the United Nations was only a means to an end and that the facts themselves were not established for any other reason than to furnish the United Nations organ concerned with relevant material and information.

A recent example is provided by the Security Council Commission composed of Bolivia, Portugal and Zambia established under resolution 445(1979) in response to a Jordanian request of 23 February 1979 to examine the situation relating to the most

> ominous and accelerating erosion of the status of Jerusalem and the rest of the occupied Arab territories in consequence of the Israeli occupation authorities' systematic, relentless and deliberate policy and practice of

settlement and colonization of those territories which constitute a grave threat to international peace and security.[21]

The Commission's mandate as defined in operative paragraph 4 of resolution 446(1979) adopted at the close of the eighth meeting on the subject, was to "examine the situation relating to settlements in the Arab territories occupied since 1967, including Jerusalem". This rather broad mandate appears to be appropriate to a problem of such girth and complexity as the one the Commission was asked to examine; to set forth the elements of the problem in the context in which it arose, to separate fact from fiction, to ascertain the juridical anchorage of the conflicting assertions and to evaluate the evidence of the different hypotheses advanced over the years, needed a mandate of the widest latitude. In reality, however, the Commission's mandate was a very modest one; it was to make a point rather than reveal the truth, even though the point itself had already been made in the resolution which created the three-member Commission.

Thus operative paragraph 1:

Determines that the policy and practices of Israel in establishing settlements in the Palestinian and other Arab Territories occupied since 1967 have no legal validity and constitute a serious obstruction to achieving a comprehensive, just and lasting peace in the Middle East;

Operative paragraph 2:

Strongly deplores the failure of Israel to abide by Security Council resolutions 237(1967) of 14 June 1967, 252(1968) of 21 May 1968 and 298(1971) of 25 September 1971 and the consensus statement by the President of the Security Council on 11 November 1976 and General Assembly resolutions 2253(ES-V) and 2254(ES-V) of 4 and 14 July 1967, 32/5 of 28 October 1977 and 33/113 of 18 December 1978:

Operative paragraph 3:

Calls once more upon Israel, as the occupying Power, to abide scrupulously by the 1949 Fourth Geneva Convention to rescind its previous measures and to desist from taking any action which would result in changing the legal status and geographical nature and materially affecting the demographic composition of the Arab territories occupied since 1967, including Jerusalem, and, in particular, not to transfer parts of its own civilian population into the occupied Arab territories.

Unless it was able and willing to examine the settlements issue as but one aspect of the broader problem of Israel's security and risk, if necessary, taking exception to the views on the subject widely held throughout the United Nations, there was little the Commission could add to what was already contained in resolution 446(1979). But this was not to pass. The Commission regarded its mission as one of assisting the Security Council, inter alia, by:

> (a) bringing up to date the basic information already at the disposal of the Council; (b) determining the consequences of the settlement policy on the local Arab population; and (c) assessing the impact of that policy and its consequences with regard to "the urgent need to achieve a comprehensive, just and lasting peace in the Middle East" stressed by the Security Council in the preambular part of resolution 446(1979), under which the Commission was created.[22]

Clearly, the Commission's conclusions, as Israel's Ambassador to the United Nations suggested to the Security Council on 18 July 1979, "were determined in advance in both the preambular and operative parts of the resolution in question.[23] Thus, for example, the Commission concluded that

> the pattern of that settlement policy, as a consequence, is causing profound and irreversible changes of a geographical and demographic nature in those territories, including Jerusalem;[24]

and that it had

> no doubt that those changes are of such a profound nature that they constitute a violation of the fourth Geneva Convention relative to the Protection of Civilian Persons in Time of War of 12 August 1949 and of the relevant decisions adopted by the United Nations in the matter, more specifically: Security Council resolutions 237(1967) of 14 June 1967, 252(1968) of 21 May 1968, and 298(1971) of 25 September 1971; the consensus statement by the President of the Security Council on 11 November 1976; as well as General Assembly resolutions 2253(ES-V) and 2254(ES-V) of 4 and 14 July 1967, 32/5 of 28 October 1977, and 33/113 of 18 December 1978.[25]

Consequently,

> After examining the situation relating to settlements in the Arab territories occupied since 1967, including Jerusalem, the Commission wishes to reaffirm the determination made by the Security Council in resolution

446(1979), according to which "the policy and practice of Israel in establishing settlements in the Palestinian and other Arab territories occupied since 1967, have no legal validity and constitute a serious obstruction to achieving a comprehensive, just and lasting peace in the Middle East.[26]

On 20 July 1979 the Security Council adopted by a vote of 14 to none, with the United States abstaining, resolution 452(1979) in which it commended the Commission for its work in preparing the report and adopted its recommendations without reservation. It also charged the Commission with the task of keeping "under close survey the implementation of the present resolution and to report back to the Security Council before 1 November 1979".

From time to time resort to consensus has been suggested as a means of arriving at reasonable decisions and of averting unreasonable ones. Professor Sohn referred to a procedure developed at the Caracas Conference on the Law of the Sea, which provided for maximum efforts to reach agreement on substantive matters until all quests for consensus had been exhausted.[27] It was agreed, for example, that any vote on matters of substance be deferred for a period not exceeding ten days, if such a delay was requested by at least fifteen representatives. If, after ten days, agreement had not yet been reached, another decision was to be taken to determine whether further efforts at agreement was warranted. The Caracas procedure also sought to safeguard against surprise elements by providing that votes be scheduled not earlier than two days after the announcement of the vote was made.

The Helsinki Conference on Security and Cooperation in Europe in 1973 agreed to reach all its decisions by consensus, which it defined as the absence of any objection expressed or put forward that constituted an obstacle to adopting the decision in question.[28] In the United Nations system, according to UNESCO's Director-General Amadou-Mahtar M'Bow, the term denotes both a process of negotiation and its result, and is designed to achieve the elaboration of a text by means of negotiation and its adoption without taking a vote. Dr. M'Bow told the International Diplomatic Academy in Paris on 21 March 1978[29] that, thanks to the use of consensus, the United Nations and the specialized agencies were able to take a number of far-reaching decisions and that the search for consensus had become in practice the habitual working method of the General Assembly, the Economic and Social Council and various other United Nations bodies.

Tracing the growth of consensus in the United Nations bodies, the Director-General of UNESCO attributed it largely to the need of arriving at decisions in areas where division between majority and minority rendered all decisions nugatory. "Since the mission of an international organization", Dr. M'Bow said,

> was to seek and translate into action solutions which can contribute inter alia towards the maintenance of a just and durable peace between nations and to the progress of all countries, it thus appears difficult to imagine such solutions being adopted merely by applying the majority principle, when their implementation will require the active participation and commitment of all peoples and all States.[30]

Another fact which enhanced the importance of consensus as a way of decision making, Dr. M'Bow continued, has been the increase in the share represented by voluntary contributions toward the resources made available to international organizations, in particular for activities linked with development. The States which make the most substantial contributions, he noted, inevitably seek to be associated in one way or another with decisions as to how these funds are used. This, he said, is an area where confrontation makes little sense; he quoted from an address which Paul Prebisch, UNCTAD's first Secretary-General, delivered at the first session of UNCTAD in 1964 as follows:

> There is obviously no immediate practical purpose in adopting recommendations by a simple majority of the developing countries but without the favorable votes of the developed countries, when the execution of those recommendations depends on their acceptance by the latter.[31]

The same, of course, applied to all other bodies entrusted with difficult negotiations in the economic field and those which manage funds constituted from voluntary contributions, such as the Governing Council of the United Nations Development Program.

After admitting that it was very difficult to pin down and analyze the notion of a consensus, particularly in legal terms, Dr. M'Bow stated that UNESCO proposed to carry out studies "to explore the political, sociological, cultural and legal bases of consensus as a method of formulating the position of the international community and as a means of resolving or bypassing conflicts of opinion and interests by tying in consensus with certain traditional practices and institutions".[32]

The basic issue is whether consensus, any more than voting, is a substitute for genuine deliberation and compromise. "Too often", former British Prime Minister James Callaghan told the General Assembly in 1974,

> we use the United Nations as a whipping-boy for our inability to act in concert in response to a common problem. The weaknesses in international cooperation which exist today are not U.N. weaknesses. The responsibility rests with us, the Member States, that have willed that the U.N. should work on the basis of the lowest common denominator or agreement between the Member States. This negative consensus—for that is what it is—sometimes means little more than a wafer-thin formula to paper over our differences without any real meeting of minds. Such a consensus cannot be construed as universal approval. Indeed, because it happens in this way, there are occasions when the words in which we express this negative consensus have no chance of being translated into action because the action proposed does not correspond with realities. What we need in order to be able to act together is positive consensus: a determined effort to reach common ground and an equal determination to work together to overcome the political and economic threats to our people.[33]

Indeed, the consensus on which the whole United Nations is built is very brittle and narrow. Consensus is possible only in respect to matters which, as Dr. M'Bow indicated, engage the interests of all States Members; it cannot be achieved at the expense of third parties. The condemnation, for example, of a country by consensus may no more serve the cause of justice and equity than condemnation by majority vote. On the contrary, it may offer States an opportunity to evade their responsibilities by sparing them the burden and agony of stating their positions and declaring their judgments.

It is to such questions as due process, impartiality and moral and intellectual integrity that the United Nations must address itself before it can hope to restructure the political sector and plug the leaks which are draining its lifeblood. Temperance is an admonition worth heeding even by the United Nations, perhaps especially by the United Nations. In a world in which evil is not neatly confined, it is risky for States Members to override all rules and decency in dealing with third parties in the belief that they will not be affected in the future by the decisions they make today. As long as its actions and decisions are demonstrably shaped by political bias, the United Nations will not be thrust beyond the accepted image of it, as the seat of uncaring nihilism disguised as moral outrage, into the front-ranks of power and influence. As long as it indulges in the selective application of moral judgment and ministers to the sore spots of particular groups or interests, the United Nations will be denied the opportunity of performing the great tasks for which it was created. There should never be more evil in the means than there is good in the ends sought. Not until the actions and decisions of the United Nations are intrinsically sound and freely accepted by the majority and minority alike will the world body be entrusted with the power to pronounce binding judgments and serve as a sure bridge between the reality of interdependence and the vision of international community.

The United Nations is adrift and it is in the best interest of all Member States that the world body steer clear of the shoals toward which it is heading. The vitality and effectiveness of the United Nations depends not so much upon changing its basic structure and rewriting its Charter as upon the resolve of the States Members to come to terms with a reality that offers a choice between cooperation in areas of mutual interest or confrontation in areas of divergent interest. And therein lies the opportunity for bringing about benevolent change in the world Organization. It is better to recognize the weaknesses of the United Nations and seek to remedy them than to mistake posturing and empty assertions for signs of strength and burden the world body with tasks which it cannot possibly fulfil. For example, as may be recalled, the United Nations has had little success in mediating or conciliating disputes among nations. The reasons are many and varied. Aside from the fact that its moral right to sit in judgment over third parties was forfeited when it lent itself to partisan purposes, the United Nations is ill-equipped to deal with the complex sets of interest and concern and to pronounce itself on the rights and wrongs of a dispute with a detachment that is alien to its present structure. Without prejudice to its constitutional responsibilities, it is a disservice to the world Organization to make demands upon it that it cannot meet or to try to make it a party to pretension. It is not for the United Nations, as for other human institutions to finish the job. On this subject Secretary-General Kurt Waldheim had this to say:

> There is one source of disillusionment with the United Nations as an instrument of international cooperation which is due in some degree, I believe, to the way we are accustomed to speak of great problems. In the United Nations, as in the world at large, we speak much of settlements—usually just and lasting—and solutions—usually long-term and comprehensive. This habit of speech gives the impression that, with sufficient application and ingenuity, a total solution can and will be found even to the most intractable of problems. The assumption that a total solution can always be achieved can lead to disillusionment. The problems which come to the United Nations are usually immensely complex questions. Many of them also constitute a potential threat to international peace and security. The United Nations provides a political framework where such problems can be contained, defused and treated. It also provides a place where all can agree to work together for a solution or a settlement. Very often, however, such a settlement can only come slowly through a period of evolution, during which the problem must be treated and positive forces constantly channeled in the right direction. This is a vital practical function of the United Nations which should not be overshadowed by the frustrations which arise from a failure to achieve quick and comprehensive solutions.[34]

Nondestructive change, Claude Levi-Strauss observed, can evolve only from inside a society itself. Change for the better in the structure and orientation of the United Nations will evolve from constant challenge and response. The United Nations must be challenged whenever and wherever its vulnerabilities have been bared and unerringly probed. It must be challenged for its deductive logic, which rigorously derives the most outrageous conclusions from premises whose correctness are rarely examined; for its claims to a higher ethic of universalism that are no more than a denial of others' claims in favor of one's own; and for solutions which ignore the connections between the different factors which enter into the equation. The United Nations must also be faulted for seeking to impose simplistic cures on complex difficulties; for seeking to obtain interpretation before fact, and for succumbing to situations rather than controlling them. And it must also be called to account for the ease with which it permits itself to be drawn into the corrupting vortex of diplomatic maneuvering; for taking the simplicity of its notions as a guarantee of their self-evidence, and for its ability to offend when the requirement is for leadership. Above all, the United Nations must be challenged for surrendering its integrity and sense of justice; for straining arguments beyond evidence; for being partial, ready to accept the half-truth and to look no further to the realities of the larger world, and for its blatant abdication of even the most elementary moral standards.

NOTES

1. See, for example, *Report of the Ninth Conference on the United Nations of the Next Decade*, sponsored by the Stanley Foundation in Vail, Colorado, 9–16 June 1974. The Conference concluded that United Nations decision-making processes were both procedural and political and that without spirit, dedication and political will, the best decision-making procedure was at best an efficient but useless machine.

2. Rule 28 of the provisional Rules of Procedure of the Security Council provides:

> The Security Council may appoint a commission or committee or a rapporteur for a specified question (S/96 Rev.3, 1948).

As to the General Assembly, the *Yearbook of the United Nations*, 1947–48, states that:

> In addition to main, procedural and standing committees, the General Assembly may appoint such ad hoc committees or commissions as may be required from time to time for special purposes (p. 25).

In the period between September 6 and 29 November 1947, the General Assembly appointed the following ad hoc committees and commissions: Interim Committee; United Nations Temporary Commission on Korea; United

Nations Special Committee on the Balkans; United Nations Palestine Commission; Special Commission on Information Transmitted under Article 73e of the Charter (ibid.).

For listing of Security Council ad hoc bodies see ibid., p. 337.

3. For an extract from the Report of the Committee on Standing Orders and the Application of Conventions and Recommendations to the 202nd session of the Governing Body, see *International Labour Conference, Sixty-Third Session, Geneva 1977, Record of Proceedings*, Appendix I, pp. 20–21; for extracts from the Minutes of the 202nd session of the Governing Body, see ibid., Appendix II, pp. 21–29.

4. For text, see *Record of Proceedings*, op. cit., pp. 19–20.

5. See Minutes of the 202nd session of the Governing Body, op. cit., passim; see also the records of proceedings for the Sixth Sitting of the Conference on 3 June 1977, *Record of Proceedings*, op. cit., pp. 108–121.

6. Ibid., passim.

7. Ibid., p. 25.

8. Ibid., p. 120.

9. Ibid., pp. 779–788.

10. For text of letter of 5 November 1975 addressed by Secretary of State Henry Kissinger to the Director-General of the International Labour Organization, see GB 198/22/111.

11. See, for example, "The Quest for Collective Security", an address delivered by Benjamin V. Cohen at the Sixty-Third Annual Meeting of the American Society of International Law, *Proceedings*, 1969, pp. 55–66; "The United Nations Charter: 1945 and 1962", an address delivered by Ambassador James Plimsol of Australia at the Fifty-Sixth Annual Meeting of the American Society of International Law, *Proceedings*, 1962, pp. 162–170; Remarks by Ambassador James F. Leonard and others at a panel on "The United Nations: Reorganizing for World Order", at the Seventieth Annual Meeting of the American Society of International Law, *Proceedings*, 1976, pp. 139–152; Ramatullah Khan, *Implied Powers of the United Nations*, Vikas Publications, Delhi, Bombay, Bangalore, 1969.

12. *Due Process in the United Nations*, American Journal of International Law 69, July 1975, pp. 620–622.

13. Ibid., p. 621.

14. *Enabling the U.S. to Contest Illegal U.N. Actions*, ibid., October 1975, pp. 852–854. For a critique of Professor Sohn's views, see Dan Ciobanu, *Could the Use of the Contentious Procedure of the International Court of Justice have any Impact upon the Practice of the United Nations?* Reply to Professor Louis B. Sohn, American Journal of International Law, April 1976, pp. 328–338.

15. See above, pp. 22–23.

16. See Goodrich, Hambro and Simons: *Charter of the United Nations*, 3rd revised edition, Columbia University Press, N.Y. 1969, pp. 12–17.

17. Ibid., pp. 569–570.

18. Ibid., pp. 101–104 (Article 7 of the Charter of the United Nations): pp.

186–191—Article 22 of the Charter; pp. 236–239—Article 29 of the Charter; and pp. 435–441—Article 68 of the Charter.

19. "Partiality and Impartiality of Human Rights Enquiry Commissions of International Organizations", a chapter contributed by Professor Ermacora to Vol. I of a Festschrift in honor of Professor Rene Cassin published by Editions A. Pedone, Paris, for the International Institute of Human Rights and entitled: *René Cassin, Amicorum Discipulorumque, Liber I, Problemes de Protection Internationale des Droits de L'Homme, 1969.*

20. Ibid., p. 69.

21. S/13115, 23 February 1979.

22. Report of the Security Council Commission, established under Resolution 446(1979), S/13450, p. 39.

23. S/PV 2156, p. 22.

24. Report of the Security Council Commission, op. cit., p. 41.

25. Ibid.

26. Ibid., p. 42.

27. The Caracas Conference on the Law of the Sea agreed that every effort should be made to reach agreement on substantive matters until all efforts at consensus have been exhausted. It was agreed, for instance, that any vote on a matter of substance should be deferred for a period not exceeding ten days, if this was requested by at least fifteen representatives, for the purpose of enabling the President of the Conference to make every effort to facilitate achievement of a general agreement. If at the end of ten days general agreement has not been reached, the Conference is obliged to take another decision on whether further consultations were desirable before all efforts to reach agreement are abandoned. For details see Rules of Procedure of the Conference of the Law of the Sea, A/ConF/62/2 and Add 1 to 3.

28. Rules of Procedure, Final Recommendations of the Helsinki Consultations, Helsinki 1973, p. 22, Rule. 6.

29. From an address entitled "Consensus in International Organizations", UNESCO, DG/78/01.

30. Ibid., p. 3.

31. Ibid., p. 5.

32. Ibid., p. 6.

33. A/PV.2240, p. 81.

34. Introduction to the Report of the Secretary-General on the Work of the Organization, General Assembly Official Records, Thirty-Third Session, Supplement No. 1.A/33/1, p. 1.

GENERAL INDEX*

* *The letter-by-letter system has been followed.*

ABOUT THE AUTHOR

Moses Moskowitz is at present Secretary-General of the Consultative Council of Jewish Organization, which is an organization in consultative status with the Economic and Social Council of the United Nations, Council of Europe, UNESCO, UNICEF and other inter-governmental bodies.

The author contributes to a variety of national and international journals and has written three other books to date: "Human Rights and World Order" (1958), "The Politics and Dynamics of Human Rights" (1968) and "International Concern with Human Rights" (1975).

COLOPHON

letter: times 11/13 and 9/11
setter: William Clowes
printer: Samsom Sijthoff Grafische Bedrijven
binder: Callenbach
cover-design: Jan Jonkers